THE COLLAGE AESTHETIC IN THE HARLEM RENAISSANCE

The Collage Aesthetic in the Harlem Renaissance

RACHEL FAREBROTHER
University of Swansea, UK

ASHGATE

Published by
Ashgate Publishing Limited
Wey Court East
Union Road
Farnham
Surrey, GU9 7PT
England

Ashgate Publishing Company
Suite 420
101 Cherry Street
Burlington
VT 05401-4405
USA

www.ashgate.com

British Library Cataloguing in Publication Data
Farebrother, Rachel.
   The collage aesthetic in the Harlem Renaissance.
   1. Harlem Renaissance. 2. American literature – African American authors – History and criticism. 3. American literature – 20th century – History and criticism.
   4. Modernism (Literature) – United States. 5. African American aesthetics.
   I. Title
   810.9'896073–dc22

Library of Congress Cataloging-in-Publication Data
Farebrother, Rachel.
   The collage aesthetic in the Harlem Renaissance / Rachel Farebrother.
       p. cm.
   Includes bibliographical references and index.
   ISBN 978-0-7546-6198-6 (hardback : alk. paper)
   1. American literature—African American authors—History and criticism. 2. American literature—20th century—History and criticism. 3. African American aesthetics.
4. Literature and anthropology—United States—History—20th century. 5. African Americans—Intellectual life—20th century. 6. Modernism (Literature)—United States.
7. African Americans in literature. 8. Harlem Renaissance. I. Title.

   PS153.N5F37 2009
   810.9'896073—dc22

                                                                    2009015786

ISBN 9780754661986 (hbk)

Mixed Sources
Product group from well-managed
forests and other controlled sources
www.fsc.org Cert no. SGS-COC-2482
© 1996 Forest Stewardship Council
FSC

Printed and bound in Great Britain by
TJ International Ltd, Padstow, Cornwall

Contents

List of Figures

Acknowledgements

It has taken me longer than I care to admit to complete this project. I would never have managed it without the support, advice and generosity of mentors, friends, colleagues and family. I would like to thank the Arts and Humanities Research Board for funding my research. I would also like to express my sincere gratitude to Jay Prosser, whose patient and encouraging guidance kept me going. For all its omissions and mistakes, I hope that this book captures something of his urge to reach beyond familiar interpretive frameworks. I owe a huge debt to Mick Gidley. Without his critical insights, wise counsel and kindness, I would certainly have given up on academia long ago. Thanks are also due to mentors who helped and inspired me along the way, especially Elleke Boehmer, Shirley Chew, Hermione Lee and Hugh Stevens, who introduced me to Hurston in the first place.

I count myself lucky to have studied at the University of Leeds where I benefited from the advice and support of colleagues and friends. Special thanks are due to Gillian Roberts, Rob Stanton, David Stirrup, Jayne Waterman and Andrew Warnes, whose work on African American culture has been an inspiration. Thanks for things too many to mention must go to Claire Chambers, Mike Goff, Bee Marriott, Nicola McClellan, Ellen Murray and Colin Winborn.

Beyond Leeds, I would like to acknowledge the many individuals who helped me develop my ideas. I am particularly grateful to Maria Lauret, whose perceptive, searching questions redefined the focus of my project. Thanks are also due to my former colleagues at Leeds Metropolitan University, especially Andrew Lawson, Rachel Rich and Ruth Robbins. Heartfelt thanks to Emma Robertson for wise words and astute feedback on portions of the manuscript. Colleagues in American Studies at Swansea have been very supportive. I gratefully acknowledge the University's contribution towards copyright and reproduction costs, and Hayley Elliott's help with finance matters. A special thank-you to Catherine Clarke and Hilary Brown for moral support and perceptive feedback on parts of the manuscript. It has been a genuine privilege to share my interest in African American studies with Daniel Williams, whose acute insights reshaped my ideas at a critical juncture. I am also grateful to Ashgate's reader for a challenging, heartening report and to my commissioning editor Ann Donahue who has been unfailingly helpful in the face of my glacial progress. A condensed version of Chapter 3 appeared in *Journal of American Studies* (© Cambridge University Press, 2006) and a section of Chapter 5 appeared in *Comparative American Studies* (© Maney Publishing, 2007, www.maneypublishing.co.uk/journals/cas and www.ingentaconnect.com/content/maney.cas). Permission to reprint this material is gratefully acknowledged.

I would also like to thank the editors and anonymous readers at these journals for interventions that have had a major impact on my thinking.

Last but not least, I thank my family who have supported me in so many ways during the course of the project. I couldn't have done it without them. As a token of my gratitude, I dedicate this book to them.

Rachel Farebrother

List of Abbreviations

C	Jean Toomer, *Cane*
F	Edward Said, *Freud and the Non-European*
J	Zora Neale Hurston, *Jonah's Gourd Vine*
M	Zora Neale Hurston, *Moses, Man of the Mountain*
MM	Zora Neale Hurston, *Mules and Men*
N	Alain Locke, ed. *The New Negro*

Introduction

In her account of a Harlem jazz club in *Quicksand*, Nella Larsen presents the dancing African Americans in striking visual terms. She describes a sliding spectrum of colours, a 'moving mosaic', which is both imbued with possibility, as suggested by a dynamism that undercuts strict racial categorization, and fraught with the danger of self-obliteration (Larsen 1995, 60). Larsen's use of collage-like imagery to highlight the complexity of race is by no means unique: this trope also features in the writings of Jessie Fauset, Langston Hughes, Zora Neale Hurston, Claude McKay, George Schuyler and Jean Toomer, to name only a few. Furthermore, a number of aesthetic statements from the Harlem Renaissance mark collage, or the juxtaposition of distinctive cultural pieces, as a significant form.[1] The challenge for this study is to interpret the historical, aesthetic and political burdens of these recurring patterns.

The dynamic interplay between word and image in key Harlem Renaissance anthologies and magazines, such as *The New Negro* (1925), *The Crisis* and *Opportunity*, has provoked much recent research. In *Word, Image, and the New Negro* (2005), Anne Elizabeth Carroll considers collaborative illustrated volumes of the Harlem Renaissance, including *Opportunity*, *The Crisis*, *Fire!!* and *The New Negro*. She pays detailed attention to the dynamic interplay of text and illustration in these magazines and anthologies, exposing complexities and ironies that animate the New Negro search for a distinctive African American voice. Martha Jane Nadell's *Enter the New Negroes* (2004) explores these 'interartistic' texts to different effect, showing that writers like Alain Locke and W.E.B. Du Bois mobilized form to counter prevailing stereotypes, revealing the heterogeneity of black experience. Much less critical attention has been focused upon techniques of juxtaposition and stylistic incongruity deployed within other Harlem Renaissance writing. This book seeks to address this critical lacuna by analysing

---

[1] A number of Harlem Renaissance authors drew attention to their deployment of patchwork forms, which not only combined American, African and European cultural elements, but also crossed disciplinary boundaries. Here are just a few examples. In a letter to his agent, Claude McKay likened *Home to Harlem* (1928) to 'a mosaic that puzzles and yet intrigues and holds the reader' (North 1994, 118). In her only exclusively interpretive anthropological essay, 'Characteristics of Negro Expression', Zora Neale Hurston identifies a collage-like pattern as the guiding principle of African American culture. She claims that 'the white man thinks in a written language and the Negro thinks in hieroglyphics' (1995b, 831), developing a visual motif that is reminiscent of collage, or at least stylistic incongruity. Finally, Countee Cullen described his poetry, which recasts conventional forms such as the sonnet, as '[a] variety within a uniformity' (Early 1991, 41).

the collage aesthetic in a selection of texts by Alain Locke, Zora Neale Hurston and Jean Toomer.

Techniques of juxtaposition and stylistic incongruity do not only shape those New Negro texts that include art on their pages. On close inspection, it is clear that many Harlem Renaissance texts are characterized by the patching together of diverse sources, which can be identified and held in view by the reader. The pages of Harlem Renaissance fiction abound with fragmentary cultural pieces, which are combined and revised to make something new, whether that be the orchestrated patterns of formal discord in *Cane*, or the textual synthesis achieved in Hurston's lyrical novels. With its emphasis upon technical innovation, this study contributes to a burgeoning field, especially in its sustained attention to the politics of form.

Perhaps the strongest argument for gathering these writers together under the umbrella term 'the collage aesthetic' emanates from the texts themselves. Jean Toomer's *Cane*, for example, a difficult, avant-garde text, which adopts an aesthetic of assemblage by splicing together genres and splitting open traditional literary forms, invites sustained formalist analysis. Approaching the text as a version of collage captures the vital essence of Toomer's project, drawing out the political implication that undergirds his formal experimentation. Likewise, Alain Locke's *The New Negro* manipulates the anthology form for political ends, orchestrating his chosen contributions to reconfigure democracy, making an argument for African American 'culture-citizenship' (Locke 1992b, 99). A formalist interpretation of Hurston may appear to be more surprising, given her apparently simple, limpid prose style. Yet, close attention to Hurston's diverse *oeuvre* reveals a wealth of stylistic and thematic references to European and African art, anthropology and music.

Why choose collage as a metaphor for such formal innovation? Emphasis upon early twentieth-century developments in anthropology and visual art brings to light transatlantic cultural exchanges that underpinned modernist experimentation among black and white writers and artists of the period. Taking collage in Harlem Renaissance and modernist art as my point of departure, I mine visual art for a critical vocabulary through which to analyse literary patterns of synthesis and fragmentation. This search for ways in which the visual and the literary might illuminate one another is alert to a dynamic flow of ideas and techniques across the Atlantic, which inspired European and American writers and artists to experiment with collage-like forms.

Visual art, however, is not the only source for my formulation of the collage aesthetic. The writings of the anthropologist Franz Boas and his students abound with accounts of cultural development, which describe culture in collage-like terms, as a thing of reconstructed fragments. Since all the writers featured in this book were deeply immersed in Franz Boas's anthropology, it seems appropriate to consider their formal choices in the light of a Boasian framework. Recourse to anthropology is crucial to any assessment of the politics of collage form, not least because Boas conceived of anthropology as a means of intervening in contemporary political concerns.

Such attention to transatlantic discourses about race and nation complicates recent critical assessments of the relationship between the Harlem Renaissance and modernism, which have tended to fall into two broad camps: those who identify a unique African American modernism and those who emphasize interracial collaboration. In his influential book *Modernism and the Harlem Renaissance* (1987), for instance, Houston A. Baker describes the Harlem Renaissance as a distinctive kind of modernism that was necessarily subversive, deploying '*the mastery of form* and *the deformation of mastery*' (1987, 15). On the other hand, Ann Douglas's *Terrible Honesty: Mongrel Manhattan in the 1920s* (1995) and George Hutchinson's *The Harlem Renaissance in Black and White* (1995) pay close attention to the interracial quality of aesthetic experiment during the period. I find space in between these two positions, exploring neglected, often transatlantic, connections between modernism and the Harlem Renaissance, while remaining alert to the ways in which African American writers mobilized such techniques from a particular cultural and historical perspective. In short, Harlem Renaissance writers drew inspiration from vernacular forms *and* modernistic formal experimentation.

Focusing on Harlem Renaissance writers' formal choices in the light of transatlantic discourses about race and nation necessitates a shift in the critical framework through which we regard the Harlem Renaissance, placing it beyond the confines of American race politics into a broader, international context. My formulation of the collage aesthetic, with its crossing of geographical and disciplinary borders, puts cultural exchange right at the heart of any consideration of the Harlem Renaissance, paving the way for discussion of international cultural and political trends. Attending to the formal aspects of Hurston's writing, for example, not only sheds light upon her complex engagement with Euro-American modernism, but it also exposes the internationalist scope of such works as *Moses, Man of the Mountain* (1939), a novel that has been somewhat left behind in the recent resurgence of interest in her work.

In pairing sustained formalist analysis with an internationalist framework, my approach owes much to Brent Hayes Edwards's efforts to 'move against the grain of much of the scholarship on African American culture in the 1920s, which has tended to emphasize U.S.-bound themes of cultural nationalism, civil rights protest, and uplift in the literary culture of the "Harlem Renaissance"' (2003, 2-3). Focusing on Paris, the transcultural capital of black modernism and internationalism, Edwards pays particular attention to links between New Negro and Francophone intellectuals, an approach that yields a sophisticated account of tensions generated when such discourses as Négritude, European colonialism and Communism interact. More pertinent to my purposes is the connection Edwards establishes between 'the transnational contours of black expression between the world wars' and formal innovation (2003, 3). To take only one example, he contends that the elaborate 'framing strategies in [James Weldon Johnson's] *The Autobiography of an Ex-Colored Man* [are] anchored not just in the form of the novel but also by its transatlantic journey out of the nation-space' (2003, 41).

This crucial insight that new transnational conceptions of identity necessitated a break from conventional literary forms accords with my emphasis upon the politics of form. However, while Edwards focuses upon transactions between black intellectuals across the African diaspora, *The Collage Aesthetic in the Harlem Renaissance* addresses African American writers' engagement with Euro-American modernism, especially Boasian anthropology.

With this in mind, I now turn to selected paintings and collages by Pablo Picasso, Loïs Mailou Jones, Aaron Douglas and Benjamin Péret to outline some of the thematic and stylistic effects of an aesthetic of assemblage. At this juncture, it is worth acknowledging some of the difficulties generated by a theoretical model that moves between visual art and literature. Any direct correlation between visual and textual collage is, of course, impossible, given differences in technique and genre. For one thing, a literary text cannot replicate the literal assemblage of disparate materials that is so fundamental to artistic collage. Next, there are important distinctions to be made between how we read a written text and how we interpret a visual collage. Chief among them is the issue of interpretation and time. A viewer can see an entire collage in a single instant, registering intricacies of texture and relationships between fragments. While writers can mimic such effects through inventive typographical layout, they remain constrained by the fact that meaning, in a literary text, can only be disclosed gradually, with the passage of time. As Wolfgang Iser explains, '[i]n every text there is a potential time sequence which the reader must inevitably realize, as it is impossible to absorb even a short text in a single moment. Thus the reading process always involves viewing the text through a perspective that is continually on the move, linking up the different phases, and so constructing what we have called the virtual dimension' (1980, 56). Even a narrative that describes a single moment is governed by this temporal dynamic since it relies upon a reader's ability to remember and reconstruct.

Such differences of media undoubtedly pose challenges for this study. Nevertheless, it seems to me that collage, a technique that makes room for integrative representation and disorientating fragmentation, offers a useful conceptual framework for analysing the formal choices made by Harlem Renaissance writers. For the most part, collage functions as a metaphor in the pages of this book. It is my intention to develop a set of reading practices, which focus attention upon productive juxtapositions between divergent registers and styles, and word and image.

At the same time, my discussion of modernist collage carries a larger significance because critics have so often described 'montage and collage of the image as the dominant avant-garde aesthetic mode' (Goldman 2004, 163). In his influential study *Theory of the Avant-Garde*, for instance, Peter Bürger writes that '[a] theory of the avant-garde must begin with the concept of montage that is suggested by the early cubist collages. What distinguishes them from the techniques of composition developed since the Renaissance is the insertion of reality fragments into the painting, i.e., the insertion of material that has been left unchanged by the artist' (Bürger 1984, 77). For Bürger, collage is a specifically Euro-American artistic practice, which enabled Picasso and others to subvert western aesthetics from within the tradition. More recently, commentators have convincingly demonstrated that collage forms drew much of their subversive energy from an engagement with non-European cultures. Helen Carr, in a subtle account of imagism, explains that '[t]he collages of modernism came out of a hybrid, multiracial world' (Carr 2000, 87). Sieglinde Lemke also emphasizes the galvanizing effect of intercultural exchange during the period. In *Primitivist Modernism: Black Culture and the Origins of Transatlantic Modernism*, she trains her critical gaze on 'a phenomenon that has itself been "the invisible man" of cultural criticism: that black, or African-inspired, expressions have played a seminal role in the shaping of modernism' (1998, 4).

Such critical reappraisals shed light on the interplay of ideas between cultures that is a salient feature of modernist collage. In an untitled surrealist collage of 1929, for instance, Benjamin Péret pasted a representation of an exploitative, sexualized relationship between a white male and a black female slave into a detailed drawing of a European country house, which is bursting with visual markers of wealth and cultural refinement. Through the unexpected juxtapositions of his collage, which cross geographical boundaries to introduce the history of the United States to Europe, he pieces together a history of racial and sexual exploitation that remains unspoken in "realistic" national narratives (see Figure 1).

Figure 1   Benjamin Péret, *Collage* (untitled) (1929) © Librairie José Corti, Paris

Manipulating collage technique to challenge dominant, bourgeois values, Péret juxtaposes the abuse perpetuated through slavery with luxurious products of European social and economic power. Indeed, every available space on the walls and ceiling of this country house is covered with ornate art in gilded frames. Establishing a link between violence against slaves and the European country house, which was designed to mask all evidence of exploitative sources of wealth, Péret exposes the oppression exercised in the name of "civilization". His image endorses André Breton's claim that the innovatory quality of collage rests in the combination of diverse pieces, which stages an encounter between disparate realities. For Breton, such juxtapositions resulted in a challenging transformation of reality that had the capacity to '"nous dépayser en notre propre souvenir" or disorientate both producer and viewer' (Adamowicz 1998, 4). But Péret stresses European and American interdependence, placing special emphasis on making visible "truths" that have been silenced or denied. It is precisely because of such transatlantic stylistic and thematic connections that my conceptualization of the collage aesthetic begins with visual art.

Between 1912 and 1914, Pablo Picasso, who is credited with making the first deliberately executed collage, produced a large number of *papier collés* by gluing wallpapers, hand-made and mass-produced coloured papers, newspaper, magazine illustrations, pieces of string and alcohol labels onto his canvases (Poggi 1992, 6). Through his bold mixing of high art with the bric-à-brac of everyday reality, he questioned assumptions about the role of the artist and what art should be. In *Guitar and Wine Glass* (1912), he uses an array of materials to suggest the shape of a guitar: a cubist drawing of a wine glass, *faux bois* wallpaper, a crudely cut circle of white paper, a strip of bright blue paper, a corner of a musical score and a fragment of newspaper (see Figure 2). All these pieces are pasted onto mass-produced wallpaper. Through analysis of this painting, I want to introduce several key themes that will be central to my formulation of the collage aesthetic: the tension between fragmentation and synthesis; how we read collage; the politics of collage; and the use of collage forms to transform dominant historical narratives.

Picasso's collage is animated by a tension between fragmentation and synthesis. When the picture is viewed as a whole, the fragments, which have been orchestrated according to principles of symmetry and balance, cohere into the shape of a guitar. Yet, such synthesis is disrupted if viewers focus upon individual pieces that comprise the collage. Taking this close-up view, elements of the composition remain disconnected from each other and appropriated materials 'retain their former identity within the new pictorial context' (Poggi 1992, 1). As a consequence, newsprint can either be read, quite literally, as text describing specific contemporary events, or merely as an artistic backdrop that creates a particular mood. In breaking apart an image we initially read as a whole, Picasso brings together strikingly different representations of the "real" world, from apparently banal found objects to carefully composed sketches, only to muddy the aesthetic categories that prize some fragments over others. Subverting expectations, he 'individualize[s] and humanize[s]' mass-produced objects that are supposed to conform to a regular pattern, cutting or tearing paper in a way that 'inflect[s] everything … with his sensibility and hand' (Staller 2001, 236).

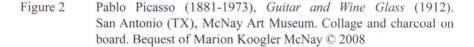

Figure 2   Pablo Picasso (1881-1973), *Guitar and Wine Glass* (1912). San Antonio (TX), McNay Art Museum. Collage and charcoal on board. Bequest of Marion Koogler McNay © 2008

As we shall see, the Harlem Renaissance writers featured in this study also exploit a variety of interpretive modes, or reading spaces, opened up by collage form. Reading *Cane*, for instance, is analogous to viewing a Picasso collage from afar: above all, viewers notice jarring juxtaposition of high art with strange and unfamiliar objects, debris from the everyday world. Such disjunctions are less obvious in Zora Neale Hurston's writing because she often adopts an extreme close-up technique, inviting readers to focus attention on each cultural fragment that she isolates. What both writers share, however, is their refusal to allow readers a comfortable, complacent position in relation to their texts. In *Cane*, point of view is hardly a settled matter; perspectives veer from bird's eye views to extreme close-ups. As Mark Whalan has demonstrated, gaps in the narrative force readers to become more involved: '[f]illing those silences removes any readerly distance that may exist, pushing the reader against the "tactile" surfaces of the lynched, abused, and murdered bodies that the text frequently omits to mention' (2007, 216). Odd shifts of perspective are also common in Hurston's writing. Consider, for instance, Hurston's taste for what Alice Gambrell has called 'versioning' (1997, 14), an aesthetic method whereby she revised existing fragments of her published writing for incorporation into new works. While such repetition can create a sense of coherence across a diverse *oeuvre*, it also initiates a process of defamiliarization. Recontextualization requires readers to reassess well-known material from a new angle of vision. In this sense, there are striking correspondences with the process of interpreting collage. In particular, these multiple perspectives are reminiscent of what we might call the double take, that crucial instant of recognition when we realize that a collage is at once a collection of disparate parts and an integrated whole.

This brings me to a key theme for the book: the question of how we read collage. Given that disparate elements remain 'in a dynamic process of multiple meanings and hovering significations constantly reactivated', viewers are assigned an active interpretive role (Adamowicz 1998, 25). Picasso's aesthetic of assemblage casts viewers as researchers, who must follow through the implications of his indirect, oblique form. His disruption of the canvas with actual words, for instance, directs us beyond the confines of the image itself: we are encouraged to track down sources, and then to puzzle out relationships with other fragments in the picture. In *Guitar and Wine Glass* (1912), Picasso not only cuts up newsprint to communicate the violence of war, but he also includes motifs that are familiar from other collages he produced in the period. By including text from the 18 November edition of *Le Journal* alongside coloured paper and patterned wallpaper, he puts the picture into conversation with *Siphon, Glass, Newspaper and Violin* (1912) and *Glass and Bottle of Suze* (1912). Such roaming motifs create considerable uncertainty. On the one hand, they generate disorientation because the images are twice removed from their original context. On the other hand, such repetition holds out an unfulfilled promise of unity: viewers are tempted to identify underlying themes and preoccupations, a quest that can only end in frustration. As Natasha Staller explains, Picasso's collages 'challenge us to imagine images that never can be organically whole, which shimmer forever as fragments, but which evoke and suggest a series of unnameable wholes' (2001, 228).

Since collages are characterized by material heterogeneity and incongruous juxtaposition that break the continuity of discourse, they alter the way that we read. Faced with collage, viewers are forced to piece together meaning actively: they must tease out relationships between parts – each fragment is perceived in relation to other fragments, to the whole (and possibly to other collages) and to its origin. These meanings remain suspended in dynamic play. It is the viewer's task to identify cultural pieces and to hold them in view, never suppressing the heterogeneity of elements. Of course, active interpretation is even more crucial in verbal collage because 'the encoded intent is often less visible than in pictorial collage'; its identification often depends on a reader's ability to decode intertextual fragments (Adamowicz 1998, 15).

Another major theme is the political significance of collage form. Since collage subverts aesthetic hierarchies, it often articulates 'a generalized stance of opposition' (Staller 2001, 246). Picasso's collages, for instance, 'rail against authority, against the Church, against the Law, against the Academy, against every imaginable stripe of "expert"' (Staller 2001, 246). For many commentators, collage technique, with its democratic mixing of disparate components, is inevitably subversive: '[b]uilt into the nature of the technique is an argument against purity, newness, and unlimited progress' (Levin 1989, xix-xx).

More specifically, the sense of defamiliarization generated by rearrangement of familiar elements on the canvas offered a means of fixing attention on uneasy realities about contemporary society. In a discussion of his collages, Picasso explains that his juxtaposition of diverse materials was a deliberate attempt to disorientate the viewer:

> The purpose of the papier collé was to give the idea that different textures can enter into a composition to become the reality in the painting that competes with the reality in nature. We tried to get rid of 'trompe l'oeil' to find a 'trompe l'esprit'... And this strangeness was what we wanted to make people think about because we were quite aware that our world was becoming very strange and not exactly reassuring (Hoffman 1989, 7).

The substitution of 'trompe l'esprit' for 'trompe l'oeil' indicates subversion of the old status of painting as an illusion of reality. Given the unsettling nature of modern life, Picasso implies that 'reality' is far more complex and strange than realistic representations could ever indicate. More important for my purposes is Picasso's claim that it is collage's capacity to shock, its jarring rearrangement of previously familiar elements, which carries political implications for the present. In creating a sense of 'strangeness' that would 'make people think' about a world which 'was becoming strange and not exactly reassuring', Picasso challenges viewers to face up to the unsettling character of their contemporary society. In this sense, collage becomes a means of addressing the difficulties and complexities of modern life.

It is worth pausing here for a moment to establish the political possibilities and limitations of collage form. Of course, Picasso's formulation hardly amounts to a detailed political programme: the implications of his new perspective on contemporary society remain unspecified. As Thomas P. Brockelman has astutely pointed out, '[t]here's little to take away from collage, no portable doctrine or ideology with which to settle your affairs' (2001, 14). This is a kind of politics that proceeds by analogy, juxtaposition and suggestion rather than explicit announcement. Nevertheless, collage has the potential to complicate unquestioned assumptions: 'collage [forces] us to acknowledge a dimension of experience resistant to the very categories by which thought organizes relationships' (Brockelman 2001, 160). Benjamin Péret's untitled collage of 1929, for instance, is a striking example of how modernist artists deployed collage forms to unsettle dominant historical narratives. Furthermore, in *Cane*, Jean Toomer shatters 'whitewashed' histories to expose racial proximity and racial mixing in America. *Cane* provides a stark portrayal of the 'godam nightmare' of American history:

it is a representation of a 'whole damn bloated purple country', which has been bruised and bastardized by its slave past, a shameful past of exploitation, violence and violation (1993, 110).

Picasso and Péret's collages are part of the transatlantic phenomenon that was modernism. As many commentators have pointed out, cultural exchange between Europe and America, Africa and America, and Africa and Europe often stimulated aesthetic innovation during this period. The collaborative use of African models in the work of Picasso, a European visual artist, and Gertrude Stein, an American expatriate writer, is archetypal in this respect. Picasso's encounter with African art at the *Musée d'Ethnographie* at the *Palais du Trocadéro* in Paris inspired him to transform inherited forms. Indeed, a Grebo mask purchased during one of his *chasses aux nègres* in Avignon during the summer of 1912 led him to explore new codes of representation and to disrupt the canvas with actual words (Poggi 1992, 5-6). More recently, Natasha Staller has convincingly demonstrated that Catalan images of the black Madonna and Moorish cultural influences were a catalyst for the 'emphatically dissonant tonality' that is so characteristic of Picasso's work (2001, 336). Gertrude Stein's 'Melanctha', a portrait of an African American woman's emotional life, also turns to non-European sources in quest of new styles. She synthesizes the fragmented perspective of post-impressionist art with an attempt to represent "black" dialect as a rebellion against Standard English, creating a new stylistic mode, which straddles aesthetic divisions. As Michael North explains in his incisive discussion of Picasso and Stein, 'the step away from conventional verisimilitude into abstraction is accomplished by a figurative change of race' (1994, 61).

Given the complex patterns of intercultural exchange that characterized the early decades of the twentieth century, it comes as no surprise to learn that Harlem Renaissance visual artists manipulated collage-like forms. In fact, many influential African American artists, including Palmer Hayden, Loïs Mailou Jones, Elizabeth Prophet, Archibald J. Motley, Jr., Laura Wheeler Waring and Hale Woodruff, studied in Paris during this period (Leininger-Miller 2001; Stovall 1996). As Theresa Leininger-Miller has noted, 'Paris played a pivotal role in the development of some of the leading Harlem Renaissance artists' (2001, xvi). Since Paris was the transcultural capital of modernism and internationalism, such artists were exposed to 'traditional European art, African art, modern art, and proto-Négritude ideas' (Leininger-Miller 2001, xvi). A brief account of Loïs Mailou Jones's *Les Fétiches* (1938) sheds light on the complex engagement with Euro-American modernism that resulted from such hybrid influences. Combining geometric abstraction with a thematic exploration of her African heritage, Jones was at once inspired by modernist experimentation and critical of the shallow exoticism that often characterized European engagement with African art. As Sieglinde Lemke explains, 'Jones's reclamation of her legacy was mediated through European modernism. *Les Fétiches* flaunts the sources of influence for Jones's art and, simultaneously, parodies the *vogue nègre*' (1998, 51).

Considering European modernists like Picasso and Péret alongside African American artists exposes the interplay of ideas and styles across the Atlantic. Nevertheless, it is important to register that African American artists differed from European practitioners of the form, not least because they used collage to express the hybrid character of African American cultural identity. Crucially, such hybridity does not function as a celebratory means of confounding essentialism; rather, artists introduce violent disjunctions that encapsulate the discontinuities of African American history.

In the hands of African American artists, collage becomes a means to subvert accounts of American history which are, in Toni Morrison's words, characterized by 'obfuscation and distortion and erasure, so that the presence and the heartbeat of black people has been systematically annihilated in many, many ways' (Davis 1994, 224-5). Attention to the later African American artist Romare Bearden, who experimented with collage in the 1960s, demonstrates the radical potential of such assemblage. Bearden's collages, with their jarring arrangements of diverse cultural referents, drew inspiration from jazz to create tension and disorientation. In his introduction for a 1968 catalogue of Bearden's collages, Ralph Ellison characterizes the collages as an attempt to expose 'that which has been concealed by time, custom and our trained incapacity to perceive the truth', namely the richness of African American culture (1994, 685-6). Ellison's account of Bearden's indirect approach proves helpful for understanding visual and textual collages of the Harlem Renaissance period. According to Ellison, Bearden does not make 'explicit comment', 'telling' the viewer what to think; instead, he creates interplay between collage fragments 'to make the unseen manifest' (1994, 691-2). Such a strategy could be likened to Benjamin Péret's manipulation of collage to make visible uncomfortable "truths" that have been silenced.

A comparable, if less dissonant, revision of dominant historical narratives guides Aaron Douglas's mural *Aspects of Negro Life: From Slavery Through Reconstruction* (1934) (see Figure 3). Douglas displays his debt to modernist experimentation, but he also manipulates such assemblage to question received accounts of the Reconstruction. To this end, he juxtaposes a handful of historical images: a representation of the Ku Klux Klan; an orator speaking to doubtful African Americans about the promise of what is, quite literally, a city upon a hill; the departure of the Union soldiers; and a growing sense of elation at the prospect of freedom, which is represented symbolically through a musician, a dancer and a man in broken chains. In this way, Douglas challenges influential historical accounts, such as Ulrich B. Phillips's *Life and Labor in the Old South*, first published in 1929, which criticized the Reconstruction because African Americans were allegedly 'more or less contentedly slaves, with grievances from time to time but not ambition' (1948, 196). Douglas articulates a more expansive and yet provisional history, which represents 'aspects' of African American experience to convey a message of rebirth, rediscovery and possibility.

Figure 3   Aaron Douglas, *Aspects of Negro Life: From Slavery Through Reconstruction* (1934). Oil on canvas. Arts & Artifacts Division, Schomburg Center for Research in Black Culture, The New York Public Library, Astor, Lenox and Tilden Foundations

When this picture is viewed alongside the collages I have already discussed, it becomes clear that Douglas deploys modernist techniques of fragmentation and stylistic incongruity. Yet, although Douglas received his training in these techniques from the German-born painter Winold Reiss, it would be a mistake to run a direct line of influence from Europe to America. In fact, like Picasso, Reiss was profoundly influenced by African art, and he encouraged Douglas to introduce African styles and themes into his art. In this sense, the collaboration between Reiss and Douglas, which came to fruition in the illustrations for Alain Locke's *The New Negro*, accords with the dynamic model of cultural exchange that Sieglinde Lemke locates at the heart of modernism, whereby intercultural encounter, 'learning about "oneself" through a cultural other', becomes a catalyst for formal innovation (1998, 7).

While Douglas deploys techniques that imply a debt to Euro-American modernism, he mobilizes them for rather different ends. If Picasso takes aim at the formal conventions of western art, Douglas seeks to capture the specifics of African American culture and history. He utilizes Picasso's method of rhythmic disruption, breaking up temporality to invoke a violent past of enslavement and economic exploitation, a past that threatens to disturb the mural's celebratory tone. Notice, for instance, the slave in the bottom left-hand corner whose body merges with the Southern landscape, a landscape that has become an ancestral graveyard for African Americans. Patterns of repetition, such as the recurring circles, are cut short by images of violence. More specifically, Douglas orchestrates the segments of his layered image to formulate an implied critique of the limitations of American democracy. His inclusion of the Capitol building, for instance, is laced with subversive intent. Such an allusion harnesses the obliqueness of collage form, which proceeds by implication, to identify a need for direct political action. Ultimately, he underlines the particularity of African American experience, especially with regard to material inequalities between whites and African Americans.

Historical revisionism is also a governing concept in Loïs Mailou Jones's painted collage *The Ascent of Ethiopia* (1932). Emphasizing the hybrid character of African American cultural identity, Jones patches together thematic and stylistic features from European, American, African American and African art to represent figuratively African American cultural identity. She explores cultural fusion in America, gathering together representations of an imposing Pharaoh figure, the urban jazz scene, the pyramids and the American cityscape. This thematic mixing of recognizably American, Egyptian and African American elements is mirrored in her technique. The Pharaoh figure is stylized in a manner that resembles Egyptian art – his shoulders are parallel with the picture frame – yet Jones adds a touch of "western" realism through her careful delineation of his facial features. Moreover, she alludes to both black and white modernists in terms of content, symbolism and style: her slanted, angular skyscrapers recall the crisp abstraction of the precisionists (Kirschke 1995, 84); the panels of light echo Aaron Douglas's work; and Jones's title pays tribute to the African American sculptor Meta Vaux Warwick Fuller, who produced *The Awakening of Ethiopia* in c.1914. In short, Jones forges a bold artistic expression of African American identity, which celebrates its rich hybridity. She uses collage to rethink inherited concepts of the American nation, locating African and African American influences at its heart.

The internationalist scope of Jones's picture, with its Pan-African Pharaoh, underlines how centrally transnational discourses of race and nation impacted on Harlem Renaissance artists and intellectuals as they made formal choices about how to represent African American culture. Yet, this picture is animated by a revealing tension between internationalism and nationalism. In her recent book *Spectres of 1919: Class and Nation in the Making of the New Negro*, Barbara Foley makes the case that many Harlem Renaissance writers expressed a blind faith in nationalism as a 'fundamentally transformative politics' that could 'emancipate those bearing the yoke of oppression and exploitation' (2003, viii). Few African American thinkers could resist the lure of nationalist arguments as a means of combating racism; consequently, Harlem Renaissance writers often unwittingly repeated the essentialism they intended to challenge (2003, ix). With this in mind, the formal hybridity of Jones's painting, which displays a debt to black and white, ancient and modern modes of representation, is, to some extent, at odds with her efforts to huddle these traditions inside a specifically African American cultural identity.

As Sieglinde Lemke has shown, primitivism often acted as a catalyst for African American innovation with form, as African Americans learned about themselves 'through a cultural other' (1998, 7). Such interplay of black and white across aesthetic boundaries created complex webs of interconnection. For example, African art influenced white European modernists, such as Picasso, who in turn influenced the writing of such prominent Harlem Renaissance figures as Alain Locke (Lemke 1998, 8-9).

My approach does not amount to a quest for origins, which might run the risk of making such modernists as Picasso loom too large for the Harlem Renaissance. Instead, attention to adjacencies or points of contact between art and literature at a cultural moment that witnessed unprecedented collaboration between artists and writers (one thinks, for instance, of Picasso and Gertrude Stein, and Langston Hughes and Aaron Douglas) facilitates the development of a set of reading practices through which to interpret the complex patterning of cultural pieces in the pages of Harlem Renaissance texts.

In developing an account of collage practice, it is very important not to lose sight of the particularity of African American experience. For African American artists and writers, collage form, with its odd tonal shifts and unsettling juxtapositions, could be shaped to communicate the discontinuities and ruptures of African American history. As an artistic trope, the fragmentation and defamiliarization that are constituent to collage allow for the formulation of 'an understanding of African American identity as something that has itself been "collaged" by the vicissitudes of modern history' (Mercer 2005, 125).

Of course, the collage impulse that is so central to much Harlem Renaissance writing draws inspiration from African American vernacular culture. Stylistic and thematic incongruity is a strong feature of such forms as jazz and blues. As Paul Oliver explains, the blues are inherently paradoxical, not least because lyrical beauty collides with violence and pain: '[b]lues is the wail of the forsaken, the cry of independence, the passion of the lusty, the anger of the frustrated and the laughter of the fatalist' (Oliver 1969, 3). Jorge Daniel Veneciano addresses dynamic interplay between visual and musical forms more directly, likening to collage the practice of incorporating musical quotations into early American jazz (2004, 270). Yet, he is careful to point out that such techniques must be assessed in the context of specifically African American aesthetics: '[t]he practice of quotation and collage become musical and visual means of engaging in or *performing* a dialogue. Traditional jazz is, after all, essentially dialogic, not simply between performing ensemble musicians but also, and precisely, between musicians and their "materials and means of execution": i.e., with the music, songs, instruments, rhythms, and orchestrations of Western and African musical traditions' (2004, 270).

In the light of this description, it seems to me that collage is a fruitful metaphor for the jarring discordances in the pages of Harlem Renaissance texts. In particular, I wonder if my analogy to visual art might counter the possible reductiveness of notions such as the jazz aesthetic, which, as Maria Lauret has shown, threaten to classify all formal experimentation in African American texts as 'literary riff[s]', underplaying the significance of other literary, visual and theoretical models (1996, 59). Collage may be useful as a metaphor precisely because it incorporates aspects of the jazz aesthetic without restricting our understanding of African American texts to an exclusive focus on vernacular styles.

With this in mind, it is my double task to track the features of the collage aesthetic, as practised by Alain Locke, Jean Toomer and Zora Neale Hurston, and to tease out the aesthetic, cultural and political significance of such formal choices. Why did so many African American writers turn towards a form that could communicate synthesis and violent rupture during the Harlem Renaissance? What did it allow them to articulate? What made the collage aesthetic so important at this particular historical moment?

One element of my response to these questions involves tracing how centrally transatlantic discourses of race and nation impacted upon Harlem Renaissance writers. To some degree, the collage aesthetic was an intervention in early twentieth-century debates about American and African American identity. As Desmond King has demonstrated, the U.S. government fashioned a static and fundamentally Anglo-Saxon ideal of Americanness in the 1920s: they introduced increasingly restrictive immigration legislation and instituted programmes of Americanization through the Bureau of Education, which attempted to mould immigrants into 'preexisting Americanism' (King 2000, 106). However, the government's racial exclusivity was met with dissent among a prominent group of cultural critics. The Young America group, which included Randolph Bourne, Van Wyck Brooks, Waldo Frank and Horace Kallen, rallied to promote a distinctively American artistic tradition. Their discussions of American identity, which were published in widely disseminated periodicals, such as the *The Nation* and the *Atlantic Monthly*, as well as avant-garde publications, such as *The Seven Arts*, regarded Americanness as a fluid concept, which could be adapted and reshaped. Many of these critics made room for an element of cultural and racial diversity. In his important essay 'Democracy versus the Melting-Pot: A Study of American Nationality' (1915), for instance, Horace Kallen tackles the issue of how to create a national identity out of assorted individuals who possess very different cultural, ancestral, geographical and linguistic backgrounds. Posing the question of how to balance the need to avoid a 'cacophony' (83) with the demands of democracy, he rethinks American identity to figure the nation as an orchestra divided into sections, 'a multiplicity in a unity' (Kallen 1996, 92).

Reading the collage aesthetic in the light of these debates, it is my contention that collage form became a kind of figurative vocabulary through which African Americans could intervene in, and transform, debates about cultural and racial identity. Piecing together various cultural fragments, they contested dominant national narratives to register cultural difference and/or syncretism and interchange. It is in this sense of the production of proximities, analogies, juxtapositions, frictions and distinctions that collage became a way of expressing African American identity. In Nella Larsen's *Quicksand*, for example, a vision of African Americans as a kaleidoscope of racial types offers a visionary, if fleeting, alternative to the stereotypes of primitivism, which have been internalized by the novel's protagonist, Helga Crane:

> For the hundredth time she marveled at the gradations within this oppressed race of hers. A dozen shades slid by. There was sooty black, shiny black, taupe, mahogany, bronze, copper, gold, orange, yellow, peach, ivory, pinky white, pastry white. There was yellow hair, brown hair, black hair; straight hair, straightened hair, curly hair, crinkly hair, woolly hair. She saw black eyes in white faces, brown eyes in yellow faces, gray eyes in brown faces, blue eyes in tan faces. Africa, Europe, perhaps with a pinch of Asia, in a fantastic motley of ugliness and beauty, semi-barbaric, sophisticated, exotic, were here. But she was blind to its charm, purposely aloof and a little contemptuous, and soon her interest in the moving mosaic waned (1995, 59-60).

For Larsen, the defining feature of African Americans is diversity: she provides an inventory of hair shades, skin colour, hair texture and geographical origin and then notices the intersections between types. She figures this collage of distinct and overlapping types as a sliding spectrum of colours, a 'fantastic motley' and a 'moving mosaic', to imbue it with dynamism and fluidity. Through her use of repeated phrases, such as 'there was', Larsen separates her narrative voice from Helga's disgust and 'contemptuous' attitude towards 'this oppressed race of hers', who can only command Helga's fleeting attention because she is so desperate to assure herself that she is not 'a jungle creature' (1995, 59). By opposing Helga's internalization of white primitivism with a collage-like reality, Larsen exposes the ridiculousness of a concept of American identity that is organized through binaries of black and white, and primitivism and civility. In distinction to Helga's sense of utter isolation as a figure who is 'singularly apart' from her community (1995, 58), blinded by the propaganda of a black and white view of the world, Larsen's 'moving mosaic' represents a dynamic and inclusive, if transient, model of identity.

Larsen uses collage-like imagery to highlight the complexity of race. This directs us to an early twentieth-century discourse that attempts to describe and analyse the reality that Larsen represents figuratively, namely Boasian anthropology. My investigation of Harlem Renaissance collage forms consistently points towards an allusion to anthropological ideas. It is appropriate, then, to begin in Chapter 1 with Franz Boas's ground-breaking spatial culture concept, teasing out its significance for the Harlem Renaissance. Boas's rejection of an evolutionist, linear model of cultural development in favour of a dynamic model, 'a multiplicity of converging and diverging lines' of development (1974a, 34), opened the way for 'a newly relational, contextual, and often critical' mode of thinking about the American nation, not only in anthropology, but also in literature and cultural criticism (Hegeman 1999, 4). For Boas, cultural analysis was a way of 'unravel[ling] the processes that are going on under our eyes', a means of intervening in the concerns, tensions and complexities of his contemporary moment (1940, 285).

Boas's role in the formulation of a discourse that attempted to describe cultural and racial reality is brought to bear on my reading of aesthetic versions of collage and I expose the interleaving of collage forms with their cultural context. *The Collage Aesthetic in the Harlem Renaissance* juxtaposes these cultural and aesthetic strands in each chapter to reveal that Alain Locke, in Chapter 2, Jean Toomer, in Chapter 3, and Zora Neale Hurston, in Chapters 4 and 5, deploy collage form in order to delineate a specifically African American culture. My two chapters on Zora Neale Hurston are emblematic of this approach. As a writer and an anthropologist, who completed her training with Boas, Hurston moved between the disciplines of anthropology and fiction. Even though in separate chapters, my analysis of Hurston's anthropology and her fiction complicates any straightforward separation of cultural and aesthetic collage.

In focusing on the collage aesthetic of the Harlem Renaissance, I take literary form as my starting point, paying close attention to formal properties, such as genre, revision, intertextuality, pastiche, parody, allusion, rhetoric and mode of narration. Influential critics, such as Henry Louis Gates, Houston A. Baker and Michael North, have argued that readers do not always pay enough attention to African American work formally, as literature. North criticizes readers who 'focus rather single-mindedly on subject matter' (1994, n. p.) and Gates laments the narrow focus upon identity, which has resulted in a 'lack of sophisticated scholarly attention' to African American 'formal traditions' (1988a, xii). My approach follows these critics to reinstate the importance of form as a point of critical departure. This is not an attempt to inhabit the abstract, philosophical realm of aesthetics; rather, each chapter moves from form to subject, from collage to culture.

By beginning with form, I am able to explore levels of meaning and expression that might otherwise remain unnoticed. Attention to the honeycombed form of *The New Negro* anthology, for example, exposes contradictions that underpin Locke's efforts to document African American heterogeneity.

In contrast to critical terms referring to cultural and racial identity, such as hybridity, that are often applied to world literature without an appropriate awareness of specific cultural context, my theorization of the collage aesthetic grows from a direct engagement with the literature and art of transatlantic modernism. As I have suggested, collage was a modernist creation; hence, my method takes its cue from Harlem Renaissance artists. Likewise, the repeated movement from the aesthetic to the cultural that is so characteristic of my approach is derived from Boasian anthropology and Zora Neale Hurston's restlessly dynamic, amphibious position between fiction and anthropology. With this in mind, it is to the Harlem Renaissance engagement with Boasian anthropology that I turn next.

Chapter 1
Boasian Anthropology and the Harlem Renaissance

George Hutchinson's *The Harlem Renaissance in Black and White* (1995) was the first major study to offer a sustained analysis of the impact of Boasian anthropology upon Harlem Renaissance techniques of cultural description. Since then, a number of commentators have elaborated upon his assessment that Boas 'bequeathed a dual, even contradictory, legacy to the 1920s' (Hutchinson 1995, 76). Vernon J. Williams pays detailed attention to what he terms 'the 'Boasian paradox' – the contradiction between his philosophical egalitarian sentiments and his recontextualization of traditional European and American physical anthropology' (1996, 6). More recently, Barbara Foley has addressed the conceptual limitations of Boas's thinking on race, contending that his tendency to analyse racism in emotional or psychological terms fails to account for 'the material foundations of racism' (Foley 2003, 153). She finds comparable limitations in key Harlem Renaissance texts, not least Alain Locke's landmark anthology, *The New Negro*. Michael A. Elliott suggests an alternative point of entry to the issue, arguing that Boas's work 'crystallizes the possibilities and the dilemmas of the documentation of culture' (2002, 3). Although Boas consistently challenged the racist logic of social Darwinism, his culture concept 'suffered from a crucial limitation, the inability to account for cultural change' (Elliott 2002, xxvi).

In line with these critics, I am centrally concerned with the tensions and contradictions that made Boasian anthropology a malleable, transitional discourse. Toomer, Locke and Hurston were careful readers of Boas, and all three of them responded to his ideas in print. To date, critics have underestimated the extent to which African American writers' revision of Franz Boas's ideas allowed for a move from evolutionist determinism towards an intervention in early twentieth-century debates about American culture. Reading Toomer, Locke and Hurston alongside Boas reveals that these writers developed Boasian anthropology's mode of thinking culturally to critique American society and to envision a political future.

This chapter will pave the way for detailed exploration of Harlem Renaissance writers' substantial revision of Boasian anthropology in subsequent chapters. Building on Susan Hegeman's insightful analysis of the Boasian culture concept as a spatial pattern, I offer a detailed account of the collage sensibility that underpins Boasian cultural description. In contrast to the evolutionists who arranged cultures into 'a time series' demonstrating humanity's progress from simple to complex civilization, Boas accounted for differences in populations by identifying historical processes of contact, migration, trade and exchange as the vehicle of cultural change (Boas 1938, 177). This shift of emphasis from race to culture paved the way for a critical mode of thinking about the American nation. Indeed, for Boas, cultural analysis was a means of intervening in contemporary political debates about race and immigration.

For the most part, this collage pattern remains implicit in Boas's thinking, but it does occasionally surface in particular metaphors and images. An important early essay 'The History of Anthropology' (1904), for instance, challenges the evolutionist assumption that a developmental distance separates 'primitive' and 'civilized' cultures. Deploying uncharacteristically striking visual imagery, Boas describes culture as a tangled web composed of diverse elements:

> The grand system of the evolution of culture, that is valid for all humanity, is losing much of its plausibility. In place of a simple line of evolution there appears a multiplicity of converging and diverging lines which it is difficult to bring under one system. Instead of uniformity, the striking feature seems to be diversity (Boas 1974a, 34).

This is a moment when the collage-like pattern that lies underneath Boas's reorganization of the culture concept comes into view. Countering prevailing evolutionist conceptions of cultural development as a single line of progress, he achieves what Susan Hegeman has called 'a *spatial* reorganization of human differences' (1999, 32). What emerges is a complex understanding of 'converging and diverging lines' of development, which highlights independent development of cultural traits *and* diffusion. With Boas's acknowledgement that all cultures are composites of foreign and native elements comes an abandonment of the evolutionist cultural time series.

The pertinence of this collage pattern to Boas's anthropological contribution becomes clearer later in the essay. Adding colour and animation to his usually spartan, if not plodding, prose, he employs a striking visual image that challenges the 'ill-concealed teleological tinge' of evolutionism:

> The grand picture of nature in which for the first time the universe appears as a unit of ever-changing form and color, each momentary aspect being determined by the past moment and determining the coming changes, is still obscured by a subjective element, emotional in its sources, which leads us to abscribe the highest value to that which is near and dear to us (Boas 1974a, 26).

Analysis of the specifics of cultural interchange and independent development lays bare realities obscured in evolutionist accounts of cultural development. '[F]or the first time' culture is exposed as a mobile collage with shifting forms, colours and parts, a kaleidoscope of fluctuating shapes that are reconfigured according to the needs of a particular historical moment. In a move that is perhaps analogous to interpreting reconstructed fragments in a collage, anthropologists can only begin to understand a culture's dynamic form by recognizing it as a hodge-podge of past and present, old and new, foreign and familiar. Rather than smoothing over such complexity in a sweeping 'subjective' interpretation, Boas fixes attention upon the various pieces that comprise each culture to stress dynamism and multiplicity.

Boas's emphasis upon cultural complexity, especially his insistence upon difficulties that prevent anthropologists from arriving at certainties about individual cultures, has led Arnold Krupat to classify his work, with its investment in the 'ironic mode', as modernist in character (Krupat 1992, 88-9). In keeping with Krupat's theory, Boasian anthropology is riddled with hesitation; it is certainly not an objective science that can provide a static, reliable 'picture' of organic cultural wholes. Instead, scientists should map complex internal relationships since cultures are an accretion of elements from their specific past, 'determined by the past moment and determining the coming changes'. What Boas registers is an historical process of collaging that renders cultures dynamic and unstable, always 'subject to change and drift' (Stocking 1974, 8). It is partly for this reason that cultures cannot be neatly arranged into a hierarchy that prizes 'that which is near and dear to us'.

In his images of tangled 'lines' and 'ever-changing form[s]', Boas reproduces the latent collage pattern that animates his culture concept. Admittedly, his meticulous investigations of language, racial mixing and cultural development seem to be a long way from the creative energy generated by Toomer's orchestration of jarring forms or Hurston's bold experimentation with the vernacular. Nevertheless, it is the task of this chapter to interpret the collage sensibility in Boasian anthropology, a discussion that will establish the coordinates for my analysis of the Harlem Renaissance collage aesthetic throughout the book.

Language: 'diverse sources ... gradually worked into a single unit'

The dynamic interplay between the Harlem Renaissance and Boasian anthropology has provoked recent research. Even so, it is still quite rare to find sustained analysis of Boas's writing in the pages of critical studies of the New Negro movement. The two best accounts of African American engagements with Boas, George Hutchinson's *The Harlem Renaissance in Black and White* (1995) and Barbara Foley's *Spectres of 1919: Class and Nation in the Making of the New Negro* (2003), are broadly synoptic, offering little in the way of sustained textual analysis. Since Boas's writing lacks the energy and verve that abounds in early twentieth-century literature, it is hardly surprising that literary critics have neglected such detailed reading. Still, a closer look at Boas's work proves helpful in understanding the possibilities and limitations of the Boasian culture concept, a formulation that was to undergo substantial revision in the hands of African American writers like Hurston and Toomer. To this end, I now turn to Boas's discussions of language and racial mixing.

For Boas, the study of language carried particular significance. In his introduction to the *Handbook of American Indian Languages* (1911), he identifies a primary difference between studying language and other ethnological phenomena: 'linguistic classifications never rise into consciousness, while … other ethnological phenomena … often rise into consciousness, and thus give rise to secondary reasoning and to re-interpretations' (1966, 63). Such statements contrast 'the unconscious character of linguistic phenomena' with secondary explanations and rationalizations that cluster around cultural customs and rituals (1966, 63). To take only his most famous example, the modern European practice of putting the fork in one's mouth, but not the knife, is rationalized as a way to avoid cutting one's lips and tongue, even though this justification is hardly logical (1966, 65). For Boas, investigation of linguistic development promised a virtually unobstructed view into the inner workings of culture; he believed that such analysis would remain unclouded by existing interpretations and his own preconceptions.

At its core, Boas's investigation of language development is governed by a sustained questioning of evolutionist approaches that held sway in early twentieth-century America. Boas's pronouncements on language declared opposition to J.W. Powell's influential evolutionist study 'Indian Linguistic Families of America North of Mexico' (1891), which identified 58 American Indian languages using brief vocabularies to define relationships. In his major works on language – *Handbook of American Indian Languages* (1911), 'The Classification of American Languages' (1920) and his introduction to the *International Journal of American Linguistics* (1917) – Boas maintains this challenge to the definition of distinct linguistic families, not least because the haphazard results of cultural contact mean that languages are 'alike in some features' but not in others (1938, 156).

Attention to the complexity of linguistic development disputes Powell's theory that there are 'distinct languages', which can be categorized into 'linguistic families' (1966, 54). Boas tackles this issue directly in a section of his introduction to the *Handbook* entitled 'Uncertainty of Definition of Linguistic Families' (1966, 54). When anthropologists notice similarities between languages, Boas contends that there is often insufficient evidence 'to prove [a] genetic relationship' (1966, 54). Even when a relationship can be proved by historical evidence, the notion of parent languages and offspring languages is complicated by the presence of 'independent elements', which may be the result of either new developments in the dialect or foreign influence (1966, 54). In some cases, 'new tendencies and foreign influences', which deviate from the 'ancestral language', may become so prominent that a new language can no longer be categorized as 'a branch of the older family' (1966, 54).

Analysis of such linguistic grafting reveals language to be a patchwork of elements from the ancestral language, foreign influences and new developments. In contrast to Powell, Boas describes a dynamic process whereby the exact relationship between foreign elements and the native culture remains imperceptible without detailed historical knowledge. In fact, Boas isolates three distinct stages to acculturation: 'there is a gradation beginning with a slight amount of borrowing and extending through more intensive intermingling, to a complete change of language' (Boas 1940, 225). Foreign elements are gradually absorbed into the existing linguistic structure until it becomes impossible to isolate either the original language or imported foreign elements.

This nuanced account of intercultural exchange, which makes room for cultural synthesis *and* jarring discordance, also informs Boas's discussion of linguistic encounter between western cultures and what he calls primitive cultures. In his highly influential essay 'On Alternating Sounds' (1889), he contests prevailing theories about language's evolutionary development from the apparently haphazard complexity of 'primitive' languages to the simplicity of English, with its absence of inflection. According to anthropologists such as Daniel G. Brinton and Powell, the 'alternating sounds' or apparently random variations in primitive languages indicated the low developmental stage of these cultures.

Boas turns such analysis on its head by addressing the cultural biases that limit participant observation. Of course, unconsciously transmitted elements determine the behaviour of anthropologists as well as the peoples they analyse. To this end, Boas's careful study of anthropologists' fieldnotes demonstrates that their transcriptions of native languages 'bear evidence of the phonetics of their own languages. This can be explained only by the fact that each apperceives the unknown sounds by the means of the sounds of his own language' (Boas 1974d, 76). Hence, investigation of the scientist's position in relation to his or her material becomes the platform for a sophisticated account of cultural contact. Inevitably, anthropologists interpret the unfamiliar sounds of American Indian languages through the structures and patterns of their native tongue. Consequently, inconsistencies and misspellings in anthropologists' notebooks are not evidence of primitivism, but 'are in reality alternating apperceptions of one and the same sound', created by the scholar's attempt to collate sounds in accordance with their own phonetic system (Boas 1974d, 76).

Boas's use of the word 'apperception' in connection with this phenomenon links his insights to psychologists such as Johann Friedrich Herbart, who regarded 'apperception' as the process whereby a new mental representation entered consciousness and was assimilated to familiar representations (Mackert 1994, 359). In other words, anthropologists, for Boas, are trapped within the bounds of their own culture, even if this perspective can shift in accordance with a growing familiarity with the language observed.

Both models of linguistic development that Boas challenges – 'alternating sounds' and 'linguistic families' – are Darwinian in implication, clinging as they do to the idea that languages can be traced back to a single point of origin. In 'The Classification of American Languages' (1920), he articulates an alternative theory of linguistic development, a theory that depicts culture as a spatial pattern:

> If these observations regarding the influence of acculturation upon language should be correct, then the whole history of American languages must not be treated on the assumption that all languages which show similarities must

be considered as branches of the same linguistic family. We should rather find a phenomenon which is parallel to the features characteristic of other ethnological phenomena – namely, a development from diverse sources which are gradually worked into a single cultural unit. We should have to reckon with the tendency of languages to absorb so many foreign traits that we can no longer speak of a single origin, and that it would be arbitrary whether we associate a language with one or the other of the contributing stocks (Boas 1940, 217).

Taking issue with the evolutionist model of identifiable and separate 'stocks', Boas contends that languages are radically transformed by contact with other linguistic structures. Highlighting a continuing process of cultural exchange and assimilation upsets any connotation of 'origin' in the word 'stock'. Instead, linguistic borrowing is the norm; various languages exist in a dynamic web of interdependence because they share 'contributing stocks'.

As in his preface to the first volume of the *Handbook* where he promises to reveal 'the essential psychological characteristics of American languages' and shed light on 'the probable historical development of grammatical forms' of 'various "linguistic stocks"', Boas begins to depart from the Darwinian conception of stock as root, origin or radical to a sense that empties it of its hierarchical, originating meaning (Bunzl 1996, 66). In this case, the existence of 'contributing stocks' exposes progressive models of founding origins and 'linguistic families' as 'arbitrary' theoretical extrapolations. Furthermore, Boas's description of linguistic development as a process of collaging whereby 'diverse sources … are gradually worked into a single cultural unit' is a pattern for, and a paradigm of, other ethnological phenomena. In other words, the Boasian culture concept announces a move away from an evolutionist idea of race as origin towards a much more complex understanding of historical processes. Even so, this remains a transitional discourse, tinged with possibility. In spite of his recognition that cultures are a combination of disparate elements, Boas still deploys technical vocabulary derived from physical anthropology.

Racial Mixing

If his discussion of language development challenges the classification of a rigid 'genealogical scheme', Boas's investigation of miscegenation is characterized by a similar attempt to complicate racial typology (1940, 225). The stigmatization of racial mixing, of course, was foundational to anthropology. During the Civil War, surgeons such as Sanford B. Hunt and Benjamin A. Gould catalogued soldiers' body measurements, interpreting their data in such a way as to assert that racial mixing led to physical debility and sterility. Comparable arguments were articulated by subsequent 'race scientists', from Josiah Nott, in his scientific justification of slavery, and Frederick L. Hoffman, to Boas's contemporaries Nathaniel Southgate

Shaler and Charles Davenport (Mencke 1979, 37-56).[1] Anthropometry became the method of choice for scientists who sought to establish fundamental differences between races. To take only the most famous example, Josiah Nott and George Gliddon's *Types of Mankind* (1854), which ran to ten editions by 1900, charted species variation to construct a hierarchical pyramid of the races (Baker 1998, 15). By the time Boas wrote his 'Report on the Anthropometric Investigation of the Population of the United States' in 1922, he could note that the assertion of 'mulatto' inferiority was an 'ever-repeated claim' (1940, 51).

Boas played a crucial role in challenging such claims as a product of 'emotional clamor' (261), 'sensational formulations' (1938, 265) and 'common saying[s]' rather than scientific fact (1921, 390). Much of his work on racial mixing is underpinned by an anti-racist agenda to counter ill-informed prejudice and 'much-read propaganda' with biological and historical facts (1925, 89). To this end, Boas's populist works, such as *The Mind of Primitive Man* (1938) and *Anthropology and Modern Life* (1929), and his essays, 'What is a Race?' in *The Nation* (1925), 'The Problem of the American Negro' in *The Yale Review* (1921) and 'The Real Race Problem' in *The Crisis* (1910), reiterate the message that racial mixing was forging biological connections between 'the component elements of our people', namely African Americans, Anglo-Americans, American Indians, Asians and various European immigrants (1938, 260).

Furthermore, Boas refutes the idea 'that the phenomenon of mixture presented in the United States is unique' (1938, 262). He marshals extensive historical evidence to prove that racial mixing has been a constant presence in human civilization, including ancient Greece and Rome, and modern European countries, such as Spain, England and Italy. In *The Mind of Primitive Man*, for example, he traces Spanish ancestry, listing a tangled lineage that includes Venetian, Carthaginian, Roman, Visgoth, Vandal, Jewish, Arabic and Moorish influences (1938, 256-60). Through his broad cultural appeal in widely disseminated journals and public speeches, Boas embarked on a mission to educate the American public about the centrality of racial crossing to human development.

In short, Boas accumulates a wealth of statistical data that identifies racial mixing as a constant feature of human civilization. Rather than deploying physical anthropology to confirm a fixed racial hierarchy, such statistics throw rigid racial categorization into doubt. Attention to historical processes of contact, migration, trade and exchange enables him to challenge any conception of racial purity or unity of descent. Take, for instance, a lecture Boas delivered in 1895 to a largely non-academic audience at the U.S. National Museum. Speaking of 'the history of the peopling of the earth', he contends that a 'slow mixture of blood through intermarriage has taken place constantly' as a consequence of migration and 'fluctuating' populations (Liss 1995, 126). Since populations are dynamic and

---

[1]   In *The Mind of Primitive Man*, Boas captures the feverish tone of these discussions by quoting Lothrop Stoddard: 'the valuable specializations of both breeds cancel out and the mixed offspring tends strongly to revert to generalized mediocrity' (1938, 27).

always in motion, it is inevitable that 'ethnical types ... merge into each other through a long series of intermediate forms' (Liss 1995, 126).

Such statements capture the ambivalence that characterizes Boas's discussions of racial mixing. His conceptualization of race remains transitional, caught between deterministic assumptions on the one hand, and a more complex account of social and environmental factors on the other.

Boas's historicist account of the 'variability in each race' goes some way in shifting the focus of physical anthropology away from comparison of distinct types towards analysis of racial complexity (1921, 385). In his later writings, he follows these ideas to their logical conclusion, identifying race as a cultural construct, a crucial recognition in the context of Nordicism. Boas's important essay 'The Problem of the American Negro' (1921) scuttles the question of common descent; instead, he identifies race as a construct, a political concept born of 'the consciousness of the outsider' and 'prejudice' towards underprivileged social groups (1921, 392). Given this, Boas regarded it as his task as a scientist to illustrate 'that the concern that is felt by many in regard to the continuance of racial purity of our nation is to a great extent imaginary' (1938, 264).

At the same time, Boas's thinking about race does not come without limitations. For one thing, he never steps beyond the empirical limits established by physical anthropology. To many, Boas's unswerving commitment to physical anthropology introduces into his thinking a 'schism between the values of cultural determinism and the values of racial determinism, a direct product of his methodological rigor' (Williams 1996, 10). In the first edition of *The Mind of Primitive Man*, for example, he holds back from completely ruling out a correlation between brain weight and intelligence because he had yet to gather a full data set. As many readers have noted, such tentativeness seems unnecessarily cautious given Boas's own acknowledgement that his contemporary scientists had been 'influenced too often by racial, national and class prejudice' (1938, 19).[2]

More problematic is Boas's contention that the 'race problem' could be solved by 'the progressive absorption of blacks and foreign immigrant groups into a uniform American culture' (Lorini 1999, 88). In *Anthropology and Modern Life* (1929) and his essays, 'The Real Race Problem' (1910) and 'The Problem of the American Negro' (1921), Boas explicitly advocates racial assimilation. Prejudice against 'outsiders' was so ingrained, he claimed, that 'the negro problem will not disappear in America until the negro blood has been so much diluted that it will no longer be recognized just as anti-Semitism will not disappear until the last vestige of the Jew as a Jew has disappeared' (Boas 1921, 395). In promoting a 'mongrel' nation, he counters the racial chauvinism of race scientists like Madison Grant and Lothrop Stoddard and of the newly invigorated Ku Klux Klan, who wanted to build 'an army of Protestant Americans' (MacLean 1994, 11). As Susan Hegeman explains, 'Boas was advocating not so much assimilation as the antiracist point

---

[2]   See Vernon J. Williams (1996, 10) and Michael A. Elliott (2002, 16-17, 192-3).

that assimilation was *possible* within the context of racial diversity' (Hegeman 1999, 49).

Even so, it is difficult to overlook the fact that Boas's contention that racial amalgamation would create 'more and more fruitful co-operation' between the races (1910, 25) is 'ultimately conditioned by his interests as a white American of European ancestry' (Kadlec 2000a, 45). His pro-amalgamation stance does unsettle a biracial view of America, but it also necessitates erasure or 'dilution' of racial and cultural distinctiveness. He claims that '[t]he less Negro society represents a party with its own aims and its own interest distinct from those of the members of the white race, the more satisfactory will be the relation between the races' (1910, 25). In the final analysis, Boas's conclusions sideline political and social realities that made a celebration of African American cultural distinctiveness such a significant gesture for so many Harlem Renaissance writers.

The Significance of Boas's Culture Pattern

In Boas's anthropology, meticulous study of connections between apparently distinct races, languages and cultures becomes the platform for a theory of cultural development, in which 'diverse sources ... are gradually worked into a single cultural unit' (1940, 217). It is to the significance of this collage-like pattern that I now turn.

As Boas notes in 'The Methods of Ethnology' (1920), evolutionist anthropology 'held almost complete sway' in the second half of the nineteenth century and 'investigators like Spencer, Morgan, Tylor, Lubbock, to mention only a few, were under the spell of the idea of a general, uniform evolution of culture in which all parts of mankind participated' (1940, 281). Working with the hypothesis that 'the same cultural features must always have developed from the same, single causes' (184), these scientists arranged cultures into 'a time series' that demonstrated humanity's progress from simple to complex civilization (Boas 1938, 177). Furthermore, evolutionists assumed that 'anatomical form, language, and culture are all closely associated, and ... each subdivision of mankind is characterized by a certain bodily form, a certain culture, and a certain language, which can never become separated' (Boas 1966, 3).

Boas's spatial culture concept mounts an attack upon the dominance of such thinking. One element of this challenge involved subjecting evolutionist ideas to rigorous historical analysis, a quality lacking from influential studies such as E.B. Tylor's *Primitive Culture* (1871). To this end, *The Mind of Primitive Man* assembles evidence to counter 'a systematic, all-embracing application of a theory of evolution of culture' (1938, 181). Boas describes instances of 'convergent evolution' when diverse customs and beliefs converge towards similar forms (185); he argues that classification of cultures into a sequence of developmental stages is hampered by 'the frequent lack of comparability of the data' (186); and the principle of a single line of evolution is undermined by 'development of customs in divergent directions' (1938, 189).

Much valuable work has been done to establish Boas's credentials as an opponent to evolutionist thinking, especially in relation to his 'spatial articulation of the culture concept' (Hegeman 1999, 12). What follows synthesizes these insights with close analysis of a particular essay, 'The Mythologies of the Indians' (1905), in order to provide a clearer sense of the significance of the Boasian culture concept.

To begin then with a brief description of Boas's essay. 'The Mythologies of the Indians' is a narrowly focused interpretation of a specific Tlingit folktale about Alexander Baranoff, manager of the Siberian Trading Company at the turn of the eighteenth century.[3] In many respects, Boas's reading is exemplary of his approach to cultural analysis. What appears to be a timeless and universal folktale is, in fact, a tight weave of diverse cultural elements. Although it begins with a realistic account of Nanak's (as the Tlingits called Baranoff) military adventures, it also bears the shaping influence of Tlingit mythology. When Nanak sails to a place where 'the water of the ocean rushes during the ebb-tide in a terrible whirlpool down into the under-world' (138), for instance, the narrative falls into a pattern derived from what Boas calls the 'common stock of Indian folk-lore' (Boas 1974f, 139). Other noteworthy narrative components, including the visit to an island where women are married to logs, are drawn from neighbouring cultural traditions.

By picking apart the tale and identifying sources, Boas undermines any conception of original (new and not derivative) or originary (native) expression: the tale, he tells us, is 'almost entirely a combination of well-known elements' and '[t]here is very little in it that is original invention' (Boas 1974f, 140). At the same time, he clings to the assumption that individual cultures are governed by a distinctive spiritual identity or 'genius'. Boas's debt to Johann Gottfried Herder is evident when he explains, in a summary of his fieldwork for the British Association from 1888 to 1897, that foreign elements are 'adapted and changed in form according to the genius of the people who borrowed it' (Boas 1974e, 96). In accordance with Herder's Romantic concept of the *Volksgeist*, particular cultural forms and important social institutions are expressions of a unitary force, usually referred to as the soul, mind or spirit of a people (Guibernau 1999, 23).

Given these complex factors, 'it becomes difficult to decide where borrowing must be assumed as a cause of sameness of myths, and where other causes may have been at work' (Boas 1974f, 144). As Marc Manganaro has astutely observed, Boas was 'content to undertheorize' the relationship between the 'genius of a people'

---

[3]		Baranoff laid the foundations for Russian colonization of the Americas. In 1801, he returned to Russia, leaving a small garrison in charge of his fort. After a period of quiet, the Tlingits attacked the fort and killed its Russian occupants. When he heard of these events, Baranoff returned to America to launch an attack on the Tlingits. Following a long struggle, in which Baranoff was wounded, the Tlingits made their escape in the night and Baranoff regained control (Boas 1974f, 135-6).

and processes of cultural transmission; consequently, diverse elements remain suspended in creative, unpredictable play (Manganaro 2002, 31). Nevertheless, a complex theory of development is implicit here, which challenges evolutionist efforts to tell the complete developmental story through a narrative sequence of cultural stages shared by all human cultures. Attending to 'differentiation' resulting from the interaction of a unique culture with 'neighboring cultural centers' *and* gradual processes of assimilation, or 'leveling down' of differences (Boas 1940, 286), Boas presents '"culture" as a fluidly processual alternative to more static and essentializing conceptions of group identity' (Kadlec 2000a, 37).

The Politics of Collage

There is undoubtedly a political implication to Boas's collage-like culture concept. Of prime importance is his criticism of an evolutionist approach underpinned by the logic that 'our modern Western European civilization represents the highest cultural development towards which all other more primitive cultural types tend' (Boas 1940, 282). Boas identifies his work as an alternative to the 'ill-concealed teleological tinge' of evolutionist ethnography, which described development from 'simple forms to more complex forms' as progress 'from the less valuable to the more valuable' (Boas 1974a, 26).

One element of Boas's critique of evolutionist cultural description is that its rhetoric of observation, privileging as it does the detached, omniscient anthropologist, renders primitive cultures 'static' (Boas 1938, 177). Not only that, but such methods have been 'selected for the purpose of obtaining a consistent picture of cultural development' (Boas 1940, 282). An evolutionist approach generated representations of non-European cultures that fixed them in what Johannes Fabian has termed the 'ethnographic present' (1983, 80). The temporal logic of evolutionist anthropology distanced 'those who are observed from the Time of the observer', without making room for the vital energy of everyday practices (1983, 25).

Evolutionist ethnography, in Fabian's discussion, is informed by a politics of time that runs the risk of reducing anthropological subjects to the status of scientific specimens. Classification of separate cultures rests upon an idea of 'evolutionary Time'; past and living cultures become 'irrevocably placed on a temporal slope, a stream of Time – some upstream, others downstream' (1983, 17). This meant that "savage" and "tribal" cultures could be categorized as outside or before history, fixed in their difference. Such modes of interpretation trapped primitive culture in the past: these cultures provoked scientific interest precisely because they could explain the origins of modern western civilization. Consequently, synchronic temporality served to reinforce a hierarchy that prized the anthropologist's 'present' culture above the cultures under scrutiny. What emerges is a rhetoric that endorses the anthropologist's objectifying, ordering gaze. Anthropologists, the logic goes, are capable of transcending or suspending their culture while their subjects remain irredeemably static, locked within particular cultural parameters.

In his forceful critique of this tendency to view cultures as 'static phenomena' (Boas 1940, 282), Boas could certainly be accused of downplaying his own part in 'reorient[ing] anthropology from *diachronic* (and universal) history to *synchronic* (and culturally specific) description and analysis' (Elliott 2002, 20). Faced with page after page of transcribed folktales, it is difficult to disagree with Michael A. Elliott's assessment that 'Boas leaves us with texts that portray culture as a synchronic, static entity' (Elliott 2002, 22). Although Boas theorized an interpretive framework that emphasizes the shaping influence of historical processes, his 'division and arrangement of the texts [in his ethnographies] asserts their status as descriptive acts that produce a taxonomy of tribal life' (Elliott 2002, 22).

Yet, it seems to me that Elliott goes too far when he claims that '[t]he sheer difficulty of comprehending a single cultural system precludes, in turn, the Boasian anthropologist from discerning how cultures *change*' (Elliott 2002, 25). At the very least, Boas's spatial theory of cultural development, with its emphasis upon points of contact between cultures, is governed by an awareness of the fluidity of cultural traits. Indeed, Boas claims that 'primitive society loses the appearance of absolute stability which is conveyed to the student who sees a certain people only at a certain given time' when analysed through the lens of his broadly historicist method (1940, 284).

What I am calling Boas's collage sensibility promised new ways of thinking about cultural difference. Indeed, Susan Hegeman has argued that Boas's most important gesture was his 'critique of progressivist visions of human difference', which opened the way for a 'spatial articulation of the culture concept' in investigations of American identity by modernists such as Waldo Frank, W.E.B. Du Bois, Randolph Bourne and Horace Kallen (Hegeman 1999, 12). Above all, Harlem Renaissance writers drew inspiration from Boas's account of cultural analysis as a means through which to grapple with contemporary issues. His synchronic or spatial approach catches culture in its dynamics:

> In short then, the method which we try to develop is based on a study of the dynamic changes in society that may be observed at the present time. We refrain from the attempt to solve the fundamental problem of the general development of civilization until we have been able to unravel the processes that are going on under our eyes (Boas 1940, 285).

Such statements may be at odds with the ahistorical quality of Boas's own ethnographies, but these theoretical pronouncements introduce a logic and lexicon of critique into anthropological discourse. This crucial shift towards using anthropology to intervene in issues facing contemporary American society is a distinguishing feature of Boasian anthropology. Rather than addressing 'the fundamental problem' of global cultural development, investigation of 'dynamic changes' is primarily a critical gesture that has implications for the present.

With this move, anthropology is re-imagined as a method of critique; scientists can deploy what Zora Neale Hurston called 'the spy-glass of Anthropology' to 'unravel' contemporary problems (Hurston 1990a, 1). A comparable gesture underpins Boas's 1911 review of Fritz Graebner's *Methode der Ethnologie* when he contends that anthropologists should turn their attention away from 'purely mechanical concepts of transmission' towards 'the innumerable cases of transmission that happen under our very eyes and try to understand how transmission is brought about' (Boas 1940, 302). In short, such analysis becomes a mode of interpretation that facilitates examination of uncomfortable processes that are 'going on under our eyes'. While Boas still considered himself primarily as a social scientist, his account of anthropological description as political gesture came to fruition in Harlem Renaissance writing that unsettled established disciplinary boundaries between anthropology and fiction.

Although his effectiveness as a public activist was, to some degree, hobbled by an unswerving commitment to 'methodological rigor' (Williams 1996, 10), Boas believed that he 'could use the authority of objective scientific procedure to dispel deep-seated beliefs about the nature of biologically inherited race' (Elliott 2002, 17). Boas's report for the U.S. Immigration Commission in 1911, which provided substantial anthropometric data to undermine Nativist efforts to curb immigration, is only the best-known example of such endeavours.[4] More broadly, Boas held that empirical anthropological data could 'guide us in many of our policies' (1929, 235).

Any account of Boas's vision of a political role for anthropology must begin with his sustained criticism of a Nativist nationalism founded upon myths of racial purity.[5] In opposition to what he called the 'Nordic nonsense' of white supremacists like Madison Grant and Lothrop Stoddard (Foley 2003, 154), Boas demonstrated that '[t]he earlier concept of nationality has been given a new meaning by identifying nationality with racial unity and by assuming that national characteristics are due to racial descent' (1938, 253). Not only that, but he documents the social and political consequences of such ideas. In particular, he mentions a number of laws banning miscegenation, laws based upon 'assumption[s]' and 'fears ... of a modification or deterioration of national character on account of the influx of new types into the population of our country' (1929, 18-19). Summing up 'the general character of the growth of this movement', Boas indicted the extremism, racism and dogmatism of Madison Grant's 'much-read propaganda' (1925, 89).

Boas's key work, *The Mind of Primitive Man*, gathers historical examples of racial mixing from across the globe in order to expose how the contention that 'national characteristics are due to racial descent' is a damaging ideological construct, based upon prejudice rather than scientific fact (1938, 253). Throughout his career, he sought to challenge 'imperialistic nationalism' (1919b, 236)

---

[4]   See Michael A. Elliott (2002, 17).

[5]   See Foley (2003, 122-47) for an illuminating discussion of the widespread appeal of Nordicism, which tended to yoke Americanism with racial purity.

by drawing attention to the gap between dangerous myths of racial purity and scientific fact. Making clear his opposition to the 'imperialistic tendencies' of modern nationalism (236), Boas fleshed out an alternative concept of 'nationality', which celebrated the mixing of 'distinct racial elements' (232) as a challenge to 'unwholesome uniformity of thought' (1919b, 237).

In attending to the realities of racial mixing, Boas uses anthropological cultural description to fix the nation's gaze on uneasy realities that do not chime with the myths that the nation tells itself about democracy. To borrow a phrase from David Richards, anthropology challenges controlling ideologies by 'butchering sacred cows and remaking our culture afresh' (1994, 189). Boas's empirical study of miscegenation launches an attack upon essentialist notions of race, not least because 'the well-being of so many millions of citizens of our country' is at stake (1940, 51). Balanced analysis of the 'facts' of racial mixture would, Boas hoped, 'clear up these problems, which are of vital importance for the future of our nation' (1974h, 330). Moreover, Boas does not shy away from exposing scientific complicity in perpetuating racist ideologies: 'I think we have reason to be ashamed to confess that the scientific study of these questions has never received the support either of our government or of any of our great scientific institutions' (1938, 271). Such embarrassment is indicative of anthropology's radical potential: scientific analysis here becomes a way of facing shameful inequalities maintained by the state and rich scientific establishments.

Boas's use of the words 'citizen' and 'nation' in connection with scientific research reveals a utopian strain in his thinking; science could, he suggests, help America live up to its democratic ideals. With regard to African Americans, these ideas reach fruition in his preface to Mary White Ovington's sociological study of African Americans in New York, *Half a Man: The Status of the Negro in New York* (1911). Scientific attention to social and economic realities could, he tells us, gradually erode fundamental inequalities between diverse ethnic groups: '[e]very demonstration of the inequality of opportunity will … help to dissipate prejudices that prevent the best possible development of a large number of our citizens' (1911, viii). With a nod to America's mythic status as a land of opportunity, Boas trains his gaze upon his fellow 'citizens', a gesture that alters the focus of anthropological analysis from geographically distant cultures to America's 'melting pot'.

On a separate front, Boas countered racist views by educating Americans about African cultural achievements. Boas's best-known effort of this kind was his commencement address at Atlanta University in 1906, given in response to an invitation from W.E.B. Du Bois, which documented the achievements of African civilizations. Challenging the widely-held belief that 'slavery as an institution had the beneficial effect of turning savage Africans into disciplined laborers' (Lorini 1999, 86), Boas aimed to persuade his audience that there were few obstacles to stop them becoming 'useful citizens' (Boas 1974g, 314). After all, he said, 'the evidence of African ethnology is such that it should inspire you with the hope of leading your race from achievement to achievement' (Boas 1974g, 312). Arming African Americans with anthropological facts, 'he manifested an explicit will to give African-American students a usable past with which to fight against racism' (Lorini 1999, 86).

Given the prevalence of evolutionist accounts that associated Africa with savagery and barbarity, it comes as no surprise that Boas's speech had a galvanizing effect upon African American intellectuals. In his autobiography *Black Folk Then and Now* (1939), for instance, Du Bois recalled the speech as a paradigm-shifting moment:

> Franz Boas came to Atlanta University where I was teaching history in 1906 and said to a graduating class: You need not be ashamed of your African past; and then he recounted the history of black kingdoms south of the Sahara for a thousand years. I was too astonished to speak. All of this I had never heard and I came then and afterwards to realize how the silence and neglect of science can let truth utterly disappear or even be unconsciously distorted (Hutchinson 1995, 63).

Ultimately, Boas's reassessment of African history was written with an eye to the present: he looks to the past in order to improve race relations in his contemporary America. This gesture of critique was to prove Boas's most enduring legacy. His interventions in broader debates about collective American identity among cultural critics, race scientists and politicians created a discourse tinged with possibility, which moved beyond a biracial account of race relations. As Hegeman has convincingly argued, Boas developed 'a newly relational, contextual, and often critical' way of thinking about American identity (1999, 4).

In this context, it is significant that Boas's best-known book, *The Mind of Primitive Man*, culminates with a cosmopolitan vision, which celebrates racial and cultural difference:

> Freedom of judgment can be attained only when we learn to estimate an individual according to his own ability and character. Then we shall find, if we were to select the best of mankind, that all races and all nationalities would be represented. Then we shall treasure and cultivate the variety of forms that human thought and activity has taken, and abhor, as leading to complete stagnation, all attempts to impress one pattern of thought upon whole nations or even upon the whole world (Boas 1938, 272).

Challenging the identification of 'nationality with racial unity' (Boas 1938, 253), Boas articulates an alternative concept of identity, founded upon diversity. Through the image of a showcase of various racial types, Boas insists that '[t]he cultures of different groups should be studied synchronously, as instances of different, rather than hierarchical, human activities' (Foley 2003, 149). Furthermore, intercultural contact galvanizes new developments: cross-cultural exchange promises to stave off 'stagnation'. Even so, it is difficult to miss the irony that Boas's celebration of cultural 'variety', which he associates with 'freedom' from prejudice, reproduces a method of cultural description that produces a taxonomy of racial types. By casting himself in the role of curator to a museum crammed with racial and national types, he introduces a static racial typology, and a quality of stillness, which is at odds with his broader argument about cultural dynamism.

Such tensions mark out Boasian anthropology as a transitional discourse, poised between racial determinism and cosmopolitanism. For Karen Jacobs, it is 'Boas's retention of the cultural category of the primitive' that complicates his anti-racist credentials (2001, 117). In a perceptive reading of *The Mind of Primitive Man*, she identifies 'a wealth of criteria' that uphold the distinction between primitive and civilized, data that contradicts Boas's explicit attack upon these categories as ideological constructs (Jacobs 2001, 117). In a similar vein, Barbara Foley and Julia E. Liss have addressed the conceptual limitations of Boas's thinking on race. According to Liss, his tendency to analyse racism in emotional or psychological terms, 'as a survival of a primitive tendency of hatred of the stranger', means that he never gets to grips with ideological structures that underpin racism (Liss 1998, 148). More pertinent to this book is Foley's sharp analysis of the tensions that animate Boas's thinking on the relationship between race and culture: 'his Herderian definition of culture as folk genius implied an essentialist notion of group collectivity that threatened to let in through the ontological back door the linkage of culture with race that had been ushered out the epistemological front door' (2003, 156).

Collage Patterns in Subsequent Anthropology

Although Boas paved the way for a newly politicized method of anthropology, it was only in others' hands that his gesture of cultural critique reached full form. George Stocking is right on the mark when he describes Boas's anthropology as a 'spare discipline', which opened up interpretive possibilities without drawing out their implications (1974, 15). Much of Boas's work on race and racism, for instance, is broadly theoretical; he never really gets to grips with the specifics of American race relations. It was, in fact, Boas's students who gave full expression to the political possibilities latent in a spatial culture concept. Ruth Benedict's *Patterns of Culture* (1935) and Margaret Mead's *Coming of Age in Samoa* (1928), for instance, manipulate 'cultural estrangement for the purposes of social critique' (Hegeman 1999, 46).

It is not hard to find collage-like culture patterns in ethnographies by Boas's students. Some of them even pursue an analogy with collage as they strain to capture complex processes of cultural development on the page. Consequently, new metaphors that describe a cultural hybridity in which disparate sources retain their material heterogeneity supersede Boas's two-dimensional account of 'diverging and converging lines' of development (Boas 1974a, 34). When she speaks of the 'rags and tatters of cultures', Ruth Benedict gives shape to a configurational theory that emphasizes complexity and integration (Babcock 1992, 61). Robert

Lowie's account of 'that planless hodge-podge, that thing of shreds and patches' in *Primitive Society* (1921) goes further: his theory of random cultural accretion represents a significant departure from Boas's investment in the Herderian concept of a *Volksgeist* (Lowie 1949, 428). Furthermore, such emphasis upon the diverse textures that animate individual cultures developed in tandem with a renewed stress upon anthropologists' role as 'cultural critics who brought anthropology to bear on the political and social controversies of their time' (Handler 1990, 253).

Nowhere is this connection more apparent than in Edward Sapir's influential essay 'Culture, Genuine and Spurious', which was first published in *The Dial* in 1919. Generally speaking, Sapir's article has been discussed with reference to a broader anthropological debate about the relationship between community and individual. As Mark Whalan puts it, Sapir 'proposed a dialectic, with individuals capable of shaping and developing the "genuine" culture, just as that culture worked to shape the tastes, views, and aesthetics of individuals' (Whalan 2007, 135). It is less often remembered that Sapir's formulation of culture as a 'mosaic', in which cultural fragments harmonize into a cohesive whole, enables him to extend Boas's gesture of cultural critique (Sapir 1963, 326). Making a qualitative distinction between 'genuine' and 'spurious' cultures, Sapir takes aim at the capitalist social system of his contemporary America. When Sapir asserts that the American individual now exists 'as a mere cog, as an entity whose sole *raison d'être* lies in his subservience to a collective purpose that he is not conscious of or that has only a remote relevancy to his interests and strivings', he departs from Boas by focusing upon the cultural consequences of modern working practices and patterns of consumption (1963, 315).

Sapir's essay is significant because it extends Boasian anthropology's mode of thinking culturally to envision an alternative future. 'A healthy national culture is never a passively accepted heritage from the past', he tells us, 'but implies the creative participation of the members of the community' (1963, 321). With this ideal of a 'genuine culture' in his sights, Sapir sets out to 'build' a new collective spirit in America (1963, 331). As Susan Hegeman explains, 'Sapir advocated undertaking something like an archaeological dig of the American psyche, to find the buried, "genuine", fragments of cultures, to shore against the ruins of our spurious existence' (Hegeman 1999, 91). In short, Sapir not only turns a critical gaze on his contemporary America (like Boas), but he also imagines an alternative cultural order, which would foster a dynamic relationship between culture and individual.

Of more immediate relevance to this study is Melville Herskovits's narrowly focused study of racial mixing in the African American communities of Harlem and Howard University: *The American Negro: A Study in Racial Crossing* (1928), a project on which Zora Neale Hurston worked as a research assistant.[6] Given that

---

6 Langston Hughes describes Zora Neale Hurston's role as Herskovits's assistant in his autobiography, *The Big Sea* (1940): '[a]lmost nobody else could stop the average Harlemite on Lenox Avenue and measure his head with a strange-looking, anthropological

this research answers Boas's frequent call for fuller analysis of miscegenation (Boas 1940, 18-59, 138-48; 1938, 271-2), it comes as no surprise that Boas played a fundamental role in securing funding for the project (Baker 1998, 152).

For the most part, Herskovits follows the parameters established by Boas's physical anthropology. In accordance with Boas's work for the U.S. Immigration Commission, for instance, he gathered statistical information in an attempt to overturn enduring ideas about African American physical inferiority. This helps to account for Herskovits's exhaustive cataloguing of African American physical characteristics, such as '[i]nterpupillary [d]istance', '[w]idth of [n]ostrils', '[h]eight of [e]ar', [l]ength of [m]iddle [f]inger' (32), 'stature' and 'height sitting' and 'cephalic index' (1985, 46). Herskovits uses such data to confirm Boas's hypothesis about the ubiquity of racial mixing; indeed, he contends that racial crossing has led to the emergence of 'a definite physical type' (1985, 19). An account of African Americans as an '[a]malgam' of 'all of the principal racial elements of which humanity is composed – White, Negro, and Mongoloid' (19) culminates in the Boasian point that 'race' is a sociological fiction devoid of any biological reality (1985, 82).

At the same time, Herskovits reiterates certain limitations that characterize Boas's treatment of racial mixing. For a start, the study is underpinned by an assumption that the African American 'will, by and large, succeed only in so far as he adapts himself to the patterns of the dominant culture' (1985, 54). Yet, there is a revealing contradiction between Herskovits's emphasis upon assimilation to white American values and his account of the emergence of a newly vitalized black culture. What is new is the implied correlation he establishes between the consolidation of a distinctive African American physical 'type' and New Negro cultural confidence:

> The movement has been of no little social significance, for it means that the American Negroes – or, in any event, a small group of them – are claiming a portion of their heritage as Americans, and are identifying themselves more and more closely with the culture of this country which is theirs by birth (Herskovits 1985, 18).

On one level, this statement simply reads like an endorsement of cultural assimilation. Within the context of the book, however, it adds to a continuing emphasis upon the parallel emergence of a new physical 'type' and hybrid modes of African American cultural expression. Indeed, Herskovits specifically argues that the New Negro movement's quasi-anthropological focus upon culture is transforming conceptions of America. Echoing Alain Locke's argument in *The New Negro* (1925) that African Americans are simply 'an interesting and

---

device and not get bawled out for the attempt, except Zora, who used to stop anyone whose head looked interesting, and measure it' (1993, 239).

significant segment of the general American scene', he describes America as a patchwork of diverse cultures (Locke 1992a, xxvi).

Herskovits retains an investment in assimilation: he cannot imagine any alternative to conformity to American structures. Nevertheless, his discussion of the aesthetic possibilities of racial mixing and cultural crossing opens up alternative possibilities. Not only does his approach suggest that 'cultural traits traversing racial classifications, and racial groups crossing cultural boundaries' (Hegeman 1999, 49) might alter accepted ideas of what it is to be American. A shift of emphasis from a nation-state founded upon common racial descent to a collective identity based upon a shared culture and geography also strikes a chord with 'the efforts of black intellectuals to transform African-American identity from a teleological racial concept, into a spatially-conceived cultural one' (Hegeman 1999, 50).

Wheeling forward to consider more recent anthropological theorizations allows for a sharp assessment of the possibilities and limitations of the Boasian culture concept. James Clifford's turn to surrealism in search of a 'helpful paradigm' for writing ethnography in *The Predicament of Culture* provides an illuminating point of comparison (1988, 146). Of course, Clifford's account of anthropology must be considered within the context of a broader debate in the 1980s about the politics of anthropology in a postmodern, postcolonial world, a debate that is a far cry from Boas's efforts to establish anthropology as an academic discipline. Nevertheless, juxtaposition of these two influential thinkers brings into focus the possibilities opened up by Boas's emphasis upon intercultural exchange.

Clifford's collage method resists a familiar pattern of ethnographic interpretation, in which disjunctions generated by cross-cultural comparison are 'smoothed over in the process of ethnographic comprehension' (1988, 146). He aims to hold such discordance in view:

> The surrealist moment in ethnography is that moment in which the possibility of comparison exists in unmediated tension with sheer incongruity. This moment is repeatedly produced and smoothed over in the process of ethnographic comprehension. But to see this activity in terms of collage is to hold the surrealist moment in view ... Collage brings to the work (here the ethnographic text) elements that continually proclaim their foreignness to the context of presentation. These elements – like a newspaper clipping or a feather – are marked as real, as collected rather than invented by the artist-writer (Clifford 1988, 146).

A comparison of Clifford and Boas reveals convergences and divergences between the two writers. It is difficult to imagine that Boas would have approved of Clifford's emphasis upon the aesthetic qualities of ethnography, but this description of the anthropologist as collector recalls Boas's emphasis upon fieldwork. In this context, Boas's legendary 'five-foot' shelf of materials on the Kwakiutl is relevant (Krupat 1992, 83). As part of the professionalization of anthropology, Boas encouraged his students to collect specimens, alongside informants' explanations of the specimens and grammatical information, when undertaking fieldwork (Jacknis 1996, 199-200). Such practices certainly invested ethnography with authority, laying stress upon anthropologists' skilled interpretation. Yet, this 'imperative for preservation' also introduced contradictions into Boas's writings (Elliott 2002, 10). For one thing, the theoretical implications, and potential uses, of such data, which often appeared without explanation or analysis, remain unspecified (Krupat 1992, 82). Next, as Michael A. Elliott has demonstrated, the overarching 'salvage story' that frames Boas's ethnographies effectively transformed folktale transcriptions into static artifacts so that 'the texts themselves stand alone as an authoritative, "pure and trustworthy", ahistorical depiction [of a particular culture]' (Elliott 2002, 21).

Clifford's account of the anthropologist, however, resolves some of these tensions to question 'ethnographic authority'. For Clifford, the fact that 'collected' data cannot be integrated into an overarching schema of interpretation indicates anthropology's limitations. Rather than smoothing over incongruity by adopting the pose of an 'artist-writer' (a privileged and apparently objective outsider who can allegedly rationalize a culture and identify thematic consistencies), he contends that anthropologists must cede mastery by highlighting 'foreignness' and disjunction.

The impetus for Clifford's collage method is to expose implicit cultural hierarchies that underpin participant observation. As Mark Whalan explains, participant observation 'encouraged a kind of panoptic vision, whereby the ethnographer was supposed to see everything and yet remain a subject who was not observed, who did not disturb the social interactions or patterns of the culture under study' (2007, 139). By contrast, Clifford wants to preserve the ruptures created by cultural observation, not least because such unmediated tensions 'render the investigator's own culture newly incomprehensible' (1988, 147). In other words, he values comparative cultural analysis precisely because it generates an estranged mode of perception, which prompts us to recognize that all cultures are arbitrary systems guided by ideological values (1988, 147).

Like Clifford, Boas envisaged cross-cultural comparison as a means through which to defamiliarize American culture. In 'The Aims of Ethnology' (1889), for example, Boas claims that anthropology 'alone opens to us the possibility of judging our own culture objectively, in that it permits us to strip off the presumably self-evident manner of thinking and feeling which determines even the fundamental part of our culture' (Boas 1974c, 71). For Boas, immersion in another culture provokes a searching reappraisal of one's own cultural outlook. Such analysis 'forces anthropologists ... to realize that all patterns of thought, including their own, are contingent upon the dense contextual web called culture' (Elliott 2002, 8). In distinction to Clifford, Boas stops short of turning this self-reflexive gaze upon his own status as an anthropologist. Instead, he makes grand claims for the trained scientist's ability to suspend cultural bias, offering a supposedly objective view of the world.

It is with reference to the issue of colonialism, however, that the most striking differences emerge between Clifford and Boas. When he describes his collage method, Clifford uses literary terms, such as metonymy and metaphor, to establish parallels between fiction and anthropology. With this move, anthropology itself becomes a stylized form that invites sustained analysis. It is but a short step from this insight to interrogation of ideological assumptions that undergird the discipline. In this context, Clifford demonstrates that anthropological accounts are always governed by asymmetrical power relations between the observer and the observed. Clifford explains, for example, that Bronislaw Malinowski's selection of '[r]itual exchange valuables' to symbolize Trobriand Islands culture introduces a vocabulary that is at odds with the islanders' belief system, a vocabulary that aligns anthropological description with imperialist ambition (1988, 146). Addressing this point, he adumbrates an alternative mode of cultural description, which refuses to assimilate 'foreignness' into the western 'conceptual domain' (1988, 146). In so doing, he short-circuits a narrative coherence that is, to some degree, complicit in an imperialist logic of divide and rule.

According to Clifford, his collage method rejects an imperialist strategy of subsuming difference into western structures of understanding. Indeed, he litters his ethnography with carefully chosen motifs, which invite readers to apply their interpretive skills. Such images force readers to recognize the unequal power dynamic between anthropologists and their anthropological subjects. Hence, it is hardly a coincidence that Clifford juxtaposes the crown jewels, a glittering symbol of imperial sovereignty, with '[r]itual exchange valuables, *vaygu'a* (shell necklaces)' when he introduces his anthropological method in the passage I quoted above (1988, 146).

Clifford's insistence upon the subversiveness of his approach, however, threatens to smooth over complexities that animate his treatment of colonialism. To some extent, Clifford's celebration of hybridity as necessarily radical is undercut by his discussion of specific examples of cross-cultural exchange, including 'the penetration of the Third World by Coca Cola Company and Hollywood' (Michaelsen 1999, 22). As Scott Michaelsen demonstrates, 'Clifford's example temporalizes colonial relations in highly familiar ways, play[ing] on established stereotypes (drums versus television, primitive versus modern), in order to specify the results of hybridization' (Michaelsen 1999, 22).

Notwithstanding such provisos, Clifford's avowed opposition to anthropology's complicity with colonialism exposes Boas's inadequate response to the issue. Clifford's anti-colonialist stance stands in marked contrast to Boas's equivocal pronouncements on colonialism, which introduce ideological cross-currents into his anti-racist thought. In 'Colonies and the Peace Conference' (1919), for example, his criticism of European greed and racism is compromised by his refusal to condemn colonialism and his plea for Germany to be allowed to maintain its position as an imperial power (1919a, 247). Boas was by no means alone in his failure to take the apparently logical step from anti-racism to anti-colonialism. In a fascinating account of the Races Congress held in London in 1911, for instance,

Alessandra Lorini demonstrates that the organizing committee for this anti-racist conference made a deliberate effort to muzzle criticism of colonialism (Lorini 1999, 145-6). Even so, Boas's ambivalent attitude demonstrates that any account of Boasian anthropology and the Harlem Renaissance must be framed very carefully, addressing the possibilities and limits of anthropological discourse for African American authors.

Boas's Collage Sensibility and the Harlem Renaissance

My concern in this book is not simply to establish a direct line of influence between Boas and Harlem Renaissance writers. Rather, analysis of Boas's culture concept paves the way for an investigation of Hurston, Locke and Toomer's substantial revision of Boasian concepts. Such an approach inevitably accentuates particular aspects of the Harlem Renaissance while relegating others to the background. Consequently, my examination of the collage aesthetic in subsequent chapters will pay close attention to other literary, visual and musical models that inspired writers to innovate with form.

That said, any account of Harlem Renaissance writers' engagement with Boasian anthropology must begin by acknowledging the widespread currency of these ideas among modernist, avant-garde circles. Consider, for instance, the frequent appearance of essays with an anthropological bent in little magazines such as *The Double Dealer* and *The Dial* (Whalan 2007, 136). With specific reference to the Harlem Renaissance, George Hutchinson contends that '[e]choes and paraphrases of [Boas's] work reverberate through novels as diverse as Jessie Fauset's, Wallace Thurman's, and George Schuyler's' (Hutchinson 1995, 70).

Toomer, Locke and Hurston were careful readers of Boas, and all three of them responded to his ideas in print. Boas, of course, is often mentioned in the same breath as Zora Neale Hurston because she studied under him from 1925 to 1927. Evaluations of Hurston's writing have often hinged on an assessment of her investment in, or subversion of, anthropological discourse, with several influential critics making the case that anthropological inquiry inevitably established limiting parameters for an African American writer (Baker 1991, 95-7; Carby 1994, 28-44). Sustained analysis of Hurston's engagement with Boasian ideas, however, opens up an alternative assessment of this question, which sees anthropology as a transitional discourse, which she could adapt for her own ends.

If Hurston drew inspiration from Boas's emphasis on cultural documentation, Locke valued his anti-racist pronouncements. In 'The Eleventh Hour of Nordicism' (1935), he named Boas as one of 'just a few strong dissenting voices' amid a tide of racist extremism (1983c, 232). Elsewhere, Locke revised Boasian ideas for his own purposes. An essay entitled 'The Concept of Race as Applied to Social Culture' (1924), for instance, mounts a vigorous challenge to Boas's pro-amalgamation stance, but it also reiterates certain limitations that characterize Boasian anthropology, not least 'the lack of a comprehensive notion of ideology around which to organize his various insights into the functioning of "race antipathy"' (Foley 2003, 211).

Locke's most significant departure from Boas in the essay involves his conceptualization of the term 'race'. For Locke, complete refusal of any relationship between race and culture, a position espoused by Robert Lowie in *Culture and Ethnology* (1923), misses something fundamental about the 'relative constancy' of connection between physical characteristics and cultural mores (425), and 'the sense of race' that creates 'perhaps the most intense of the feelings of commonality' (1983d, 428). With this in mind, Locke contends that cultural contact actually results in a hardening of racial boundaries, even as processes of acculturation occur. Having established that all cultures are 'composite', he still emphasizes cultural distinctiveness: '[a] diversity of cultural types temporarily at least accentuates the racial stresses involved, so that even when a fusion eventuates it takes place under the conditions determined by the resistance developed and the relative strength of the several cultural components' (Locke 1983d, 428). Within America, he avers, ethnic groups are bound together by a shared culture, but this larger whole is made up of distinctive cultural 'components'. Such a model not only moves away from a concept of race rooted in biology; it also makes room for 'resistance' to dominant values within the context of shared national values. This culture pattern, with its unstable investment in acculturation and distinctiveness, features in a number of Harlem Renaissance texts.

Finally, Toomer's 'Race Problems and Modern Society' (1929) and the unpublished essays 'The Negro Emergent' (1924) and 'The Crock of Problems' (1928) engage with Boas, Melville Herskovits, Alfred Kroeber and Ales Hrdlicka's ideas. Of particular interest to Toomer were anthropological investigations of racial crossing demonstrating 'that so-called race problems are not due to biological causes, but to the superimposed forms and controversies of our social *milieu*' (Toomer 1996c, 174). In *Cane*, Toomer revises Boasian historicism to locate mixed race histories at the heart of his contemporary America. But Toomer's engagement with Boasian anthropology is not limited to subject matter. As Michael A. Elliott has astutely pointed out, 'the shift from cultural evolution (which understood culture as a uniform, global process) to Boasian culture (which understood culture as an aggregation of the practices and beliefs specific to a particular group) involved a radical change in the *narrative* organization of knowledge about group-based alterity' (2002, xxiii). Perhaps we can begin to account for Toomer's aesthetic of assemblage, in which he splices together forms and warps received generic conventions, in the light of Elliott's insight that 'problems of narrative structure were intimately bound to the representation of cultural difference' (2002, xxiv).

Even a brief overview of Hurston, Locke and Toomer's treatment of Boasian anthropology scuttles any notion of linear influence. In their engagement with anthropology, these writers deploy strategies of appropriation and revision that could be likened to Henry Louis Gates's notion of Signifyin(g) – or repetition 'with a signal difference' (1988a, xxiv). What is at stake when these three writers revise Boas is something to which I shall return in subsequent chapters.

For the moment, I want to address the question of African American engagement with anthropological discourse more broadly by assessing Du Bois's championing of Boas in the pages of *The Crisis*, the National Association for the Advancement of Colored People (NAACP) magazine that he edited from 1910 until 1934. Such analysis is important because, as Christa Schwarz has demonstrated, *The Crisis* and *Opportunity*, a monthly magazine funded by the National Urban League (NUL), 'contributed significantly to the definition, interpretation, and development of the Harlem Renaissance' (2003, 26). Since these magazines played a fundamental role in generating a market for African American writers, *The Crisis* provides a revealing snapshot of engagement with Boasian anthropology.

Before turning to *The Crisis*, it is worth pausing for a moment to note that Du Bois's turn to Boasian anthropology was, at least in part, a response to scientific racism. In the early decades of the twentieth century, writers who mobilized eugenics and evolution to bolster a static racial hierarchy enjoyed widespread popularity. Madison Grant's *The Passing of the Great Race* (1916), for instance, ran to multiple editions and Lothrop Stoddard wrote a regular column for the *Saturday Evening Post*, which gave scientific legitimacy to a narrative of decline that coupled racial mixing with 'the "destruction of civilization"' (Foley 2003, 149).[7]

Du Bois was bitterly aware of the threat posed by such scientists: '[s]ocial science in America has so long been the foot ball of "nigger"-hating propaganda that we Negroes fail to get excited when a new scientist comes into the field' (Du Bois 1928, 202). In this context, Boas's sustained efforts 'to decouple the primitive from the atavistic' by explaining cultural difference in historical rather than biological terms meant that his ideas were a valuable resource for Du Bois's anti-racist project (Foley 2003, 149). George Hutchinson even goes so far as to claim that Boas was 'virtually the house anthropologist for *Crisis* magazine subsequent to the paper he delivered at the Second National Negro Conference of May 1910, through which the NAACP was founded' (1995, 63).

Du Bois harnessed Boas's work to advance his political project of improving the social, economic and political status of African Americans. In December 1910, he printed Boas's essay 'The Real Race Problem', which marshals evidence from physical anthropology to demonstrate that racial prejudice has no basis in scientific fact; in reality, it is the product of ingrained social attitudes. Although recent commentators have criticized Boas's eagerness to explain racism in emotional rather than ideological terms, Du Bois prefaces the article with a glowing editorial comment: '[t]he editor of *Science* reports that the leading scientists of America regard this department of Columbia as the strongest in the country. This gives a peculiar weight to Dr. Boas' words, which were first delivered at the Second National Negro Conference in May, 1910' (Boas 1910, 22). Boas, whose status as a professor is highlighted in the essay title, is cast as a legitimizing voice

---

[7]   The *Saturday Evening Post* was, as Barbara Foley points out, one of the most popular magazines of the period, with at least two million readers (2003, 152).

whose academic credentials lend 'a peculiar weight' to his call for racial equality. With this move, Du Bois aligns *The Crisis*'s agenda of nurturing 'earnest, active opposition' to increasing racism by 'doing away with the excuses for prejudice … showing the unreasonableness of prejudice … [and] exposing the evils of race prejudice' with the cutting edge of science (Du Bois 1910a, 16).

The magazine's sustained use of Boasian anthropology to educate readers and alter attitudes is illustrated by an advertisement in May 1911, which promotes the purchase of 'The Real Race Problem', 'by America's foremost anthropologist', in pamphlet form. The sale of a single copy for five cents and a thousand copies for three dollars suggests that Du Bois envisaged mass circulation of Boas's essay. An advert featured from July 1911 until November 1912 demonstrates the success of such promotional initiatives. Advertising for Mary White Ovington's *Half a Man* devotes as much space to Boas, who contributed a foreword of only a single page, as it does to Ovington, a founding member of the NAACP (see Figure 4). Rather like the prefaces Boas later wrote for Zora Neale Hurston's *Mules and Men* (1934) and Margaret Mead's *Coming of Age in Samoa* (1928), such publicity suggests that Boas's name was familiar to American readers. An endorsement from Boas, it seems, could help to decide the fate of ethnographic texts in the marketplace.

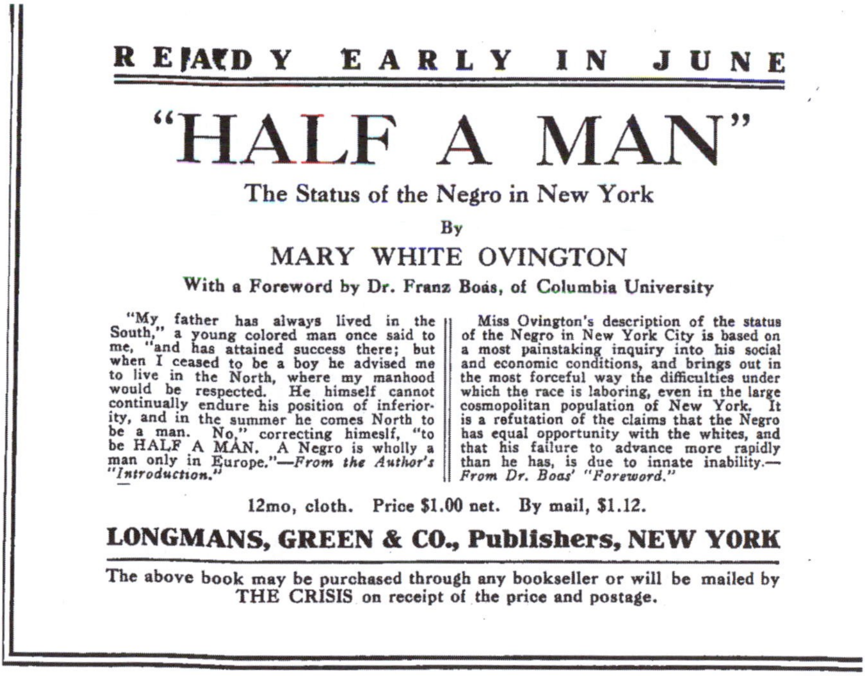

R E|A©D Y   E A R L Y   I N   J U N E

"HALF A MAN"

The Status of the Negro in New York

By

MARY WHITE OVINGTON

With a Foreword by Dr. Franz Boas, of Columbia University

"My father has always lived in the South," a young colored man once said to me, "and has attained success there; but when I ceased to be a boy he advised me to live in the North, where my manhood would be respected. He himself cannot continually endure his position of inferiority, and in the summer he comes North to be a man. No," correcting himself, "to be HALF A MAN. A Negro is wholly a man only in Europe."—*From the Author's "Introduction."*

Miss Ovington's description of the status of the Negro in New York City is based on a most painstaking inquiry into his social and economic conditions, and brings out in the most forceful way the difficulties under which the race is laboring, even in the large cosmopolitan population of New York. It is a refutation of the claims that the Negro has equal opportunity with the whites, and that his failure to advance more rapidly than he has, is due to innate inability.—*From Dr. Boas' "Foreword."*

12mo, cloth.   Price $1.00 net.   By mail, $1.12.

LONGMANS, GREEN & CO., Publishers, NEW YORK

The above book may be purchased through any bookseller or will be mailed by THE CRISIS on receipt of the price and postage.

Figure 4   Advertisement for Mary White Ovington's *Half a Man*, *The Crisis*, June 1911, p. 88

BEST BOOKS

For students of the Negro Problem and general readers. Your library will be incomplete without a selection from this up-to-date list.

These are books produced by the best writers and most able authorities on the problems affecting the races. By mail at following prices:

ESSAYS

RACE ADJUSTMENT.
Kelly Miller $2.15
SOULS OF BLACK FOLK.
W. E. B. Du Bois 1.35
CURSE OF RACE PREJUDICE.
Jas. F. Morton, Jr. .... .27

ATLANTA UNIVERSITY STUDIES

The Atlanta University Studies are an annual study of decennially recurring subjects, covering every phase of Negro-American life.

No. 7—THE NEGRO ARTISAN ......$ .75
No. 8—THE NEGRO CHURCH 1.50
No. 9—NOTES ON NEGRO CRIME .. .50
No. 10—BIBLIOGRAPHY OF THE NEGRO-AMERICAN .... .25
No. 11—HEALTH AND PHYSIQUE OF THE NEGRO-AMERICAN 1.50
No. 12—ECONOMIC CO-OPERATION AMONG NEGRO-AMERICANS 1.00
No. 13—THE NEGRO - AMERICAN FAMILY .... .75
No. 14—EFFORTS FOR SOCIAL BETTERMENT AMONG NEGRO-AMERICANS .... .75
No. 15—THE COLLEGE-BRED NEGRO-AMERICAN .... .75
No. 16—THE NEGRO COMMON SCHOOL .... .75

FICTION

QUEST OF THE SILVER FLEECE.
W. E. B. Du Bois $1.50
FLOWER O' THE PEACH.
Percival Gibbon 1.45
MARROW OF TRADITION.
Chas. W. Chesnutt 1.65
HOUSE BEHIND THE CEDARS.
Chas. W. Chesnutt 1.65
THE WIFE OF HIS YOUTH.
Chas. W. Chesnutt 1.65
THE CONJURE WOMAN.
Chas. W. Chesnutt 1.40
SPORT OF THE GODS.
Paul Laurence Dunbar 1.65
THE TESTING FIRE.
Alexander Corkey 1.35
WISDOM'S CALL.
Sutton E. Griggs .... .60

POEMS

LYRICS OF LOWLY LIFE.
Paul Laurence Dunbar $1.40
LYRICS OF THE HEARTH-SIDE.
Paul Laurence Dunbar 1.40
LYRICS OF LOVE AND LAUGHTER.
Paul Laurence Dunbar 1.40
LYRICS OF SUNSHINE AND SHADOW.
Paul Laurence Dunbar 1.40
POEMS OF PHILLIS WHEATLEY 1.10

HISTORICAL AND SCIENTIFIC

NEGRO IN THE SOUTH.
Washington and Du Bois $1.10
NEGRO IN THE NEW WORLD.
Sir Harry Johnston 6.30
MIND OF PRIMITIVE MAN.
Franz Boaz 1.65
INTER-RACIAL PROBLEMS.
Official Record, Univ. R. C.... 2.55
HISTORY OF THE NEGRO RACE.
E. A. Johnson 1.40
NEGRO EXPLORER AT THE NORTH POLE.
Matthew A. Henson 1.10
SUPPRESSION OF THE SLAVE TRADE.
W. E. B. Du Bois 1.65

BIOGRAPHIES, ETC.

JOHN BROWN.
W. E. B. Du Bois $1.40
FREDERICK DOUGLASS.
Booker T. Washington 1.40
LIFE OF HARRIET BEECHER STOWE.
By her son and grandson 1.65
UP FROM SLAVERY.
Booker T. Washington 1.65
AUTOBIOGRAPHY OF AN EX-COLORED MAN.
(Anonymous) 1.40

SOCIAL STUDIES

HALF-A-MAN.
M. W. Ovington $1.12
AFTERMATH OF SLAVERY.
W. A. Sinclair 1.65
SOUTHERN SOUTH.
Albert B. Hart 1.65
RACE PREJUDICE.
J. Finot 3.25
NEGRO AND THE NATION.
G. C. Merriam 1.92

FREE

Should you at any time require special information concerning books, authors or publishers, WRITE US.

Our location gives us the opportunity to render this service to our many patrons.

This service is FREE.

SPECIAL OFFER Add 75 cents to the regular price quoted for any of these books and we will send you THE CRISIS for one year and one CRISIS cover design, printed on plain paper, for framing. Size 8½ x 11. Address all orders to

THE DUNBAR COMPANY

26 Vesey Street New York City

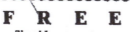

Figure 5 'Best Books', *The Crisis*, November 1912, p. 52

A closer look at such advertising reveals that Du Bois frames Boasian anthropology very carefully so that it accords with his project of racial uplift. *The Mind of Primitive Man* (1911), for instance, which represents a comprehensive overview of Boas's anti-racist arguments, was publicized relentlessly in *The Crisis* during the 1910s and 1920s. It appeared in the 'Best Books' section of the magazine, alongside such classics as *The Souls of Black Folk*, from September 1912 until July 1915 (see Figure 5). In November 1912, for instance, *The Mind of Primitive Man* was included in a list of 'books produced by the best writers and most able authorities on the problems affecting the races' (1912, 52). Such adverts construct an upwardly mobile, educated African American audience. Cheap prices, special offers and free advice to anyone interested in building a library suggest a deliberate effort to reach African American migrants who had often only recently acquired the economic means to purchase books.

An assessment of Du Bois's treatment of Boasian anthropology in the pages of his magazine offers a new perspective on the relationship between Euro-American modernism and the Harlem Renaissance. As I mentioned in the introduction, much Harlem Renaissance scholarship has tended either to emphasize the intercultural quality of the movement or to celebrate its radical departure from Euro-American modernism. Attention to Du Bois's reinterpretation of Boasian anthropology in *The Crisis* demonstrates the ultimate interdependency of these two positions. Du Bois does not simply champion Boas's work, quoting from an authoritative source. Instead, he transposes Boas's ideas to a new context, reinterpreting them in a more politicized form. Hence, Du Bois's project is vitalized by interracial exchange, but he never loses sight of the particularity of African American experience.

To examine how these apparently conflicting impulses combine, I will discuss two specific examples from *The Crisis*. First, I turn to Du Bois's editorial framing of 'The Real Race Problem', which, as I mentioned above, appeared in the magazine's second issue, in December 1910. As a whole, Boas's essay undermines misconceptions that had very real consequences for African Americans. First, he documents the achievements of African culture in an attempt to blast stereotypical associations of Africa with savagery. Secondly, he challenges a long-standing association between racial mixing and physical inferiority. At the climax of the article, these two strands converge when Boas provides examples of flourishing ancient cultures in the Sudan and Egypt that derived their richness from racial and cultural mixing. From here, it is but a short step to his call for racial amalgamation.

Du Bois employs a number of strategies to guide interpretation of 'The Real Race Problem'. For a start, he adds subheadings, which summarize Boas's ideas in very bald terms – 'The Negro Not Inferior', 'Mulatto Not Inferior', 'Handicap of Slavery'. Importantly, these titles muffle Boas's problematic claims about racial assimilation. Boas's essay, as I mentioned above, culminates with the argument that it is only the gradual 'disappearance of the most distinctive type of Negro, which will … alleviate the acuteness of race feeling', a declaration that all too easily slides into an assumption of white superiority (1910, 25). Du Bois's gloss for this section – 'Mulatto Not Inferior' – diverts attention from Boas's stance on amalgamation towards a more general anti-racist point. It is tempting to speculate that these summative headings had the potential to silence Boas's pro-amalgamation argument completely for those readers who did not find scientific prose to their taste.

A second level of editorial framing encourages readers to bring Boas's scientific ideas into contact with contemporary politics. Julia E. Liss and Barbara Foley have recently criticized Boas for his tendency to analyse racism in psychological terms without sufficient reference to political, social or economic factors. For Foley, Boas's emphasis on 'race feeling' has the unfortunate effect of rendering his analysis ahistorical, draining it of contemporary resonance (2003, 153). Du Bois's careful juxtaposition of Boas's essay with hard-hitting accounts of racial violence and discrimination, however, forces readers to think beyond Boas's abstract theoretical framework.[8]

To take only one example, an editorial with the subheading 'The Inevitable' precedes 'The Real Race Problem'. In it, Du Bois challenges the rhetoric of inevitability that often surrounded discussions of lynching, a rhetoric that absolved white Americans from any sense of responsibility for racial violence. Du Bois indicts such complacency: '[i]t is not inevitable', he says. 'It is criminal injustice. It is inhuman treatment and it is socially dangerous. It is based on the *unscientific* assumption that human beings who resemble each other in one important particular, like color of skin, resemble each other in all particulars' (1910b, 21 [my emphasis]). Du Bois chooses his vocabulary very carefully. The word 'unscientific' immediately creates a thread of connection with the anthropological essay that follows, implying that such 'scientific' evidence might be mobilized to challenge racism. Furthermore, placing Boas's essay in the midst of lengthy discussion of segregation, debt slavery, lynching and the NAACP's commitment 'to fight the wrong of race prejudice' gives Boas's ideas a new, radical edge (1910a, 16). Moving from scientific generalization towards engagement with specific social realities in the context of an urgent struggle for African American equality, Du Bois reveals the radical potential latent in Boas's anthropological data.

My second example comes from a review essay featured in Du Bois's regular column 'The Browsing Reader' in June 1928. Du Bois's notorious account of Claude McKay's *Home to Harlem* (1928), in which he claims that the novel 'for the most part nauseates me, and after the dirtier parts of its filth I feel distinctly

---

[8]   See Anne Carroll, *Word, Image, and the New Negro: Representation and Identity in the Harlem Renaissance* (2005, 20-54) for a brilliant analysis of Du Bois's '[j]uxtapositions of protest and affirmation' in the pages of *The Crisis* (2005, 43). Pairing what he calls 'the grim awfulness of the bare truth' about racial violence with a more optimistic narrative of social uplift (Du Bois 1912, 153), Du Bois provokes a sense of discomfort, which forces readers to recognize the precarious position occupied by African Americans, and perhaps even encourages active involvement in NAACP campaigns for reform (2005, 43).

like taking a bath' is now the stuff of legend (Du Bois 1928, 202). It is less often remembered that Du Bois paired his evaluations of *Home to Harlem* and Nella Larsen's *Quicksand* with an extended commentary on Melville Herskovits's *The American Negro: A Study in Racial Crossing* (1928).

With its extensive tables of physical measurements, Herskovits's study is certainly indebted to the discredited discipline of physical anthropology. Much of the book is concerned with collecting data about physical characteristics: Herskovits documents everything from height of face and height of ear to height sitting and cephalic index. Yet, Du Bois appears to be desperate to present Herskovits's study as a radical break from the racist science of the past. He champions Herskovits as 'a man who is more interested in arriving at truth than proving a thesis of race superiority' (Du Bois 1928, 202).

Any reader of *The American Negro* cannot fail to notice that this text devotes more space to data than to analysis. While Herskovits raises some provocative points, there is a continual danger that the sheer volume of raw statistics will overwhelm his analysis. In spite of this, Du Bois extracts a very clear thesis from the study, a thesis that accords with his own project of engaging in interracial collaboration while affirming a distinctive African American culture. Bypassing Herskovits's emphasis on the American character of the Harlem Renaissance, Du Bois instead gives prominence to his theory that racial mixing among African Americans has led to the emergence of a new, distinctive type.

For Herskovits, such mixing is primarily, although not exclusively, biological, but Du Bois transposes these ideas to the arena of culture, speaking of a 'singular group stability' based upon shared values (1928, 202). Du Bois emphasizes a group identity – or '"racial" … inter-thinking' as he calls it – that is 'more largely a matter of social and rational accomplishment than of mere physical descent' (Du Bois 1928, 202). Much hangs on this small but crucial shift of emphasis from a biological notion of race towards a concept of culture that makes room for intercultural exchange and cultural distinctiveness. With this move, Du Bois undermines arguments that were used to justify segregation while focusing attention upon distinctive ethnic identity.

Such insights take on a new significance when we remember that Du Bois considers Herskovits's ideas in relation to New Negro literature. Du Bois puts his anthropological discussion of cultural identity into contact with literary criticism, in which he judges fictional writers according to their ability to resist white expectations (Larsen is praised for her sincerity, but McKay is criticized because he 'has set out to cater for that prurient demand on the part of white folk for a portrayal in Negroes of that utter licentiousness which conventional civilization holds white folk back from enjoying – if enjoyment it can be called' (1928, 202)). In this context, Du Bois's assessment of Herskovits contributes to a broader debate about the relationship between politics and aesthetics, a debate best illustrated in the 1926 *Crisis* symposium 'The Negro in Art: How Shall He Be Portrayed'. When he examines Herskovits's study in relation to the New Negro movement, Du Bois stretches Boasian anthropology beyond the narrow confines of science, applying its insights in a nuanced examination of cultural politics. His theoretical extrapolations from *The American Negro* are brought to bear on the politics of literary representation.

My focus on Boasian anthropology in *The Crisis* may appear to be a marginal, or even eccentric, topic, having little to do with the avant-garde formal experimentation of Zora Neale Hurston, Alain Locke and Jean Toomer. However, these writers found it productive to pursue correspondences between literature and anthropology. Consequently, exploration of Du Bois's subtle revision of Boasian anthropology in the pages of the magazine not only allows for a useful intervention in continuing debates about the relationship between the Harlem Renaissance and Euro-American modernism. It also identifies a need for more sustained analysis of Harlem Renaissance revisions of Boasian anthropology.

Conclusion

This chapter opened with a discussion of those moments in Boas's *oeuvre* when the collage pattern implicit in much of his work comes to the surface and he describes culture as a dynamic kaleidoscope of diverse elements. Such spatial patterns are crucial to Boas's thinking, not least because they enabled him to contest evolutionism and its stratification of culture into a hierarchical time series. My analysis of these patterns is motivated by an awareness that Boas's ideas were part of the *Zeitgeist*. W.E.B. Du Bois, Jessie Fauset, Langston Hughes, Zora Neale Hurston, Alain Locke and Jean Toomer, to name only a few, incorporated Boasian cultural description and concepts into their writing. Always alert to '[t]he aesthetic possibilities of cultural documentation' (Elliott 2002, 12), they transformed anthropological discourse in the process, introducing a dynamism that was missing from Boas's ethnographies. What was at stake in such revision is the subject of the following chapters, which investigate techniques of juxtaposition and stylistic incongruity deployed within selected works by Alain Locke, Jean Toomer and Zora Neale Hurston. Anthropology is, of course, only one component of such collage forms, all of which restlessly cross disciplinary borders, especially between literature and anthropology. Nevertheless, any conceptualization of the Harlem Renaissance must engage Boas's account of anthropology as a means of intervening in contemporary political concerns, not least because he deploys collage-like imagery in his theorization of cultural development.

Chapter 2

'[F]lung out in a jagged, uneven but progressive pattern': 'Culture-citizenship' in *The New Negro*

The honeycombed structure of *The New Negro* has not gone unnoticed by critics. In one of the most detailed accounts of the volume's textual content, George Hutchinson describes the anthology as a 'diverse and self-divided text' (1995, 433). For Hutchinson, Locke's orchestration of contradictory views is at once a strategic attempt to undermine reductive stereotypes, and the inevitable product of a moment of instability when concepts of racial identity were in transition. More recently, the anthology's multimedia format has received considerable critical attention. A particular focus of such research has been its emphasis upon the editor's ability to control textual meaning. Anne Elizabeth Carroll, for instance, explores how Locke orchestrates conflicting approaches to reinforce his own views. To take only one example, she argues that African thematic and stylistic motifs in the illustrative material build a coherent narrative about African cultural retentions, which is often at odds with claims made by contributors (2005, 173-9).

It would be a mistake, however, to assume that this new scholarship on the productive juxtaposition of word and image in *The New Negro* rests upon a simplistic understanding of authorial (or editorial) intention. Anne Elizabeth Carroll and Martha Jane Nadell pose searching questions about tensions that animate Locke's efforts to give voice to the multiplicity of African American culture, which is, in Charles S. Johnson's words, '[f]lung out in a jagged, uneven but progressive pattern' (*N* 297).[1] As Carroll convincingly demonstrates, Locke grapples with a dilemma that has implications for the Harlem Renaissance more broadly: the question of how to represent African Americans socially and aesthetically as a group with a shared sense of identity while preserving a space for individual complexity. Formulated against the backdrop of the Great Migration (which marked a transition from a predominantly southern, rural culture to an urban, northern one), a tension between the one and the many, the editor and the contributors, shapes both the anthology and Locke's democratic vision of African American culture. This sense of a culture in flux speaks to the various interpretations that Harlem Renaissance writers present of potential cultural and

---

[1]   References to *The New Negro* are abbreviated to *N*.

racial identities in modern America, whether in the northern city or among the southern folk.

Building upon these foundational studies of Harlem Renaissance 'interartistic' texts, this chapter pursues an analogy with visual art to analyse *The New Negro*'s form, paying special attention to techniques of juxtaposition and incongruity. Interpreting the anthology as a version of collage opens up new interpretive possibilities. As Anders Olsson has written of the 'anthologizing' process, 'the texts selected are taken out of their original context and brought into the frame of the anthology, that is, the texts are decontextualized to become recontextualized' (Olsson 2000, 15). Such a method, of course, is reminiscent of collage-making. There are also correspondences between how we read anthologies and interpret visual collage. Faced with an anthology, readers must tease out relationships between parts: each individual contribution is examined in relation to other contributions, to the whole (especially the editorial frame) and to its origin. This sense of a perspective that shifts restlessly from close-up to overview resembles the interpretive process that I have termed the double take, that crucial moment of recognition when we realize that a collage is at once a collection of fragments and an integrated whole.

Keeping these observations in mind, this chapter explores two concepts of collage with reference to *The New Negro*. One of them is author-centred, focusing on Locke's editorial decisions, his careful patterning of contributions. The other turns to questions of reading, exploring how reviewers have dipped into the anthology, creating juxtapositions that depart from Locke's intended thematic structure. To date, critics have tended to focus on Locke's editorial vision, noting that his choice of a 'genre-bending' format is strategic. As Anders Olsson has shown, the compilation of any anthology involves selection and arrangement: the editor's task is to order a 'mass of texts', developing a paradigm for their interpretation (2000, 273).

Moving beyond such analysis, I offer a new perspective on Locke's collage aesthetic by considering the anthology's initial reception. Analysis of early reviews reveals that readers often overlooked Locke's carefully patterned structure, with its consistent emphasis upon African American heterogeneity. Employing a technique of sampling, reviewers focused on particular contributions, smoothing over the heterogeneity hard-wired into the anthology's structure.

Democracy and the Anthology Form

'He has put not merely the best foot of the new Negro forward; he has put *all* his feet forward' (2007, 224). So Carl Van Vechten describes *The New Negro* in a review for the *New York Herald Tribune Books* in December 1925. Marking the anthology as a significant departure from previous representations of African American culture, Van Vechten notices a shift from a monolithic notion of black upper-class identity towards emphasis upon African American heterogeneity.

Van Vechten's review responds to the collage aesthetic of Alain Locke's landmark anthology, which juxtaposes diverse forms in an effort 'to document the New Negro culturally and socially' (*N* xxv). Building upon Van Vechten's insights, we might describe *The New Negro* as a kaleidoscope of disciplines and genres: poetry, prose, drama, artwork, critical essays, art criticism, anthropology, folklore and sociology sit side by side. As well as incorporating various media and genres, Locke makes room for a variety of contributors. One of the most unusual aspects of the anthology is its inclusion of white writers, such as the anthropologist Melville Herskovits, alongside African American artists and intellectuals. By framing the entire anthology with a dedication to 'the Younger Generation' and the score and lyrics for a line from a traditional spiritual, 'O, rise, shine for Thy Light is a' coming', Locke implies that his wide-ranging portrait of African American culture heralds a new era.

In spite of its diverse content, the volume is carefully structured. Locke divides material into thematic sections, such as 'Negro Youth Speaks', 'The New Scene' and 'The Negro and the American Tradition', which situate his delineation of the New Negro in the context of local, national and global cultural trends. Each section comprises a variety of genres and disciplinary approaches to the topic. 'The Negro Digs up his Past', for instance, opens with Arthur A. Schomburg's call for a revisionist history of African and African American cultural achievement since '[t]he American Negro must remake his past in order to make his future' (*N* 231). Next, Arthur Huff Fauset's essay on the importance of anthropological accuracy 'based on a scientific recording' (*N* 244) challenges the damaging legacy of Joel Chandler Harris's Uncle Remus tales, which established a tradition of 'misrepresentation of the temper and spirit of Negro folk lore' (*N* 241). Fauset puts his anthropological theory into practice in two folktale transcriptions that follow, one of which crosses media boundaries through its inclusion of a musical score (*N* 244). After that, Countee Cullen's poem 'Heritage', with its refrain 'What is Africa to me?', tilts away from the scientific framework of anthropology towards a more personal, reflective exploration of the difficulties posed by any attempt to connect with African heritage given the cultural dislocation of slavery. Locke rounds off the section with his essay on African art 'The Legacy of the Ancestral Arts', which aims to challenge a prevailing association of African American culture with primitivism.

Juxtaposition of diverse media is continued in illustrative material for the section. Small Africanized decorations, featuring masks, silhouette figures and geometric patterns, nestle in the text: they appear above essay titles and often at the end of contributions. At the same time, photographic images are used to document the richness and diversity of black culture. Alain Locke's 'The Legacy of the Ancestral Arts' showcases photographs of African art from Alfred Barnes's collection and various European ethnological museums, labelled by culture group, in the style of Franz Boas; and Schomburg's essay includes a sample title page from his famous collection of African American cultural artifacts.

As a number of commentators have noted, dynamic interplay between word and image characterizes *The New Negro* more generally because the entire volume is interspersed with images by Winold Reiss and Aaron Douglas. Reiss, a German immigrant whose interest in cultural types was partly inspired by his visits to German ethnographic museums, provides what Sieglinde Lemke has called 'a visual hagiography' of African American intellectuals (these portraits were printed in colour in the first edition) and documentary portraits of 'Harlem Types', such as 'The Librarian' and 'The School Teachers' (1998, 125). If Locke's selections from Reiss's *oeuvre* assert the painter's credentials as a realist, 'a folk-lorist of the brush and palette', the African American artist Aaron Douglas is aligned with modernist experimentation (*N* 419-20). Douglas's 'black-and-white geometric designs' not only fuse African and American themes and styles, but they also eschew realistic representation in favour of a patterning of shapes, lines and silhouettes that owes much to Egyptian funerary murals (Nadell 2004, 62).

For Locke, the interdisciplinary format of *The New Negro*, with its emphasis upon interracial collaboration and individual expression, is part of a wider attempt to rethink concepts of democracy, challenging the idea that 'democracy require[s] uniformity' (1925a, 676). Brent Hayes Edwards has convincingly argued that the impetus to anthologize blackness in the 1920s and 1930s was shaped by contemporary European fascination with non-European cultures and the institutionalization of Boasian anthropology, but Locke is also alert to the political potential of collage form (Edwards 2003, 44). In fact, he uses the anthology form to reconfigure democracy, highlighting the need for African American 'culture-citizenship'. In various statements of intent, Locke emphasizes the democratic openness of his collage form, in which many voices speak for themselves.

The openness of the anthology form lends itself to expressing democratic values because the inclusion of diverse voices creates a collage-like effect of multiplicity in unity. At the end of 'Negro Youth Speaks', for instance, he makes an explicit connection between an 'emancipating vision' of democracy and his version of the anthology form, which privileges the self-expression of multiple contributors who 'speak … for themselves' (*N* 53). As in his concept of 'culture-citizenship', which binds together cultural contribution and political participation in that order, Locke's project of documenting African American heterogeneity is connected to the question of adequate political representation in a democratic nation-state, even if the precise details of this relationship remain unspecified.

Given that redefining democracy is central to Locke's interdisciplinary format for the anthology, it is worth mentioning that this concept was the subject of considerable debate in early twentieth-century America. In the wake of Woodrow Wilson's campaign to make the world safe for democracy, the concept became a political football, put to work by anthropologists, cultural critics, politicians, journalists and writers, among others. From 1921 to 1926, there were no less than one hundred and twenty books in print with the word 'democracy' or its derivatives in the title (Birch 1993, 51).

With regard to Locke's participation in this debate, one of the most important contributions is Horace Kallen's 'Democracy versus the Melting-Pot', which characterizes America as 'a chorus of many voices each singing a rather different tune' (1996, 83). Kallen felt that the nation was at a crossroads: Americans needed to decide whether the United States should be 'a unison, singing the old Anglo-Saxon theme "America", the America of the New England school, or a harmony, in which that theme shall be dominant, perhaps, among others, but one among many, not the only one?' (1996, 89).

Locke's multidisciplinary anthology can be interpreted as an intervention in this debate, giving shape as it does to an alternative concept of democracy. Rejecting the idea of a single figure speaking for the collective – '[o]ur poets have now stopped speaking for the Negro – they speak as Negroes' – Locke builds upon Kallen's multi-vocal formulation, adding a new emphasis on racial diversity (N 48). To this end, he stresses the diversity of expression and opinion among African Americans in The New Negro. In Locke's account, an acceptance of difference is fundamental to democracy: it is only through the achievement of equality between diverse racial and cultural groups that 'American ideals' can be 'progressively fulfilled and realized' (N 12).

Locke's use of the word 'representative' is central to his endeavour to 'offer through art an emancipating vision to America' (N 53). As Mick Gidley has shown, 'representation' refers both to the artistic and political spheres. As a result, there is a relationship between what W.J.T. Mitchell calls 'things that stand for other things' and 'persons who act for other persons' (Gidley 1992, 2). With this in mind, one of Locke's strategies in The New Negro is to detach 'representative' art from the 'stiltedly self-conscious, and racially rhetorical rather than racially expressive' voice of the best-foot-forward philosophy (N 48), which he connects with class elitism and '"lily-whitism"' (Locke 1983b, 161).

Locke mines a rich seam of association between cultural and political representation to make claims for New Negro poets' ability to stand for the masses. Introducing a political vocabulary into his discussion of literature, he speaks of poets as 'a new leadership' who understand what the Great Migration is 'all about' (N 5). According to Locke, these poets express the people's experiences authentically and 'represent' their 'voice', without lapsing into propaganda: '[y]outh speaks, and the voice of the New Negro is heard. What stirs inarticulately in the masses is already vocal upon the lips of the talented few, and the future listens, however the present may shut its ears' (N 47). As such, the interests of the many are uttered by 'the talented few', in a manner that resembles democracy since individuals are represented by a deputy.

Locke's notion of representation recalls '[t]he fundamental idea of democratic legitimacy ... that the authorization to exercise state power must arise from the collective decisions of the members of a society who are governed by that power' (Cohen 1996, 95). Interracial collaboration lies at the core of Locke's democratic vision for The New Negro as he explains in 'Frontiers of Culture', a retrospective account of the anthology's genesis. In an attempt to 'rule[] out' 'racial chauvinism' and exclusiveness, he claims that he avoided the espousal of a single view in *The New Negro* (1989b, 232). Instead, participation in the New Negro project 'was democratically open to all who might be interested on the basis of collaboration and mutual understanding' (1989b, 232-3). According to Locke, the anthology was founded upon a model of democratic inclusiveness, which encouraged equal participation of various cultural and racial groups. Indeed, 'five of the collaborators of *The New Negro* were whites whose readily accepted passport was competent understanding of the cultural objectives of the movement and creative participation in them' (1989b, 232).

It is difficult, however, to miss the elitism that underpins Locke's model of cultural 'representation'. Following in the footsteps of W.E.B. Du Bois, he champions the vanguard efforts of a 'talented tenth', clinging onto the assumption that the 'masses' are inarticulate, a gesture that completely disregards a vibrant vernacular culture that was transforming America's northern cities (Griffin 1995, 64). Consequently, an intriguing tension between democratic openness and editorial control animates Locke's collage form. There is a discrepancy between Locke's democratic rhetoric and his editorial choices, which tend to reinstate gender, class and cultural hierarchies. As Anne Elizabeth Carroll has noted, there are several 'disappointing omissions and hierarchies' in *The New Negro*, and some of these come into play as Locke configures his concept of democracy (2005, 158). These countercurrents cluster around the issue of 'representation'. In 'The New Negro', for instance, Locke argues that the growth of racial contact and collaboration between 'the more intelligent and representative elements of the two race groups', who have been kept apart by social mores and prejudices, is 'an augury of a new democracy in American culture' (*N* 9). There are contradictory valuations at work here. On the plus side, a 'new democracy' is being forged through cultural collaboration. But ultimately, Locke restricts such 'democracy' to an educated upper-class elite, implying that some groups are 'more representative' than others. With this move comes a reliance on cultural, class and aesthetic hierarchies that introduces an element of exclusion to his notion of cultural democracy.

Consequently, it comes as no surprise that Locke has received considerable criticism for his political conservatism in *The New Negro*. According to Henry Louis Gates, there was a direct association between the New Negro and political radicalism until Locke appropriated the concept. Making a comparison with W.A. Domingo's 1920 description of the New Negro who 'speaks the language of the oppressed' to defy the 'language of the oppressor', Gates contends that Locke 'transformed the militancy associated with the trope and translated this into an apolitical movement of the arts' (Gates, 1988b, 147). Other critics have attended to class and gender biases in *The New Negro* (Carroll 2005, 158; Dawahare 2003, 39), or condemned Locke's failure to address what Barbara Foley has termed 'the material foundations of racism' (2003, 153). Such assessments certainly seem justified given Locke's tendency to sideline various kinds of radicalism – anti-colonialism, sexual politics or class struggle to name only a few – by bringing contributions into line with 'the discourse of nationalist cultural pluralism' (Foley 2003, 238).

'Culture-Citizenship': Collage Culture Patterns in *The New Negro*

Reading *The New Negro* as a collage, in which a variety of perspectives jostle, encourages us to resist the temptation to resolve such contradictions. The relationship established between specific contributions, and between part and whole is something to which I will return. In this section, I want to focus on Locke's efforts to define African American culture, not least because he often describes it in spatial terms as a collage-like pattern. Such analysis lays the foundation for my subsequent interpretation of the anthology's collage structure since there is a close relationship between Locke's theory of culture and his careful patterning of material in the volume.

For Locke, cultural participation is a first step towards social and economic equality: 'for the present, more immediate hope rests in the revaluation by white and black alike of the Negro in terms of his artistic endowments and cultural contributions, past and prospective' (*N* 15). Acknowledgement of the New Negro's role as 'a collaborator and participant in American civilization' (15) will, he claims, herald 'a new American attitude' (*N* 10). Taking this idea of 'collaboration' as his point of departure, Locke attempts to balance a claim for a distinctive African American cultural identity with emphasis upon the need for more substantial involvement in national institutions and systems:

> America seeking a new spiritual expansion and artistic maturity, trying to found an American literature, a national art, and national music implies a Negro-American culture seeking the same satisfactions and objectives. Separate as it may be in color and substance, the culture of the Negro is of a pattern integral with the times and with its cultural setting. ... Liberal minds to-day cannot be asked to peer with sympathetic curiosity into the darkened Ghetto of a segregated race life. ... Now that there is cultural adolescence and the approach to maturity, – there has come a development that makes these phases of Negro life only an interesting and significant segment of the general American scene (*N* xxvi).

Identifying shared 'satisfactions and objectives' and common patterns in black and white culture, Locke argues that any understanding of African American culture that restricts it to a 'darkened Ghetto', which can be viewed by white Americans with detachment, is no longer appropriate. Invoking a vocabulary of cultural slices, 'portion[s]' and components that recalls Boasian cultural description, African American culture is instead depicted as an important, distinctive part (with its own 'color and substance') of a larger, more diverse cultural whole, namely America. In a visual patterning of culture that lays stress upon plurality, a variety of distinct 'segment[s]' co-exist as equally important components of the 'general

American scene'. In this way, Locke stakes a claim to American cultural and political structures without losing sight of the particularity of African American experience.

This vision of a national culture composed of ethnic 'segment[s]' chimes with Locke's thesis in 'Racial Progress and Race Adjustment', a lecture he gave in 1915 under the auspices of the NAACP and Social Science Club. Stressing that 'this is not a doctrine of racial isolation ... or even a doctrine of race integrity', he articulates 'a theory of social conservation which in practice conserves the best in each group, and promotes the development of social solidarity out of heterogeneous elements' (1992b, 98). For Locke, retaining 'heterogeneous' ethnic group identities is fundamental to the emergence of a collective national consciousness. Contesting Boas's theory that the only way to achieve 'social solidarity' in a multiracial society is to encourage physical and cultural assimilation, he insists upon the significance of distinct contributions to a shared cultural whole:

> [C]ulture-citizenship is something which is to be acquired through social assimilation, not necessarily physical assimilation [.] It is a thing which is not acquired merely in terms of social [mixing of groups or] civilization merely. <<Culture-citizenship>> must come in terms of group contribution to what becomes a joint civilization. [That] is where the consummation of the doctrine that I have just mentioned will be found, because it will enable us [,] and others who have the burden of social proof placed upon them, to qualify in terms not merely of imitation but of contribution (1992b, 99, [Stewart's editorial markings]).

What stands out in this passage is Locke's hyphenation of the phrase 'culture-citizenship', a coinage that is both unusual and far-reaching in its implications. Yoking together culture (which here refers to both cultural production and a social group) with citizenship establishes a strong link between cultural and political participation. By placing culture before citizenship, Locke implies that political enfranchisement is an extension of contribution to the national culture. It is for this reason that socially disadvantaged groups, in particular, must move beyond 'imitation' of a politically dominant culture. For Locke, creation of a 'joint civilization', in which diverse ethnic groups contribute unique expressions, is the basis for a society of political equals. In accordance with his later account of the Harlem Renaissance as 'an interesting and significant segment of the general American scene' (*N* xxvi), he calls for a 'joint civilization', in which different ethnic groups, each with their own distinctive cultures, will become interdependent, sharing a composite civilization that is the 'consummation' of cultural contact.

In keeping with this theoretical account, Locke registers growing cultural interdependence between ethnic groups in America in his essays for *The New Negro*. The contradictions that characterize his position in 'Negro Youth Speaks', the essay introducing his selections of fiction and poetry for the anthology, stem from a simultaneous attempt to assert African American cultural distinctiveness while making connections to broader American trends:

> Primarily, of course, it is youth that speaks in the voice of Negro youth, but the overtones are distinctive; Negro youth speaks out of an unique experience and with a particular representativeness. All classes of a people under social pressure are permeated with a common experience; they are emotionally welded as others cannot be (*N* 47).

At first glance, Locke's position seems to be completely paradoxical. He claims that the artistic expression of 'Negro youth' is at once 'distinctive' and representative of 'common experience'. According to Locke, shared experiences of racial oppression, described somewhat euphemistically as 'social pressure', encourage group solidarity. This, the argument goes, creates an unusually close connection between individual artists and the community, which means that African American artists are well positioned to speak of 'common experience'. Much hangs on the vagueness of Locke's terminology. Since he is at pains to stress black culture's universal appeal, he couches New Negro cultural expression in terms that accentuate its relevance to society as a whole, including the dominant white group. There is little doubt that Locke glides over the realities of racism in the 1920s as he strains towards universality. Through careful wording, he explains the curious idea of 'particular representativeness', pairing an assertion of cultural distinctiveness with an appeal to universality in a manner that exposes the compromises that such a position entails.

In accordance with his theory of the nation-state as a composite of various ethnic contributions, Locke maintains two running themes in 'Negro Youth Speaks' that are of equal importance to his democratic cultural vision. On the one hand, he emphasizes African American self-expression, laying stress upon the emergence of direct, immediate, authentic speech. Noting a departure from minstrelsy and dialect, he comments: '[o]ur poets have now stopped speaking for the Negro – they speak as Negroes' (*N* 48). This tiny but crucial shift from 'Negro' to 'Negroes' registers a movement away from adherence to a single representative model towards embracing the variety of individual self-expression. On the other hand, Locke goes some way to demonstrate the participation of African American writers in broader cultural trends. For one thing, many of the new African American artists, such as Jean Toomer, are 'ultra-modern', occupying a position at the forefront of the avant-garde (*N* 50).

Nevertheless, there is an intriguing inconsistency at the heart of Locke's rhetoric of cultural democracy. His final comment in 'Negro Youth Speaks', for instance, invokes the idea of democratic representation: he refuses to limit interpretation of artists who 'speak so adequately for themselves' (*N* 53). The irony, of course, is that Locke espouses the rhetoric of democracy, making room for individual self-expression, but he actually frames these voices in such a way as to accentuate certain aspects of African American culture, while relegating others to the background. To take only the most notorious example, his insistence upon altering the title of Claude McKay's poem 'White House' to 'White Houses' in the *Survey Graphic* and *The New Negro*, despite the poet's protests, served to blunt the political edge of McKay's indictment of American racism (Lewis 1997, 151).

Such contradictions expose the limitations of Locke's democratic vision. In statements of intent, Locke consistently emphasizes the democratic openness of collage form, in which examples are left to speak for themselves, creating space for active reader involvement. Within the pages of the anthology, he even goes so far as to present the anthology as a transparent document of African American culture in the 1920s. In introductory material, there is no obvious interpretive template or even a survey of the anthology's contents. Instead, Locke speaks as if he played little part in deciding what to include: '[t]his volume aims to document the New Negro culturally and socially, – to register the transformations of the inner and outer life of the Negro in America that have so significantly taken place in the last few years' (*N* xxv). Smoothing over the process of selection, which is crucial to the compilation of any anthology, he describes his task as exposition, not interpretation: he aims to 'register' change rather than to explain it.

In fact, this claim to randomness or complete diversity is a fiction, which masks the patterned, controlled format of *The New Negro*. For a start, Locke's theory that a democratic nation-state should possess a composite culture informs his selections, resulting in several notable omissions. As Anthony Dawahare puts it, 'Locke appropriates the rhetoric of the Left and the black nationalists – indeed, at times, representing himself as both an advocate of the rank and file and a national awakener – while he simultaneously excludes from his anthology virtually all of the writings published in radical black journals' (2003, 31). At the other end of the political spectrum, Jessie Fauset's fiction lost out because of what Locke regarded as its 'cautious moralism and guarded idealizations' (*N* 50). Notwithstanding such exclusions, Locke never admits that there may an identifiable logic governing his selections. Consequently, he obscures the fact that the structure of *The New Negro*, with its carefully managed juxtapositions, is a product of editorial control, which has been orchestrated to generate specific effects.

Anthologies and Little Magazines

Approaching *The New Negro* as a version of collage not only exposes a governing tension between the apparently democratic openness of collage form, and Locke's efforts to limit meaning in accordance with his editorial goals. It also sheds light on Locke's complex engagement with Euro-American modernist experimentation, especially the mixed media format of little magazines. A brief account of the anthology's origins demonstrates that Locke drew inspiration from both Euro-American modernist and African American sources. Some of the tensions that emerge in *The New Negro* stem from his emphasis on folk culture as a means through which 'to lay claim to the Negro's Americanism', a narrative that owes much to a discourse of American nationalism espoused by contemporary cultural critics, such as Waldo Frank and Van Wyck Brooks (Foley 2003, 199). Moving beyond a consideration of subject matter, it soon becomes clear that the formal texture of the little magazines was a shaping influence on *The New Negro*'s multigeneric format.

There is little doubt that the anthology was an important 1920s and 1930s genre. To consider at first only African American letters, the era saw the publication of several significant volumes: James Weldon Johnson's *The Book of American Negro Poetry* (1922); Robert T. Kerlin's *Negro Poets and Their Poems* (1923); Alain Locke's *The New Negro* (1925); Countee Cullen's *Caroling Dusk: An Anthology of Verse by Negro Poets* (1927); Charles S. Johnson's *Ebony and Topaz: A Collectanea* (1927); V.F. Calverton's *Anthology of American Negro Literature* (1929); and Nancy Cunard's sprawling, 'generically indiscriminate', elaborately decorated *Negro* (1934), which employs a transnational approach that encompasses Africa, the Caribbean, Europe and the United States (North 1994, 189).[2] According to Brent Hayes Edwards, such anthologies must be examined against the backdrop of a 'much wider, multilingual, Western rush to anthologize blackness' in Europe and America, a phenomenon that 'coincides with the *vogue nègre* (the acquisition-minded European fascination with black performance and artifacts) and with the institutionalization of anthropology as a discipline' (2003, 44).

Two main types of anthology are of particular relevance to Locke's formal choices. In the early twentieth century, a glut of single genre anthologies either announced or showcased a cultural movement. From 1915 to 1917, for instance, Amy Lowell edited *Some Imagist Poets*, a series of anthologies that offered a survey of imagism. Under her guidance, each selected poet was 'permitted to represent himself by the work he considers his best' (Lowell 1986, 53-4). Lowell added explanatory prefaces, which guided readers' interpretation of imagism, emphasizing shared aesthetic concerns: the use of common speech, free verse and breadth of subject (1986, 54). In short, Lowell hoped to recontextualize individual poets as a literary movement: she proposed to bring out 'our cooperative volume each year for a short term of years, until we have made a place for ourselves and our principles such as we desire' (Lowell 1986, 55).

James Weldon Johnson's influential *The Book of American Negro Poetry* fulfils a similar and yet further function. The first anthology of African American verse to be printed by a major American publisher, this collection covers a wider historical scope than Lowell's strictly contemporary selections. Johnson set out to document a rich tradition of African American poetry because, as he put it, '[t]he public, generally speaking, does not know that there are American Negro poets' (1958, 9). As well as announcing a movement worthy of critical attention, he invests his project with political significance, 'framing' his selections with a

---

[2]   For an informative account of anthologies of African American literature, see Kinnamon (1997, 22-8) and Edwards (2003, 331-2).

detailed preface that sets out to 'reshap[e] the parameters of "the Negro question" in the United States' (Edwards 2003, 46). Emphasizing African American contributions to a broader American culture, Johnson advocates a programme of cultural nationalism: 'nothing will do more to change that mental attitude [of white superiority] and raise [the African American's] status than a demonstration of intellectual parity by the Negro through the production of literature and art' (1958, 9). In other words, Johnson envisions a political purpose for his anthology, arguing that acknowledgement of African American cultural vitality could be a first step towards political and social equality.

Rhetoric pairing political and cultural aims was by no means unfamiliar in anthologies of the 1920s and 1930s. A collection of essays by another identifiable cultural group, *I'll Take My Stand: The South and the Agrarian Tradition by Twelve Southerners* (1930), for instance, launched what was immediately recognized as an anti-Left and anti-African American manifesto for the 'Old South', which opposed industrialism and modernization.

A second type of anthology, which accords with Johnson's celebration of a distinctive African American literary tradition, could be broadly defined as nationalist in its exposure of American culture as something unique, valuable in its own right. As Susan Hegeman has convincingly argued, discourses of anthropology and cultural criticism converged in the 1920s to generate a particular mode of thinking about American culture: Americans began to consider 'themselves and their allegiances in a newly relational, contextual, and often critical way' (1999, 4). Several early twentieth-century anthologies embody this new self-reflexive vision of American culture.

Harold E. Stearns's *Civilization in the United States: An Inquiry by Thirty Americans*, published in 1922, explores American culture as a 'civilization' comparable to European culture in its complexity and depth. In the preface, Stearns presents his anthology as 'the deliberate and organized outgrowth of the common efforts of like-minded men and women to see the problem of modern American civilization as a whole, and to illuminate by careful criticism the special aspect of that civilization with which the individual is most familiar' (1922, iii). In line with wider anthropological interest in cultural '*complexity* and *wholeness*' (Manganaro 2002, 7), 'careful' analysis of American culture 'as a whole' enables a 'self-conscious and deliberately critical examination of ourselves', paving the way for development of "authentic" American expression (1922, vii). For Stearns, the anthology format facilitates this kind of self-reflexive survey since different writers tackle American culture from a variety of disciplinary angles, refusing to settle on a single idea of America. To take only a handful of examples, he finds space for Lewis Mumford's 'The City'; H.L. Mencken's 'Politics'; Robert H. Lowie's 'Science'; Frank M. Colby's 'Humor'; Alfred B. Kuttner's 'Nerves'; and Elsie Clews Parsons's 'Sex'.

A survey of early twentieth-century anthologies reveals that Stearns was not alone in his manipulation of the genre to scrutinize American culture. To mention only a few examples, this approach was employed in Norman

Foerster's *Humanism and America: Essays on the Outlook of Modern Civilisation* (1930), Fred J. Ringel's *America as Americans See It* (1932) and Waldo Frank, Lewis Mumford, Dorothy Norman, Paul Rosenfeld and Harold Rugg's *America and Alfred Stieglitz: A Collective Portrait* (1934). The volume on the photographer Alfred Stieglitz warrants special attention because contributors celebrate Stieglitz, whose famous "291" gallery introduced Americans to French modernist art as well as American painters like Georgia O'Keeffe and Marsden Hartley, 'as the leader of a communal creative movement, within the march of modern thought and within the central preoccupation of our era: the creating of a new civilization, a new culture, a new world' (1975, 3-4).

The New Negro certainly shares some features with these anthologies. For a start, Locke uses his volume to launch a cultural movement, a 'Negro Renaissance' (*N* xxvii). And like Johnson, he emphasizes the contributions New Negro writers make to a broader national culture, assuming that a reassessment of African American cultural production will result in improved political and social conditions. Furthermore, Locke's emphasis upon new ways of seeing, his 'defamiliarization of old modes of perception', echoes the rhetoric of newness that characterizes cultural nationalist anthologies, a convergence that is hardly surprising given that both Locke and Young American critics like Waldo Frank drew upon anthropological discourse in their quest for a fresh lens through which to view American culture (Franke 1999, 27).

Nevertheless, Locke's anthology, with its mixing of genres and approaches, is far more eclectic than any of these books. This is, at least in part, a consequence of the collection's origin as a magazine. The overall structure of *The New Negro* and many of its individual pieces had their roots in a March 1925 special issue of the *Survey Graphic*, 'Harlem, Mecca of the Negro', which was guest edited by Locke. Although there are several significant differences between *The New Negro* and the magazine, not least a broadening of its focus beyond Harlem, the special issue did establish a template for the anthology's interdisciplinary format. As Martha Jane Nadell explains, some of the most striking 'interartistic' elements of the magazine – the illustrated articles and Winold Reiss's type sketches – were part of the *Survey Graphic*'s 'standard formula' for 'representing types' (2004, 48-50).

Locke's unease with such journalistic realism generated further generic diversity since he wanted to 'challenge Old Negro representations and include New Negro representations, especially in the realm of arts and letters' (Nadell 2004, 50). In the *Survey Graphic*, J.A. Rogers's essay 'Jazz at Home', for instance, is not only broken up by a Langston Hughes's jazz poem, but it is also illustrated by a series of Winold Reiss's paintings, which incorporate a variety of images – a cityscape, a child playing, depictions of encounters between individuals from various social backgrounds, an Egyptian-style silhouette to name only a few – to capture Harlem's cultural energy. Such stylistic incongruity led *The Survey* editor Joseph K. Hart to describe the magazine, in highly visual terms, as a 'mosaic' in his opening remarks for the issue, 'The Gist of It' (Locke 1925a, 627).

Clearly, the anthology's scope was shaped, at least in part, by *The Survey*'s goals. As Martha Jane Nadell explains, 'the interartistic logic of the *Survey Graphic* rests on the concept of the "survey" itself, the formula on which the magazine relied' (2004, 39). Governed by a commitment to social accuracy, the magazine had established a reputation for documenting new cultural movements: 'New Ireland' in November 1921, 'New Russia' in March 1923, and Mexico in May 1924. 'The Gist of It' declares a parallel focus upon cultural blossoming in Harlem, with special reference to 'the subtle traces of race growth and interaction through the shifting outline of social organization and by the flickering light of individual achievement' (Locke 1925a, 627). This contextualization of the Harlem Renaissance in the light of an international cultural awakening among marginalized peoples influenced the magazine's format, introducing what Nadell calls 'the complex dance between type and individual, social science or journalistic and aesthetic readings of the modern African American experience, and a realist visual discourse and a modernist idiom' (2004, 51).

Winold Reiss had produced pictures of 'cultural types' for the *Survey Graphic* issue on Mexico in 1924 and, later that year, Paul Kellogg, editor at the *Survey*, asked him to illustrate the Harlem issue. Kellogg gave Reiss complete responsibility for the issue's artwork, commissioning portraits of Harlem residents and New Negro leaders (Stewart 1989, 47-8). In so doing, he established a tension between Locke's project of self-representation and the 'ethnographic quality' of Reiss's 'Type Studies' (Carroll 2005, 122), which identify group characteristics in such a way as to imply that New Negroes are a group 'distinct from the readers of the magazine' (Nadell 2004, 40). Moreover, it seems likely that collaboration with Paul Kellogg opened Locke's eyes to the rich variety of layouts of image and text available to him. Kellogg, as Alan Trachtenberg reminds us, played a crucial role in developing innovative combinations of image and text in the pages of *The Survey*, not least when he worked with Lewis Hine, a photographer who 'experimented in an extraordinary variety of communicative forms – "every permutation of the picture-text marriage," observes historian Daile Kaplan: "photo montage, photo-story, photo mosaic, picture essay, centerfold, centerfold pull-out, accordian-fold leaflet, post card, and Time Exposures" – the latter a title he used for a montage panel he introduced in 1914' (Trachtenberg 1989, 198-9).

As well as considering the specifics of *The New Negro*'s textual roots in the *Survey Graphic*, Locke's multi-generic form can also be related to the eclecticism of little magazines, such as *The Double Dealer*, *Little Review* and *The Dial*, which printed artistic work that was not acceptable to commercial periodicals and presses (Hoffman 1947, 2). Of particular relevance here is the avant-garde magazine *The Seven Arts*, which served as one of the most significant forums for the so-called Young Americans, a group of cultural critics that included Paul Rosenfeld, Van Wyck Brooks and Waldo Frank. During its short print run from November 1916 to October 1917, contributors were at once highly critical of contemporary American culture and desperate to establish an authentic artistic tradition in

America, 'which shall be fundamentally an expression of our American life' ([n. d.], 51).

In his 'Foreword' to *The New Negro*, Locke connects the New Negro project of defining African American culture with a broader search for 'an American literature, a national art, and a national music' (*N* xxvi), a search that was frequently discussed in the pages of little magazines like *The Seven Arts* and *The Double Dealer*, 'a magazine with a specifically southern aesthetic to develop and promote' (Whalan 2007, 7). What was at stake in such an expression of allegiance with Euro-American modernism given that these magazines were, for the most part, produced by and for white Americans?

George Hutchinson has convincingly argued that lack of attention to the Young American critics has led to an assumption that there was considerable distance between Euro-American modernism and the Harlem Renaissance. Instead, he contends that critical essays by Randolph Bourne and Van Wyck Brooks, among others, 'precisely define the reference points to which Alain Locke alludes in *The New Negro* when he aligns his project with the search for a new America' (1995, 94). Focusing upon institutional structures that supported the Harlem Renaissance, Hutchinson is alert to the ways in which ideas disseminated in *The Seven Arts* 'helped spawn – and create audiences for – new magazines and publishers that transformed the cultural landscape and opened spaces for the emergence of African American literary modernism' (1995, 93).

It is less often remembered that the interdisciplinary format of such magazines may also have been a source of inspiration for Locke's collage form in *The New Negro*. In this context, it is significant that James Oppenheim lays stress upon multi-generic layout in his manifesto for *The Seven Arts* in November 1916:

> *The Seven Arts* will publish stories, short plays, poems, essays and brief editorials. Such arts as cannot be directly set forth in the magazine will receive expression through critical writing, which, it is hoped, will be no less creative than the fiction and poetry. In this field the aim will be to give vistas and meanings rather than a monthly survey or review; to interpret rather than to catalogue. We hope that creative workers themselves will also set forth their vision and their inspiration ([n. d.], 53).

In short, *The Seven Arts* is not a magazine for artists, but an expression of artists for the community.

Oppenheim implies that the heterogeneity of American culture requires new formal textures. The magazine's eclectic format, which at once incorporates a variety of genres and transforms conventional approaches to such genres as the critical essay, is part of an attempt at national redefinition akin to that of Harold Stearns in *Civilization in the United States*. Rather than providing a 'survey' or overview of American culture, which inevitably fixes down and limits its coordinates, the editors aim to open up a variety of interpretive possibilities. Given this, it is significant that the word 'vistas' recalls Walt Whitman's *Democratic*

Vistas (1871), which yokes sharp criticism of an American culture crippled by slavish imitation of things European with an impassioned call for 'national, original archetypes in literature' (2170) that are both 'democratic and modern' (1994b, 2171). A comparable commitment to fostering American expression in all its variety underpins *The Seven Arts* project. For Oppenheim, the magazine can only succeed as 'an expression of artists for the community' if cultural plurality is addressed through a variety of forms and styles.

Since it is inflected by the eclecticism of the little magazines, *The New Negro*'s multi-generic form does, to some extent, diverge from contemporary models of the anthology. There is clearly a connection between Locke's formal choices and his project of cultural documentation. When Locke aligns his project with Young American criticism, however, a tension emerges between his investment in American narratives of belonging and the assertions of ethnic distinctiveness made by Locke himself and some of his contributors.

Anthropological Discourse in *The New Negro*: Juxtaposition as Editorial Control

As this suggests, Locke's project of representing the New Negro is fraught with contradictions. Focusing upon the dynamic interplay between word and image in the pages of *The New Negro*, Nadell and Carroll have demonstrated that Locke establishes patterns of juxtaposition to stage tensions or connections between individual pieces. Nadell, for example, notices the orchestrated dialogue between images by Reiss and Douglas, an interplay that generates a narrative about an emergent African American modernist artistic tradition (2004, 60-67). Comparison with visual collage can shed light on such productive juxtapositions. I have already mentioned that collage and anthologies share a compositional method based upon assemblage and recontextualization. Given this, an interpretive technique analogous to the double take, that crucial moment when we recognize that a collage is both a collection of scraps and an integrated whole, promises to illuminate Locke's project of embodying the New Negro. In particular, such an approach allows for detailed analysis of individual contributions without losing sight of the overall 'picture' that these collaged fragments produce. To investigate the specifics of this reading process, I now turn to the treatment of anthropological discourse in *The New Negro*, paying special attention to Locke's juxtaposition of individual contributions.

Boasian anthropology has a significant presence in the anthology. Not only do specific pieces, such as Locke's 'The Legacy of the Ancestral Arts' and Arthur Huff Fauset's 'American Negro Folk Literature', deploy ethnographic cultural description, but the entire project follows Boas's cue in attempting to 'recreate the complete context of a single moment in time' (Elliott 2002, 6). Attention to this ethnographic paradigm exposes some of the ways in which Locke establishes patterns of juxtaposition to orchestrate multiple perspectives on black culture, capturing a moment of transition when African Americans faced the question of how to represent themselves as a people.

One of the most striking examples of Boasian cultural description in the volume is Charles S. Johnson's 'The New Frontage on American Life', which pivots on a claim that '[a] new type of Negro is evolving – a city Negro' (*N* 285). Yet, it is not only Johnson's scientific vocabulary, his rather problematic emphasis on 'types', that signals an engagement with anthropology. He also reworks Boas's emphasis upon racial mixing to describe what Werner Sollors has called 'intra-ethnic diversity' (Sollors 1986, 100): his city Negro is 'an unpredictable mixture of all possible temperaments' as 'yet in evolution' (*N* 294).

Boasian anthropology becomes a platform for the formulation of a complex, shifting conception of identity, which aims to resist reductive stereotyping through an emphasis upon fluidity:

> Thus the new frontier of Negro life is flung out in a jagged, uneven but progressive pattern. For a group historically retarded and not readily assimilated, contact with its surrounding culture breeds quite uneven results. There is no fixed racial level of culture. The lines cut both vertically and horizontally. There are as great differences, with reference to culture, education, sophistication, among Negroes as between the races. ... And just as these currents move down and across and intersect, so may one find an utter maze of those rationalizations of attitudes of differently placed Negro groups toward life in general, and their status in particular. But a common purpose is integrating these energies born of new conflicts, and it is not at all improbable that the culture which has both nourished and abused these strivings will, in the end, be enriched by them (*N* 297-8).

This passage certainly bears the mark of what has been called the Boasian 'culture concept', with its 'spatial reorganization of human differences' (Hegeman 1999, 232). Developing a collage-like pattern that recalls Franz Boas's 1904 account of 'converging and diverging lines' of cultural development (Boas 1974a, 34), Johnson describes a 'maze' in which vertical and horizontal lines 'move down and across and intersect' since there is 'no fixed racial level of culture'. Above all, such a formulation suggests cultural energy, capturing in its dynamics a moment of transition when disparate elements are in unpredictable play. In this metaphor, Johnson develops a model in which myriad particulars of identity, derived from occupation, class and culture, can reside and yet there is a level of cohesion or unity, even if it is somewhat unstable. Holding contradictions in view rather than resolving them, he contends that 'a common purpose is ... born of new conflicts': commonality develops out of diversity and representativeness out of registering differences.

In his emphasis upon identity in process, Johnson departs from Boas. Even though Boas identified historical processes of migration, trade and contact as the motors of cultural change, his commitment to portraying culture as a 'synchronic, static entity' meant that he tended to render cultural examples in ahistorical terms (Elliott 2002, 22). Consequently, he struggled with '[t]he difficulty of reconciling the documentation of culture as a static phenomenon with the necessity of accounting for cultural change' (Elliott 2002, 25). By contrast, Johnson's account of African American culture as an irregular 'maze' is rooted in a historical process of adjustment: the Great Migration. Recourse to historical developments allows Johnson to sidestep reductive stereotypes, which fix down identity, by placing emphasis upon complex historical factors that generated 'uneven' and 'jagged' results in terms of culture, education and attitude. Yet, as in the anthology as a whole, paradoxes emerge as Johnson delineates a unifying image while stressing racial diversity.

If individual pieces employ Boasian cultural description to develop a fresh lens for understanding African American identity, a more complex picture emerges as a consequence of Locke's juxtaposition of essays that bring an anthropological perspective to bear on black culture. Locke sequences contributions in such a way as to add weight to his own interpretation of African American culture. In this context, it is significant that an essay by *The Survey* editor Paul Kellogg, which interprets African American cultural and social advances in the early twentieth century as a 'belated sharing in the American tradition of pioneering', is placed next to Johnson's piece (*N* 271-2). As in a visual collage, Locke establishes relationships between apparently distinct fragments, relationships that force readers to look again, reassessing their initial assumptions.

When interpreted as a discrete essay, Kellogg's article reads as an endorsement of assimilation, with an adoption of American mores and codes being equated with political advancement. Interpreted alongside Johnson's essay, and within the context of the whole anthology, however, this piece contributes to a broader questioning of the process of cultural observation, an issue that was a key concern for Boasian anthropologists. A recurring motif in Boas's work, for instance, is his idealization of the anthropologist, who, he claims, can transcend his or her own culture to obtain an objective view of the world. In fact, participant observation masked 'the complexity of the intersubjective encounter between fieldworker and native, and its inevitable power relations' (Jacobs 2001, 115). In this context, Locke's juxtaposition of essays by Johnson and Kellogg enables him to stage a variety of perspectives on African American culture, testing their limitations.

The participant observer's capacity to unsettle cultural dynamics is of prime importance when considering Kellogg's discussion of 'the first fruits of the Negro Renaissance' (*N* xxvii):

> How to unfold it? Our number [the Harlem issue of the *Survey Graphic*] was cut from city cloth, it brought out the seams of social problems which underlie it, but also, and in all its sheen, the cultural pattern that gave it texture. It proved a magic carpet which swung the reader not across the minarets and bazaars of some ancient Arabia, but the wells and shrines of a people's renaissance. The pageant of it swept past in pastel and story, poem and epic prose, and the response was instant. In this volume, what was then done fragmentarily is now done in a way which will endure (*N* 276).

With its emphasis upon writing African American culture from outside its parameters, this passage raises a number of questions about the limitations of participant observation. Kellogg not only presumes a distance between himself and the culture he observes, but his implied reader is white. Consequently, he runs the risk of treating African Americans as 'specimens, as if they were a separate group of people, set apart and different from their viewers' (Carroll 2005, 125). Wheeling from examination of the minutiae of African American society to a quasi-anthropological bird's eye view of a "foreign" culture, he maintains a sense of distance throughout the passage.

In accordance with *The Survey*'s documentary approach, his description of the Harlem Renaissance as a homely product of 'city cloth' offers a privileged perspective of African American culture, a point of view that recalls Jacob Riis's photographic expeditions in the Lower East Side slums (Trachtenberg 1989, 170). Echoing Riis's sensational disclosure of 'how the other half lives', Kellogg promises to expose hidden 'seams' in American society by illuminating 'social problems' that affect urban America. In the next breath, however, detailed observation is supplanted by a panoramic overview. Although Kellogg pulls back from an exotic comparison with Arabian 'minarets and bazaars' to focus on the 'wells and shrines of a people's renaissance', he maintains a sharp distinction between subject and reader, positioning us on a 'magic carpet' as spectators of a stately 'pageant'. These perspectives are highly problematic since they cast the New Negro 'in the distorted perspective of a social problem' without attending to complex factors that shape individual identity, factors that Johnson places at the core of his essay (*N* 4).

It is helpful to consider Locke's juxtaposition of material in relation to a formulation of collage because his placement of individual fragments is purposeful: he places contributions side by side to establish thematic preoccupations that strengthen his case for African American cultural distinctiveness *and* participation in American cultural structures. Such manipulation of the anthology format to reinforce particular views is best illustrated by his careful framing of Melville Herskovits's 'The Negro's Americanism'. In making the case that there is little difference between white and black culture in America, Herskovits addresses the issue of perspective explicitly, inviting readers to share his outsiders' view of Harlem through such phrases as '[y]ou may look' and '[n]otice them' (*N* 354). Combining conventions from travel writing and ethnography, he positions himself as an outsider when describing his planned visit to Harlem: '[s]hould I not be able to discover there [the African American's] ability, of which we are so often told, to produce unique cultural traits [?]' (*N* 353).

In line with Boas's 'relentless drive to accumulate and publish cultural material' (Elliott 2002, 11), Herskovits documents every aspect of Harlem life, from dress codes, occupation, education and sexual behaviour to language usage, entertainment and libraries, '[a]nd finally, after a time, it occurred to me that what I was seeing was a community just like any other American community. The same pattern, only a different shade!' (*N* 353) Taking his cue from Boas, he prises apart an evolutionist, and often racist, connection between race and culture, asserting that African Americans have undergone 'complete acculturation' (360) so that there is 'not a trace' of African culture left in their cultural practices (*N* 359). Unfortunately, his argument that race does not produce culture made him 'apparently impervious to … economic hardship and demographic trauma' on the streets of Harlem (Foley 2003, 231).

A brief glimpse at the editorial history of this piece gives us a sense of Locke's aims for *The New Negro*. When Locke first wrote to Herskovits to interest him in the question 'Has the Negro A Unique Social Pattern?', his intentions were clear: 'I have been bold enough to characterize it [the question] as an analysis of the Negro's peculiar social pattern, and an estimate of its capacity in social survival and culture building' (Helbling 1999a, 65). Evidently, Locke was angling for a study that unearthed an element of African American distinctiveness. Indeed, when a version of Herskovits's article appeared in the *Survey Graphic*, Locke added editorial comments that subtly criticized its account of cultural development.

In a short editorial note, he agreed that 'Negro life' may look acculturated when '[l]ooked at in its externals', but '[i]nternally, perhaps it is another matter. Does democracy require uniformity? If so, it threatens to be safe, but dull. … Old folkways may not persist, but they may leave a mental trace, subtly recorded in emotional temper and coloring social reactions' (1925a, 676). Although he is careful to sidestep the issue of Herskovits's racial identity, Locke describes a superficial account of African American culture that does not get to grips with the complexity of intercultural contact. Alluding to Horace Kallen's 'Democracy versus the Melting-Pot', with its account of democracy as 'a multiplicity in a unity' (92) in which individuals retain an 'ancestrally determined' sense of self, Locke articulates an alternative version of American identity that makes room for African American cultural distinctiveness (Kallen 1996, 91). 'Old folkways', which derive from both the South and Africa, he tells us, leave fragmentary 'mental trace[s]' upon African American individuals and this 'ancestrally determined' sense of self 'color[s]' the dominant culture. In short, Locke challenges the idea that 'democracy require[s] uniformity', implying that a fulfilment of the concept in fact depends upon fostering a composite culture, in which cultural differences are preserved.

These editorial comments, which play off acculturation with cosmopolitanism, were excised from *The New Negro*. It is tempting to speculate that Locke allows Herskovits's argument to stand on its own terms without editorial comment because of his intention to 'document' the dynamics of a particular cultural moment (*N* xxv). However, such a reading underestimates the extent to which Locke's framing of the essay serves to muffle the impact of its assimilationist stance. For one thing, attention to the artwork that surrounds Herskovits's article undercuts his claims about African retentions. As Anne Elizabeth Carroll has pointed out, 'the essay opens and closes with Reiss's Africanist drawings, which imply a connection between African Americans and Africa that directly contradicts Herskovits's essay' (Carroll 2005, 179). Furthermore, Locke's careful sandwiching of the piece between an essay by W.A. Domingo that documents the diverse cultural heritage of West Indians in Harlem and Walter White's testimony to continuing racism in New York (which begins with an anecdote about Paul Robeson being unable to secure a restaurant table after an acclaimed performance on Broadway), undermines Herskovits's claim about the decreasing importance of racial categories on two separate fronts. Although Locke offers little in the way of explicit commentary on the article, he dramatizes the limitations of Herskovits's outsider's perspective in striking ways.

In keeping with his subtitle for the anthology, *The New Negro: An Interpretation*, Locke's declared aim is to frame debates rather than resolving them, holding multiple aesthetic and political possibilities in view. As Locke explained in 'Frontiers of Culture', a speech delivered at Howard University in 1949, there was a considered strategy behind his emphasis upon the multiplicity of African American culture. By making space for conflicting views and including white writers alongside African American artists, he hoped to supersede a superficial fixation with 'color' by developing deeper understanding of the content, or internal workings, of African American culture: '[t]he substance of Negro life was emphasized, not its complexion' (1989b, 232). This is not to say that the anthology is without tensions as Locke's sustained, if understated, questioning of white constructions of African American culture demonstrates. For a start, it is difficult to miss the irony that Locke employs a comparable vocabulary of surface and depth, of 'substance' and 'complexion' in his critique of Herskovits's contribution to the *Survey Graphic*. Such contradictions give the anthology a quality of strained plurality, which stems from Locke's desire to recognize difference without being restricted to racial categories. In reality, this ideal often breaks down in the face of cross-cultural misunderstanding so that culture lines once again coincide with racial categories.

Reading the anthology as a kind of collage allows for simultaneous attention to individual contributions and broader thematic preoccupations that give the anthology a fragile kind of unity. Taking this close-up and long-distance view, it soon becomes clear that it would be a mistake to take Locke's inclusive rhetoric at face value. There is, in fact, a tension between Locke's attempts to control meaning through a series of editorial acts and his alleged commitment to democratic openness. Ultimately, the complex, patterned structure of *The New Negro* is a product of editorial control, which has been orchestrated to generate specific effects.

When compared with other examples of the Harlem Renaissance collage aesthetic, *The New Negro* anthology lacks vibrancy, partly because Locke retreats from the incongruous shifts of tone and register that enliven the writings of Zora Neale Hurston and Jean Toomer. As Barbara Foley has noted, in the process of editing the *Survey Graphic* for publication as an anthology, Locke excised some of the starkest incongruities. He removed pieces that were 'critical of ghettoization' (227), 'eliminating an explicitly leftist voice from the anthology' in the process (2003, 225). Moreover, the vernacular African American culture that is such a rich resource for Toomer and Hurston has no significant presence in the anthology.

Drawing the Culture-Line: Artwork in *The New Negro*

Nowhere are these tensions between singularity and multiplicity, inclusion and exclusion more prominent than in the anthology's artwork. Since there is now a substantial body of work on the dynamic interplay of word and image in *The New Negro*, I will not offer a sustained close analysis of Locke's juxtaposition of images by Aaron Douglas and Winold Reiss. Instead, I want to focus on Locke's theoretical discussions of art in order to expose tensions that animate his attempt to move from a color line to a culture line. Such analysis moves beyond my central focus on techniques of juxtaposition and incongruity in order to illuminate the contradictory impulses that underpin Locke's collage form.

Interracial collaboration is central to *The New Negro*'s representational project. In 'The Legacy of the Ancestral Arts', for instance, Locke champions Winold Reiss as a model for African American artists, especially with regard to matters of style. According to Locke, the anthology's illustrative material functions as a 'path-breaking guide' for new artists: '[i]n idiom, technical treatment and objective social angle, it is a bold iconoclastic break with the current traditions that have grown up about the Negro subject in American art' (*N* 266). Only a cultural outsider, the argument goes, can challenge 'reactionary conventions of art' that perpetuate an assumption that African American subjects are not worthy of serious artistic attention (*N* 262).

As Locke tells it, Reiss occupies a position comparable to European modernists who draw inspiration from African motifs and styles, a point underlined by vocabulary readily associated with modernist experimentation, such as 'iconoclastic' and 'newness'. But, for Locke, Reiss's engagement with African American subjects is of a different order to the interest in non-European forms among modernists like Pablo Picasso, Paul Gauguin and Paul Klee since his treatment of such topics is neither superficial nor exploitative. Rather, his 'bold iconoclastic break with the current traditions' (266) will facilitate the development of 'a new style, a distinctive fresh technique, and some sort of characteristic idiom' in African American art (*N* 267).

'[S]elf-portraiture', which Locke celebrates in 'Negro Youth Speaks' by emphasizing speech, song and voice, is clearly more complicated than his focus on immediate self-expression suggests (*N* xxv). The implication is that development of 'some sort of characteristic idiom' (267) and 'a school of Negro art, a local and a racially representative tradition' can be achieved only through sustained engagement with African and European traditions (*N* 266). In a striking reversal of a contemporary modernist interest in non-European forms, Locke encourages study of European artists, such as Max Slevogt, Frank Potter and W. von Reuckterschell (who is featured in the anthology through his sketch 'Young Negro'), as 'inspiration and guide-posts', but he is careful to counter any notion of white superiority (*N* 264). Rather than advocating wholesale imitation, he recommends that African American artists revise aspects of European art for their own ends in order to 'break through the stereotypes to a new style' (*N* 267).

Locke's attempt to forge a path between dominant models of cultural value (cultural amalgamation and cultural nationalism) by featuring Winold Reiss's work in the *Survey Graphic* and *The New Negro* generated more controversy than his cool analysis implies. Some members of the Harlem elite criticized Locke for using a white artist at all while others, such as Jessie Fauset, worried about the primitivist slant of Reiss's portraits, especially 'Two Public School Teachers' (Stewart 1989, 50-54). At a forum held at the Harlem branch of the New York Public Library, attended by Elise Johnson McDougald, Reiss provoked what McDougald called a 'furore' and a Mr Williams 'wondered if the whole art side of the issue were a "piece of subtle propaganda to prejudice the white reader"' (Stewart 1989, 50). Throughout the controversy, Jessie Fauset remained Reiss's most outspoken critic. As George Hutchinson has noted, '[e]ven her contribution to *The New Negro* [which is directly concerned with African American theatre rather than visual art] initially included a critical reference to [Reiss's 'Two Public School Teachers'], a reference Locke excised' (1995, 395).

Locke's response to such criticism not only provides a clue to his motivations for featuring Reiss in the anthology, but it also exposes contradictions in his attempt to move from predetermined racial histories to a vision of a specifically African American culture. Written for *Opportunity* in May 1925, 'To Certain of our Philistines' is a justification of his decision to include Reiss's portraits of 'Harlem Types' and Harlem Renaissance leaders and artists in the *Survey Graphic*. The essay launches an impassioned challenge to a racially exclusive idea of art. Locke instead invites artists to reach beyond the 'damaging distortion of art values by color-line' towards collaborative cultural delineation: 'we shall have to draw the culture-line sharply and without compromise' (1983b, 161). The ethnographic quality of this project promises an alternative to the flattering 'representative' images generated by those motivated by a best-foot-forward philosophy.

With this emphasis upon accurate cultural description, Reiss becomes an important artist because his 'Type Studies' aspire towards accuracy and objectivity. In this context, Locke singles out 'Two Public School Teachers' for praise because, he claims, it captures 'racial aspects' through realistic representation and 'intense symbolism' without appealing to 'race pride' (1983b, 162). For Locke, such documentation of cultural types enables expression of racial distinctiveness without succumbing to what he later termed 'racial chauvinism' (1989b, 232). As he puts it in an article for *The Nation*, 'Beauty Instead of Ashes', this project depends upon the involvement of black and white artists: 'just as we are not to restrict the Negro artist to Negro themes except by his own artistic choice and preference, so we are glad that Negro life is an artistic province free to everyone' (1983a, 23).

As several critics have noted, Reiss's 'Type Studies' actually occupy a more ambivalent position in the pages of the *Survey Graphic* and *The New Negro* than Locke's commentary suggests. In a helpful account of the origins of this genre, Anne Elizabeth Carroll points out that 'Type Studies' 'often treated their subjects as specimens, as if they were a separate group of people, set apart and different from their viewers' (2005, 125). To some extent, Reiss's studies depart from these conventions, not least because his portraits depict actual individuals. Even so, certain conventions from earlier 'Type Studies' remain, such as captions that lay stress upon typical characteristics, which encourage viewers to interpret these figures as representatives of particular social groups rather than as individuals.

Faultlines also emerge when Locke attempts to abandon the 'color-line' in favour of careful delineation of a 'culture-line'. In practice, such distinctions prove difficult to maintain:

> Too many of us still look to art to compensate the attitudes of prejudice, rather than merely, as is proper, to ignore them. And so, unfortunately for art, the struggle for social justice has put a pessimism upon a playing-up to Caucasian type-ideals, and created too prevalently a half-caste psychology that distorts all true artistic values with the irrelevant social values of 'representative' and 'unrepresentative,' 'favorable' and 'unfavorable' – and threatens a truly racial art with the psychological bleach of 'lily-whitism' (1983b, 161).

Locke contends that any manipulation of art as propaganda to 'compensate the attitudes of prejudice' comes at a cost. Attempts to produce '"representative"' images, which seek equality with whites through imitation of western artistic conventions, create art drained of racial distinctiveness and reduced to a 'half-caste psychology' (1983b, 161). What is important here is not so much Locke's explicit argument as his choice of metaphors. There is a revealing tension between his emphasis upon cross-racial artistic collaboration and the racialist terms in which Reiss's art is defended, which associate the mixed race body with inauthentic expression. In this context, it is difficult to miss the irony that Reiss, a German immigrant, is hailed as the upholder of a cultural authenticity that is defended through racialized rhetoric (his portraits are celebrated as a refreshing alternative to a 'half-caste psychology' and 'the psychological bleach of "lily-whitism"').

Reference to contemporary writers who employ a comparable vocabulary when arguing for particular styles of representation demonstrates that such imagery is often expressive of '[s]plit desires' for 'a Toomeresque America beyond race' and a 'nourishing narrative of African American survival' (Warnes 2006, 379). In 'Spirituals and Neo-Spirituals', Hurston couches her opposition to concert spirituals in terms that bear a striking resemblance to Locke's defence of Reiss: she denounces the concert spiritual as a '"musical octoroon"' produced by 'squeezing "all of the rich black juice out of the songs"' (Anderson 2001, 207). Another pertinent example is Randolph Bourne's 'Trans-National America', with its condemnation of American immigrants who become 'cultural half-breeds, neither assimilated Anglo-Saxons nor nationals of another culture' (1996, 98). Like Bourne, Locke calls for preservation of distinctive ethnic cultures, but he also challenges art conceived as racial propaganda, arguing for a 'truly racial art' that does not equate beauty with whiteness. Yet, as for Hurston and Bourne, Locke's effort to open out cultural identity beyond the confines of racial separatism is compromised since an essentialist notion of racial identity resurfaces in his racial metaphors.[3] In this sense, Locke's essay bears the signs and strains of his struggle against racialist thinking that was deeply ingrained in early twentieth-century thinking.

Reading Practices and *The New Negro*: New Juxtapositions

Much of this chapter has been concerned with the creative power of the collage-maker or, in this case, the editor. I have brought my formulation of the collage aesthetic to bear on *The New Negro* not only to demonstrate Locke's purposeful juxtapositions, but also to expose contradictions that animate his project. In isolation, however, such an approach runs the risk of allowing editorial influence to loom too large. To some degree, Locke's attempts to control meaning by careful juxtaposition are limited by the way in which readers tend to approach anthologies. While fiction requires readers to read pages one by one, in a sequence, reading an anthology usually involves an element of sampling. Since there is no overarching narrative, readers are at liberty to dip into the text, creating new juxtapositions as they do so. Given the size of *The New Negro* and the presence of paratextual apparatus such as the bibliography, it is entirely logical to categorize it as a reference work that may never be read from start to finish.

With this in mind, the focus of my discussion in this section shifts from the editor's controlling vision towards new juxtapositions and points of emphasis created by various reviewers. Such an approach makes room for alternative interpretations to those envisaged by Locke. But it also reveals the ease with which readers reinstated stereotypical accounts of African American culture, overlooking Locke's consistent emphasis upon African American heterogeneity.

A brief glance at contemporary reviews of *The New Negro* in the white press reveals that readers filleted particular contributions from the anthology to bolster their own perceptions of African American culture. Individual commentators emphasize some aspects of the volume at the expense of others, isolating particular pieces for sustained comment. In doing so, they create an alternative lens on the

---

[3]   On some level, these metaphors imply that there is a connection between Locke's blueprint for cultural expression and the African American body. Such an assumption can be interpreted in the context of a broader anthropological debate about the parallel emergence of a 'new' African American body and a flourishing African American culture. In *The American Negro: A Study in Racial Crossing* (1928), for instance, Melville Herskovits argues that cultural revival in Harlem is not unrelated to historical processes of racial mixing that have created 'a definite physical type which may be called the American Negro. It is not like any type from which it has come; it is not White; it is not Negro; it is not Mongoloid. It is all of them, and none of them' (1985, 19). For Herskovits, the New Negro Renaissance amounts to a claim for the cultural heritage associated with bodily transformation into a distinctive American type.

anthology, formulating interpretive frameworks that were often sharply at odds with Locke's efforts, in the 'Foreword' and his expository essay 'The New Negro', to guide interpretation '*to ensure that the text is read properly*' (Genette 1997, 197 [Genette's emphasis]). To some extent, this tendency to distil a coherent narrative from a mass of texts is an inevitable consequence of the review, a genre that aims to reduce a book to its bare essentials. Even so, the process of recontextualization that I am describing is particularly acute in the case of *The New Negro* because of its multidisciplinary scope, and Locke's careful sequencing of material.

Generally speaking, initial reviews of *The New Negro* identify a coherent logic that underpins Locke's project. Even Carl Van Vechten, who begins his article by praising the volume's extraordinary variety, anticipates a later critical tendency to ignore sociological essays, which endorse social uplift, in favour of contributions primarily concerned with literature and culture. Furthermore, like many of his fellow reviewers, he uses the review as a platform to present his own views about African American culture. Van Vechten soon abandons detailed discussion of Locke's literary selections to make a controversial assertion that is of little relevance to the anthology's content. Taking issue with 'the old cliché that Negro novels must be written by Negroes', he argues that white writers should be free to 'exploit' 'Negro subjects' (2007, 225).

More pertinent to my argument about new juxtapositions created by the process of interpretation is a recurring preoccupation with the anthology's value as a sociological document. Howard W. Odum, in a review for *Modern Quarterly*, praises Locke for bringing together 'more than a score of examples of documentary evidence' about the cultural development of African Americans (1925, 127). In a similar vein, Dorothy Scarborough, writing in *The New York Times Book Review*, describes the anthology as an 'extraordinarily interesting page of history' (19), which 'sets forth the facts that the negro in America is developing his own racial integrity and pride' (1925, 25).

To a certain extent, this sociological, quasi-scientific vocabulary chimes with Locke's account of his project. From the outset, in his essay 'The New Negro', he contrasts representations of African Americans in the anthology with stereotypes of the 'Old Negro', which operate as 'historical fiction[s]' that are 'more of a formula than a human being' (*N* 3). Disposing of 'the dusty spectacles of past controversy' (5) in order to effect a 'reorientation of view' (4), Locke claims that *The New Negro* marks a break with 'unjust stereotypes' that have hampered 'true social or self-understanding' (*N* 4).

There is, however, an important distinction to be made between Locke's rhetoric and reviewers' emphasis upon the sociological significance of *The New Negro*. Even though he characterizes the Great Migration as 'a deliberate flight … from medieval America to modern' (*N* 6), Locke makes every effort to avoid a linear narrative of development from primitivism to civilization. Locke was conscious that delineation of African American culture in relation to a concept of development would threaten to reinscribe evolutionary theory, which tended to chart an advance from simple to complex forms in order to bolster racial hierarchies. Consequently, he characterizes the 1920s as a period of transformation when new vocabularies of race and nation were being formed. His emphasis upon an African American identity in transition stems from his interpretation of the Great Migration.[4] In this context, the convergence of African Americans from diverse backgrounds on the metropolitan centre of Harlem promises a shared consciousness: a collective identity will be created out of diversity, but the coordinates of such an identity remain unspecified.[5]

Nevertheless, his contemporary reviewers largely ignored Locke's assiduous avoidance of primitivism. V.F. Calverton's review for *The Nation* even goes so far as to take a politics of racial temporality as its structuring principle. As Paul Gilroy and Johannes Fabian have noted, notions of racial difference are often conceived in temporal terms, with racial hierarchies being supported by representations of African Americans inhabiting a time zone outside that of an exclusively white modernity.[6] Since Calverton's 'The Latest Negro' positions *The New Negro* as a specific stage in a linear narrative of cultural development, he seems to reiterate such hierarchies. In his potted history of African American experiences, Calverton tells a story of evolutionary development from 'primitivism' and emotionalism to 'refine[ment]' (761) and 'objectivity' (1925, 762). Calverton's repeated assertion that '[a] new culture is in the process of evolution' (1925, 761) echoes a number of contributions to *The New Negro*, especially Charles S. Johnson's account of the emergence of 'a city Negro' (*N* 285). There is, however, a crucial difference. For Johnson, the New Negro's arrival on the scene has been characterized by an uneven, 'ragged pattern' of development that refuses teleology (*N* 297). In Calverton's hands, however, 'evolution' retains its association with race science: he documents linear 'stages' of development that accord with the evolutionist assumption that a developmental distance separates "primitive" and "civilized" cultures.

Even Calverton's brief commentary on selected fiction in the anthology is couched in terms of a developmental time series. Calverton praises Eric Walrond for being 'more advanced' than his fellow contributors, 'earnest and sincere craftsmen', who remain 'fettered by amateurish techniques' (1925, 762). Such interpretive moves smooth over the heterogeneity of Locke's representation of

---

[4]   See, for instance, Locke's account of '[t]he tide of Negro migration' in 'The New Negro', in which his sustained analogy with the ebb and flow of the sea disrupts a linear narrative charting the emergence of the folk into modernity (*N* 6). Such emphasis upon fluidity complicates Locke's account of the Great Migration as 'a deliberate flight not only from countryside to city, but from medieval America to modern' (*N* 6).

[5]   Locke's description of the 'great race-welding' in Harlem (7), which 'has attracted the African, the West Indian, the Negro American; has brought together the Negro of the North and the Negro of the South; the man from the city and the man from the town and village; the peasant, the student, the business man, the professional man, artist, poet, musician, adventurer and worker, preacher and criminal, exploiter and social outcast', is significant in this context (*N* 6).

[6]   See Fabian (1983) and Gilroy (2000b, 57).

African Americans since Calverton incorporates the anthology into a simplistic, linear account of cultural development. In doing so, he culls a coherent narrative from the pages of the anthology, creating new juxtapositions and connections between disparate contributions in the process.

It is not my intention to offer a comprehensive history of *The New Negro*'s reception. Rather, these early reviews suggest a caveat to any account of Locke's collage aesthetic that rests upon a straightforward understanding of editorial intention. In a nuanced discussion of Locke's sequencing of word and image, Anne Elizabeth Carroll assumes that stylistic and thematic incongruity had a dramatic impact upon readers, pushing them towards acknowledgement of ideas created by juxtaposition of disparate fragments. Reviews such as the one by V.F. Calverton demonstrate that readers could easily disregard Locke's orchestration of formal discord, piecing together an alternative version of the text by selecting specific contributions for discussion in accordance with their own priorities and interests.

Few texts have provoked such an array of diverging critical responses as *The New Negro*. For Houston A. Baker, the anthology is a black nationalist text, which offers 'not only a description of streams of tendency in our collective lives but also an actual construction within its pages of the sounds, songs, images, and signs of a nation', by which he means a separate black nation within America (1987, 85). By contrast, Gerald Early contends that New Negroes defined themselves according to 'a typical American ethnic nationalism: namely, a kind of race pride and a sense of group identification that made one a distinct flavor in the American melting pot' (1991, 37). For Locke's contemporary George Schuyler, author of that biting satire of the Harlem Renaissance *Black No More*, the anthology was marred by an elitist focus on the Talented Tenth: he mocked Locke as a 'high priest of the intellectual snobbocracy', awarding him the *Messenger*'s 'elegantly embossed and beautifully lacquered dill pickle' (Lewis 1994, xxvii). More recently, Sieglinde Lemke has claimed that Locke's (unachieved) aim was to make New Negro identity readily available to the reading public: 'the anthology was meant to function as a blueprint, a manual for how to become the New Negro' (1998, 118).

Such varied critical interpretations are logical given the complex structure of *The New Negro*, in which opposing perspectives are juxtaposed. Nevertheless, these diverse responses also alert us to an abiding critical tendency for collaging particular contributions to the anthology in order to create a new, often more coherent, version of it. In this context, particular essays – Locke's 'The New Negro', Arthur Schomburg's 'The Negro Digs up His Past' and J.A. Rogers's 'Jazz at Home' among them – have come to stand for the anthology as a whole because they have been singled out for special attention as a matter of routine. Such interpretations tend to suppress the heterogeneity of elements in *The New Negro*. Given that most students now encounter Locke in *The Norton Anthology of African American Literature*, a text that situates selections from *The New Negro* in the context of an organic African American tradition while downplaying interracial collaboration, it is crucial to remain aware of the ways in which we continue to participate in this process of fragmentation and recontextualization of Locke's landmark anthology as readers and teachers.

More specifically, emphasis upon the collage construction of *The New Negro* – in terms of Locke's editorial role and the new juxtapositions created by interpretive acts – reveals a gap in existing scholarship. As several commentators have demonstrated, Locke's formal choices are motivated by his editorial aims, even if those goals remained riddled with contradictions. Most scholarship on *The New Negro*, however, misses something fundamental about Locke's inability to control how the anthology is read. In this context, any attempt to fashion a single, definitive interpretation runs the risk of smoothing over the ruptures and fragments that are the very stuff of the anthology.

Reading *The New Negro* as a version of collage, a whole composed of irreducible fragments, provides a useful counter to critical accounts that have seen the volume as a unified whole. In particular, a focus on collage form exposes the limitations of readings that represent the anthology as a landmark cultural nationalist text. *The New Negro* is, for instance, a central pillar in Houston Baker's influential argument that the Harlem Renaissance was a nationalist formulation. To make this case, Baker tidies up conflicting ideologies in the anthology, laying stress upon a shared goal 'to found a nation of Afro-Americans on the basis of RACE' (1987, 79). 'The world of *The New Negro*', he asserts, 'represents a unified community of national interests set in direct opposition to the general economic, political, and theological tenets of a racist land' (1987, 77).

There is little doubt that Baker offers a compelling model of cultural resistance, especially in the concept of '*radical marronage*' (1987, 75). Yet, it is difficult to miss the irony that Baker's account of the emergence of African American nationalist consciousness conforms with the narrative trajectory of 'nation-building', which Benedict Anderson has characterized as a linear, serial time line from folk expression to modernity. There are, of course, several moments in *The New Negro* when such a temporal dynamic of the nation 'coming into being' is invoked. One thinks, for instance, of metaphors of ripening, flowering, cultural awakening and 'cultural adolescence' in Locke's foreword to the anthology (*N* xxvi). Even so, Baker's insistence upon 'homogeneous, empty time' (30), which 'made it possible to "think" the nation', sits a little oddly with Locke's sustained efforts to scupper a linear narrative of cultural progress (Anderson 1983, 28).

More recently, there has been considerable attention to the contradictions that animate Locke's efforts to define a New Negro. Sieglinde Lemke, for instance, reads the anthology as a failed 'blueprint', which remains caught between 'two unreconciled – and paradoxical – strivings': assertions of 'cultural uniqueness' and claims of 'cultural sameness' (1998, 123-4). Even so, Lemke judges the anthology against an ideal, unified construction of New Negro identity: '[s]ince this rift is located at the ideological and programmatic foundation of the Harlem Renaissance, it could only weaken the political effectiveness of the movement's blueprint, this anthology' (1998, 124). Martha Jane Nadell and Anne Elizabeth Carroll have nuanced these critical conversations by paying detailed attention to the dynamic interplay of text and image, but they also maintain a focus on editorial control. Opening up new areas for discussion, my account of the collage construction of *The New Negro* brings together analysis of the volume's formal textures with an awareness of the ruptures and sutures that have been created by various interpretive acts. The editor cannot control how the anthology will be read, a fact that Nadell, Carroll, Baker and Lemke seem to miss. To see the text as constructing a national identity or a New Negro is to overlook the fragments and ruptures that constitute the anthology.

Conclusion

Locke's landmark anthology has featured prominently in recent reassessments of the Harlem Renaissance, which have sought to move beyond a narrow focus upon literature. Building upon such studies, I have analysed *The New Negro* with reference to concepts of visual collage, focusing upon patterns of juxtaposition. Such an approach exposes competing models of collage at work in the anthology. Although Locke reiterates his commitment to the democratic openness, or multivocality, of collage form, his anthology is, in fact, a product of authorial control. It is a patterned, controlled honeycomb, in which juxtapositions have been orchestrated to endorse particular perspectives on African American culture.

In this context, Locke's commitment to multivocality is compromised by his efforts to guide readers' interpretation of his literary selections according to his own ideas about the distinctive qualities of African American writing. Since Locke privileged innovations of style over engagement with present political realities his framing of material often muffled authors' political interventions. As we shall see in the next chapter, Locke's emphasis upon Jean Toomer's aesthetic achievements gave rise to a set of critical coordinates that have governed the reception of *Cane* until quite recently.

Further tensions emerge when a discussion of collage form is extended beyond analysis of editorial intention. Generally speaking, critics have focused on Locke's editorial agency in their discussions of his formal choices. Even a brief glance at the anthology's reception history exposes the limitations of such an approach. Initial reviews of *The New Negro* in the white press indicate that readers rarely interpreted the volume in accordance with Locke's sustained emphasis upon African American heterogeneity.

Chapter 3

'[A]dventuring through the pieces of a still unorganized mosaic': Jean Toomer's Collage Aesthetic in *Cane*

In *Cane*, the reader is immediately struck by Jean Toomer's bold manipulation of collage technique; he abandons progressive plotting, instead assembling a variety of disparate forms and genres. As well as signalling the heterogeneity of the collage elements through typographical layout, he stretches and scrambles familiar forms, breaking them, splitting them open and stitching them onto other genres. In a letter to Toomer on 25 April 1922, Waldo Frank describes the effect of these broken forms: 'in the reading the mind does not catch on to a uniformly moving Life that conveys it whole to the end, but rather steps from piece to piece as if adventuring through the pieces of a still unorganized mosaic' (Turner 1988, 159). As Frank points out, Toomer abandons linear narrative and 'uniform' progression, subjecting the reader to chaotic surprises and unexpected truths revealed through the process of piecing together the meaning of seemingly random fragments.

Since *Cane*'s publication in 1923, commentators have recognized the importance of Toomer's formal choices. However, there is a tradition of criticism stemming back to Alain Locke's claim in *The New Negro* that Toomer's motive 'in being racial is to be so purely for the sake of art' which privileges *Cane*'s aesthetic achievements over its treatment of historical or political realities (*N* 51). This lack of attention to the political significance of form is most evident in the work of Cynthia Earl Kerman and Richard Eldridge who sought to smooth over the generic disjunctions of *Cane* by interpreting it as the product of a personal quest for 'wholeness' (1987, 79).

More recently, critics have paid close attention to the politics of form in *Cane*. In *Jean Toomer and the Terrors of American History*, Charles Scruggs and Lee VanDemarr demonstrate that Toomer harnesses techniques of 'modernist indirection' to give voice to the unspoken history of miscegenation in the South (1998, 135). Anissa Wardi pursues this link between formal innovation and historical unveiling to different effect, exploring Toomer's substantial revision of the generic conventions of 'American southern pastoral' from an African American historical and cultural perspective (2003, 5). In Wardi's reading of *Cane*, southern pastoral, often associated with a romanticization of race relations in the South, is re-imagined as a highly political genre, with brutality, violence and subjugation as its central preoccupations (2003, 13). In line with these critics, this chapter investigates how *Cane*'s form allows Toomer to articulate realities and histories that remain unspoken in conventional, continuous narrative, but I will pay special attention to the orchestrated patterns of formal discord on the pages of *Cane*. In particular, I aim to link the thematic collage of the text with Boasian anthropology, demonstrating how Toomer's reworking of Franz Boas's ideas enables him to move from evolutionist determinism towards an intervention in early twentieth-century debates about American culture.

Toomer gathers an array of genres, styles and forms to produce an overt staging of the seams and material tears in his structure. *Cane* is split into three sections. The first section, set in Georgia, represents the brutality of the rural South and what Toomer calls the 'fading' of black, organic folk culture, focusing on the lives of women, from Karintha and Becky, a white woman who gives birth to two mixed race sons and is consequently ostracized by the community, to Louisa, whose life is destroyed in the apocalyptic climax of 'Blood-Burning Moon' (Rusch 1993, 24).[1] In the second section, Toomer draws upon jazz, vaudeville, imagism and spirituals to depict the developing, dynamic American culture of the urban North. Finally, 'Kabnis' explores a mixed race northerner's experience of alienation in the South to show the uncomfortable proximities of black and white, North and South, slave past and modernity. The first two sections are composed of a medley of sketches, prose poems, worksongs, stories and lyrics, while 'Kabnis' is an experimental blend of drama, prose and poetry.

In describing *Cane* as a collage, I would like to pursue parallels with the African American painter Romare Bearden. In the 1960s, Bearden experimented with collage, juxtaposing images from various historical periods and cultural sources to represent the dynamism of African American culture. Combining materials from African sculpture, Chinese calligraphy and European art with the jagged edges and improvisational patterns of jazz, Bearden creates tension and even disorientation through his jarring arrangements of multiple cultural referents. A comparison between Bearden and Toomer seems apt because these two men considered themselves as contributors to both a Euro-American artistic tradition and a specifically African American culture.

Bearden described himself as a cubist: he was interested in exploiting cubist techniques of fragmentation to explore the relations between time, vision and space (Schwartzman 1990, 109). Moreover, Bearden's use of material disjunctions on the canvas identifies him with a modernist tradition that stems back to Pablo Picasso and Georges Braque's experimentations with collage in the years before World War I, a modernist tradition that represents an important aesthetic context for Toomer's formal innovation. Picasso's description of his collages as a deliberate attempt to disorientate the reader, creating a sense of 'strangeness' that would 'make people think' about a world which 'was becoming strange and not exactly reassuring', resonates with Toomer and Bearden's use of collage

---

[1]   In an undated letter to Waldo Frank, Toomer describes *Cane* as a 'swan-song' that depicts the passing and 'fading' of Negro folk culture, particularly 'folk-song[s]' and 'the emotional church' (Rusch 1993, 24).

to challenge readers or viewers to face up to the unsettling realities of their contemporary moments (Hoffman 1989, 7). Importantly, Bearden also presented his work as part of the blues and jazz tradition: emphasizing the importance of 'call and recall' to his work, he likened his often reprised themes and motifs to the patterns of riffed repetition in jazz and blues (Berman 1980, 60-66). More specifically, he insisted that the formal structure of his work, with its striking use of colour and space, was inspired by jazz composition.

In his introduction for a 1968 catalogue of Bearden's collages, Ralph Ellison notes that Bearden has 'used Cubist techniques to his own ingenious effect', marrying vernacular forms such as the blues with the styles of high art in order to represent 'signs and symbols of a humanity that has struggled to survive the decimating and fragmentizing effects of American social processes' (Ellison 1994, 690-91). In the light of this description of the diverse cultural referents that combine in African American collage, it seems to me that collage is a fruitful metaphor for the jarring discordances in *Cane*. In particular, I wonder if my analogy to visual art might counter the potential reductiveness of such notions as the jazz aesthetic, which, as Maria Lauret has shown, threaten to classify all formal experimentation in African American texts as 'literary riff[s]', underestimating the significance of other literary, visual and theoretical models (Lauret 1996, 59). Indeed, as Bearden's work testifies, collage may be useful as a metaphor precisely because it incorporates aspects of the jazz aesthetic without restricting our understanding of *Cane* to an exclusive focus on vernacular styles. After all, throughout his life, Toomer remained wary of the ways in which reception of his work was framed by assumptions about his 'Negro' status; he frequently warned against underplaying his involvement in the formal experimentation of transatlantic modernism.[2] By uncovering a strong link between the thematic collage of the text with Boasian anthropology, I aim to show that *Cane* draws inspiration from vernacular forms *and* modernistic formal experimentation.[3]

Representing the South

To turn then to Toomer's manipulation of form in the first section of *Cane*. As I have noted, Toomer adopts an aesthetic of assemblage, combining a variety of

---

[2]   In his unpublished essay 'The Crock of Problems' (1928), Toomer argues against racial labelling: 'as far as race and nationality are concerned, I wish to be known as an American' (59). More specifically, he records his disquiet at the way in which Waldo Frank's introduction to *Cane* 'served to present [him] to the public as a Negro' (56), ensuring that his text was received in the light of assumptions about the perceived concerns of African American writers (Toomer 1996b, 55-59).

[3]   Such an approach serves to underline the importance of transatlantic cultural exchanges to both the Harlem Renaissance and Euro-American modernism. See Michael North, *Reading 1922: A Return to the Scene of the Modern* (1999) and Sieglinde Lemke, *Primitivist Modernism: Black Culture and the Origins of Transatlantic Modernism* (1998).

genres, styles and forms on the page. He shuttles from classical forms, such as the sonnet in 'November Cotton Flower' and the rhymed quatrains of 'Reapers' and 'Georgia Dusk', and modernistic, free form imagist poems, such as 'Nullo', to complex variations upon familiar forms, such as 'Face', which violently stretches the conventions of the Petrarchan blazon to represent scars on the southern landscape.

As well as creating a patchwork that is writ large in the text as a whole, Toomer uses generic mixing in individual pieces. 'Becky', the story of a white woman who is forced to live in a kind of no man's land because she has flouted the taboo of miscegenation and borne two mixed race sons, is composed of elements that derive from gothic fiction, African American spirituals, Greek tragedy and oral folktales. The sketch is framed by a lilting refrain, a summary of the action, which is reminiscent of the spirituals in its style and theme: 'Becky was the white woman who had two Negro sons. She's dead; they've gone away. The pines whisper to Jesus. The Bible flaps its leaves with an aimless rustle on her mound' (Toomer 1993, 5).[4] However, rather than containing Becky's story in accordance with the town's desire for restored racial segregation, Toomer's piecemeal technique overturns the authority of the summary through creation of ambiguities that refuse to be explained. For example, the recurring phrase '[t]he pines whisper to Jesus' takes on a slightly different meaning each time it is repeated: at times, it refers to the community's manipulation of religion to justify Becky's exclusion, but at other times, it invokes their secret attempts to assuage their guilt by providing her with food (*C* 5).

Toomer finally twists the phrase to '[p]ines shout to Jesus!' to represent the uncanny fear that the villagers feel when their unspoken desire for the suppression of Becky's story is fulfilled when she is crushed to death by her falling chimney (*C* 6). He illustrates the extraordinary fascination with Becky's situation through his melodramatic description of the apocalyptic '[u]ncanny eclipse' that occurs after her live burial, which provokes strange, confusing physical responses in the narrator, a witness at the scene: '[e]yes left their sockets for the cabin. Ears burned and throbbed. Uncanny eclipse! fear closed my mind' (*C* 6). For the narrator, the unsettling truth about miscegenation threatens to erupt in a 'shout'.

The community's need to bury the truth about Becky's transgression of racial boundaries is made explicit when the narrator's companion, Barlo, throws his Bible onto her burial place, suggesting that holiness is required to ward off her dangerous spirit. Toomer wryly exposes this attempt to seal her grave as a tabooed, unacknowledged space: Barlo throws his Bible on the pile and '[n]o one has ever touched it' (*C* 7). However, as shown by Toomer's use of repetition to complicate rather than simplify, Becky's story refuses to be fixed down. She remains unseen and unexplained, even in death, her presence pointing to a secret, hidden history that does not make sense.

---

4   Further references to *Cane* are abbreviated to *C*.

In Toomer's account, the reality of Becky's life slips between the cracks of inherited genres and narratives. She refuses to name the father of her children and the narrator, a witness of her uncanny death, is unable to relate 'the true word of it' (*C* 7). Through his deft manipulation of tropes from gothic fiction, Toomer sets up a tension between the unknown and the known, the story that the community tells itself (as illustrated by the repeated refrain that frames the story) and the hidden truths that haunt them, so that the story ends as it began, shrouded in secrecy. In contrast to the community's desire to contain Becky's story in madness, her transgression of racial taboos refuses to be fixed down by narrative: '[t]he Bible flaps its leaves with an aimless rustle on her mound' (*C* 7).

Another aspect of Toomer's collage aesthetic is patching together diverse intertextual references, preserving them as distinct, identifiable fragments. In 'Georgia Dusk', Toomer adopts a classical form, adhering to strictly rhymed quatrains. However, within this conventional form, he creates a patchwork of references to English poetry, the Bible and African survivals in African American culture, which readers must track down and identify in order to interpret the poem. He begins by transposing the conventions of Romantic poetry to the rural South:

> A feast of moon and men and barking hounds,
>   An orgy for some genius of the South
>   With blood-hot eyes and cane-lipped scented mouth,
> Surprised in making folk-songs from soul sounds (*C* 13).

Toomer twists an allusion to the figure of the poet in Coleridge's 'Kubla Khan', 'His flashing eyes, his floating hair! ... For he on honey-dew hath fed, And drunk the milk of Paradise', to outline a kind of manifesto for expression of the beauty and brutality of the South (Coleridge 1983, 565). He splits the reference from its cultural and geographical context, making it unfamiliar and unsettling. Toomer suggests that a 'genius of the South' must immerse him/herself in the realities of the South and feed upon the violent excesses of American history, even if this is a morally uncomfortable position. He/She should swallow the distinctiveness of southern life to become 'cane-lipped', an unnerving mixture of the animate and the inanimate that tips Coleridge's image into strangeness. Toomer deploys the disorientating collage effect of uprooting a familiar image from its original context to transform Coleridge's neat theory of genius as 'the imaginative synthesis of discordant or antithetic aesthetic qualities' into a means of communicating the horrors of racial conflict in the South (Abrams 1953, 119). Through such 'soul' songs, poets can represent the realities of the past, as suggested by Toomer's impressionistic portrait of a hunt for an escaped slave, but repeated images of excessive appetite imply that such writers run the risk of becoming parasitic upon violence.

In the course of the poem, Toomer alludes to 'high-priests' and the 'juju-man' of African culture and he subtly recasts the well-known opening line from Thomas Gray's 'Elegy Written in a Country Churchyard', with its lilting phrase '[t]he curfew tolls the knell of parting day' (Gray 1983, 463). By deploying the phrase '[a]nd silence breaks the bud of knoll and hill', he invokes Gray's canonization of farm labourers, suggesting that the everyday lives of southerners deserve dignified attention just as much as Gray's labourers (*C* 13). Toomer's manipulation of distinct cultural fragments and his strategy of dislocating them from their original context make the poem a microcosm of *Cane*'s form. Toomer's piecemeal aesthetic chimes with his argument in a 1921 review of Richard Aldington's essay on imagism 'The Art of Poetry'. In the essay, he quarrels with Aldington's contention that 'the old cant of a poet's "message" is now completely discredited', attacking imagism for turning its back on 'the mighty voices of the past' (Jones 1996, 4). In contrast to what he perceives as imagism's shift of emphasis from content to presentation, Toomer tries to develop a style of indirection and fragmentation that engages with the political and social realities of his cultural moment.

In the final stanza of 'Georgia Dusk', he encourages the 'genius of the South' to '[g]ive virgin lips to cornfield concubines' and to '[b]ring dreams of Christ to dusky cane-lipped throngs' (*C* 13). In this self-reflexive poem, Toomer presents poetry as a mode through which to articulate the horrors of the past in order to envisage an alternative future. Repetition of the phrase 'cane-lipped' reminds readers of his re-interpretation of Coleridge's theory of genius and he detaches biblical rhetoric from its familiar context, translating 'dreams of Christ' to the southern landscape. Twisting these 'mighty voices of the past' for his own ends, he imbues the poem with a democratic commitment to the future salvation of the 'dusky' masses or the 'throngs' of the South. In particular, Toomer gives emphasis to a concealed history of miscegenation, especially the exploitation of African American women by white slave-owners, which is, as in 'Carma', understood by the 'canefield[s]' yet remains unspoken in dominant national narratives and inherited literary forms (*C* 11). He builds on this expression of racial proximity to imagine a world where individuals are not labelled according to their colour or racial grouping, complicating racial binaries by deploying a vocabulary that eschews a direct correlation between race and colour. The phrase 'dusky', for instance, retains an element of racial ambiguity: it is hard to fix one colour with such a description.

In this context, it is important that Toomer's aesthetic of assemblage assigns the reader an active role as a researcher, who must identify sources and seek out knowledge to piece together the implications of his indirect, oblique form. In 'Box Seat', Toomer articulates a key statement of his aesthetic: '[h]is mind curves back into himself, and picks up tail-ends of experiences' (*C* 64). This method of looping back to images, motifs, words and ideas from earlier in the text occurs throughout *Cane*. Particular images crop up repeatedly: pine-needles, the sawmill, the Dixie Pike, treetops, cotton, lips, burial, burning, faces, cradles, the moon, curling smoke and windows. In contrast to the progressive development of imagery that we might expect in continuous narrative, these images are pasted into diverse contexts as fragments in a way that splinters and illuminates their original meaning. It is the reader's task to interpret the fragments, threading together a chain of 'tail-ends'.[5]

This kind of active participation in the creation of a textual meaning implied by juxtaposition rather than spelt out through explicit declaration or announcement is suggestive of the interpretation of visual collage. Ralph Ellison characterizes Bearden's collages as an attempt to reveal 'that which has been concealed by time, custom and our trained incapacity to perceive the truth' (685-6), namely the richness and vibrancy of an African American culture long obscured by 'our media-dulled perception' (Ellison 1994, 690). Crucially, Ellison highlights Bearden's indirect approach: the artist does not make 'explicit comment', 'telling' the viewer what to think and adapting an attitude of direct protest; instead, he orchestrates interplay between collage fragments 'to make the unseen manifest' (Ellison 1994, 691-2). This strategy of appropriation and revision could be likened to Henry Louis Gates's notion of Signifyin(g) – or repetition 'with a signal difference' – but it lays special emphasis on making visible 'truths' that have been silenced or denied (1988a, xxiv).

Manipulating form to highlight forgotten or repressed histories is central to Toomer's representation of the South in part one. In 'Carma', the collaging of intratextual allusions complicates interpretation of the tale. According to the narrator, the story of Carma, who takes a lover when her husband is away, fakes suicide and then provokes him to murder, is 'the crudest melodrama' (*C* 11). Toomer, however, unsettles easy categorization of the sketch, breaking the flow of the tale with an unattributed fragment, describing the Georgia dusk. This highly figurative, panoramic view of the southern landscape, written from the perspective of an outsider or an omniscient narrator who describes the sun as 'a band of gold' and smoke as a '[m]arvelous web spun by the spider sawdust pile', uses strands of colour to represent various segments of life that exist side by side: the railway, the curling silver smoke of the sawmill, a black boy, the twinkling lights, the whitewashed hut, the golden sun and the rusty cotton field (*C* 10). This accumulative layering of images and colours is enriched by various sounds, which invoke different cultures: the girl's African-derived song which suggests that '[t]he Dixie Pike has grown from a goat path in Africa', the 'chug-chug' of the gas engine and the clanging cowbells, with a breath of Switzerland (*C* 10). Toomer also juxtaposes references that have been cut and pasted from various cultures: he draws upon European fairy tales such as 'Sleeping Beauty'; 'mazda', the good principle in Zoroastrianism; and the 'juju men, greegree, witch-doctors' of African medicine (*C* 10).

---

[5] Once again, there is a correspondence between Toomer's patterning of repeated images and Bearden's collage practice. As Kobena Mercer explains, Bearden's *Photomontage Projections* 'feature patterns of generative repetition whereby certain key motifs – train, guitar, window – constantly roam between urban and rural scenes of depiction' (2005, 137).

Through his layering of segments, which are studded with glittering and sensate imagery, he indicates the complicated, tangled racial and cultural lineages of the American South. Romanticism and Zoroastrianism rub shoulders with pastoralism and the fragmentary African survivals that glitter through an African American woman's song. The hybridity of southern culture is embodied in the image of the mule, the symbol and product of miscegenation that rides into the heart of the scene: '[a] black boy ... you are the most sleepiest man I ever seed, Sleeping Beauty ... cradled on a gray mule, guided by the hollow sound of cowbells, heads ... through a rusty cotton field' (*C* 10). As Robert Young reminds us in *Colonial Desire*, throughout the nineteenth century and early twentieth century, scientists were obsessed with the question of whether the mule, the result of breeding a horse and a donkey, was infertile (1995, 8). This debate fed into a parallel discussion about the fertility of 'mulattoes' in relation to their full-blooded counterparts. Like his contemporary, the novelist and anthropologist Zora Neale Hurston, Toomer bypasses these associations with racial inferiority and sterility, reclaiming the mule as an image suggestive of the rich cultural hybridity of what Hurston calls 'uh mingled people' (1986, 210).

Yet, Toomer's exploration of hybridity is not simply a call for recognition of the cultural diversity of southern culture. By foregrounding hybridity and the image of the mule in particular, Toomer forestalls any attempt to read this poetic account of the South as sentimental romanticism. Instead, the passage must be interpreted in the light of Wardi's analysis of *Cane* as a critique of predominant modes of southern American pastoral, which eulogized the Old South as a bastion of order, harmony and dignity while repressing the history of slavery and oppression that enabled such plantations to exist (2003, 6). Toomer's pointed reference to cultural continuities across the African diaspora signals that the cultural richness described here is a direct result of the brutal history of enslavement of Africans and African Americans. In this context, the mule becomes a symbol both of the sexual exploitation of African American women in slavery and exploitative labour practices in the South. [6]

It is clear that Toomer complicates straightforward interpretation of his aestheticized, elevated gaze on the landscape through his manipulation of intratextual references. He packs the passage with images and words that refer to other moments in *Cane*, suggesting that there is more at stake here than mere pastoral. In accordance with his collage-like technique of picking up 'tail-ends', he studs the description with images that have been splintered from their original context. For example, images of 'pine-needles' and 'smoke' direct readers to several

---

[6]   Reference to Zora Neale Hurston and Booker T. Washington endorses this interpretation of the image of the mule. In *Their Eyes Were Watching God*, Hurston represents the sexual and economic exploitation of African American women figuratively through her sustained revisioning of the trope of the mule. In a speech delivered in 1915, Booker T. Washington makes a direct link to economic exploitation, arguing that the southern economy was 'based on the Negro and the mule' (Grossman 1989, 39).

flashpoints in the text. First, they invoke the oblique portrayal of Karintha's burial of her unwanted, mixed race child in the pine-needles in the opening sketch of *Cane*. This allusion marks the southern landscape as a place of intense beauty scarred by unacknowledged violence. As Scruggs and VanDemarr explain, 'Karintha's child becomes a powerful presence because it is *not* mentioned, its vanishing always associated with "bands" of pine smoke' (1998, 142). Secondly, the pine-needles recall Becky's transgression of racial taboos, her secret life outside the black and white districts. If the community tastes the shameful secret of Karintha's infanticide in the smoke from the smouldering 'pyramidal sawdust pile' (*C* 2) which saturates their drinking water for a year, then Becky's story is also bound up with a sense of communal guilt: the villagers feel partly responsible for Becky's death when their unspoken desire for the suppression of miscegenation is fulfilled and she is crushed to death by her falling chimney. Through this technique of fragmenting images from their original context, Toomer points to buried, hidden histories in the landscape, which itself is 'rusty with talk' and '[s]cratching choruses' (*C* 10).

Moreover, the unacknowledged reality of miscegenation, which remains implicit in this picturesque, even pastoral, fragment, comes to the surface in the later sketch 'Bona and Paul'. Toomer recapitulates his elevated perspective on the landscape, as Paul looks back to his roots in southern African American culture 'through a dark pane' (*C* 71). He deliberately repeats tropes from this description of the landscape in 'Carma': the segments of colour, the singing woman, the cabin and the use of an elevated, poetic vocabulary (*C* 71). In 'Bona and Paul', the stark reality of unequal power relations between black slave women and their white owners is exposed in the startling image of '[a] Negress chant[ing] a lullaby beneath the mate-eyes of a southern planter' (*C* 71). In 'Carma', Toomer stages the repression of the brutal realities of slavery which was so central to plantation fiction, a genre that tended to give the plantation house and the institution of slavery 'the immemorial status of nature itself'; while in 'Bona and Paul', he repeats the scene with a signal difference, pointing to a history of sexual and economic exploitation that has the potential to disrupt the present (Grammer 2004, 60). Toomer's emphasis on the gaze of the 'planter' could be paralleled with what Richard Godden has described as the 'primal scene of bound southern labour' in William Faulkner's fiction, the moment when the white slaveowner recognizes and represses his sense of utter dependence upon black labour (Godden 1997, 4). By choosing the word 'planter' rather than master, Toomer underlines a connection between sexuality and economy, intensifying our sense of the double exploitation of African American women during slavery.

Toomer's use of intratextual allusions to dislocate and complicate the conventions of pastoral and melodrama, pointing to secret histories, latent violence and unspoken truths, results in his refusal to authorize a single vision of the southern landscape in 'Carma'. By placing the whole description of the Georgia landscape in brackets, he questions the narrator's straightforward categorization of Carma's story as 'melodrama', labelling it as a segment that readers must interpret in relation to her life story. Toomer plays off the two sections of 'Carma' against each other, so that the one interrogates the other, leaving us questioning the reality and authenticity of both. For example, in his description of Carma riding her mule down the Dixie Pike, the narrator draws upon primitivist and exoticist tropes to represent her as a 'Nigger woman driving a Georgia chariot down an old dust road' (*C* 10). In the fragment, Toomer sends up this overblown description, substituting the woman on a mule with a 'Sleeping Beauty', a sleepy boy 'cradled' on a 'gray mule' (*C* 10). Similarly, he plays upon the contrast between the brutal violence of Carma's story, which the narrator confines to the limits of a specific genre with his admission that the 'tale as I have told it is the crudest melodrama', and the fanciful details of the fragment, with its clanging cowbells, bands of gold and polished rails (*C* 11).

To grasp the full significance of such juxtapositions, readers are forced to inhabit at least two contradictory perspectives. After engaging with each fragment in turn, we must step back to view 'Carma' as a whole, a new way of looking that compels us to reassess any initial judgements. This dynamic interpretive process, with its restless movement between various angles of vision, recalls the double take viewers must perform when viewing collage, a mode of perception that flickers between detailed examination of individual fragments and a long-distanced view that registers the reformulation of appropriated materials into an integrated whole.

Readers must interpret the fragments against each other to realize that Toomer is contesting both pastoral and melodrama as appropriate vehicles to represent the South. For Toomer, southern history refuses an escape into pastoral idyll, a genre which smoothed over the brutality of slavery, as indicated by the famous scholar of southern history Ulrich B. Phillips, who claimed in 1929 that African Americans were 'more or less contentedly slaves, with grievances from time to time but not ambition' (1948, 196). Equally, melodrama diverts attention from the realities of life in the South, allowing readers to be titillated by a familiar formula, 'a series of bloody events, sexual by implication at least, played out in the blood-heat of a "long hot summer"' (Fiedler 1968, 18).[7] Instead, as Wardi has demonstrated, Toomer 'mines the pathos of the blues' for a descriptive vocabulary tinged with paradox and contradiction, in which beauty exists cheek by jowl with exploitation, and sensuality collides with brutality (2003, 55).

Toomer gathers together threads of meaning from previous sketches and poems, forcing readers to question their assumptions. In the climax of part one 'Blood-Burning Moon', the racial violence that has been latent in the preceding sketches erupts in the lynching of Tom Burwell, who is killed for slashing the throat of his white rival for Louisa's love, Bob Stone. As Wardi has shown, 'Blood-Burning Moon' is saturated with 'evocative imagery of the sugarcane economy',

---

[7]	In the light of Toomer's exposure of the limits of melodrama, it comes as no surprise that Leslie Fiedler describes it as a form through which white writers could contain and meditate upon the 'deepest guilts and fears of transplanted Europeans in a slaveholding community' (Fiedler 1968, 18).

imagery that underlines the inescapable history of enslaved labour in the South (2003, 64). Toomer's technique of intratextual allusion heightens this connection between racial oppression during the Reconstruction, when the story is set, and the history of slavery. Toomer describes the unthinking violence of the white mob as a wordless, mechanized hum that rolls forward uncontrollably, breaking everything in its path (North 1994, 173), but he intensifies the force of his representation of the bestiality and determination of the '[w]hite men like ants upon a forage rush[ing] about' by making a link to Barlo's story of betrayal and the birth of the New World in 'Esther' (*C* 34).

In his vision, Barlo represents Africa as a giant who is 'agazin at th heavens' when

> some little white-ant biddies came an tied his feet to chains. They led him t th coast, they led him t th sea, they led him across th ocean an they didnt set him free. The old coast didnt miss him, an th new coast wasnt free, he left the old-coast brothers, t give birth t you an me. O Lord, great God Almighty, t give birth t you an me (*C* 21).

By repeating the image of whites as ants in 'Blood-Burning Moon', Toomer inverts the power relations between the lynch mob and Tom Burwell, and we are forced to reconceive of the lynching from the perspective of the African giant, who is tricked into slavery by 'white-ant biddies'. Barlo's lilting speech reminds readers of the whites' responsibility for racial conflict: white traders stole slaves from Africa, thus creating African Americans as a cultural group. By exploiting the indirectness of collage, Toomer illuminates meanings that have slipped out of view and realities that have fallen between the cracks of dominant histories, such as the direct link between explosions of racial violence and the slave past. He even suggests that Barlo's origin story has a veiled doubleness, laced with subversive intent. His story inspires a 'Negress, of wide reputation for being sanctified', to draw a 'portrait of a black madonna on the courthouse wall' (*C* 21). She inscribes the wall of a building that symbolizes white legal power with a figure that represents the suffering of black women, calling into question the courthouse's legitimacy.

The Significance of *Cane*'s Form

Having established some of the stylistic features of *Cane*, it is worth considering Toomer's comments about his chosen form. In his copious correspondence with Waldo Frank, he worked hard to transform the volume from a miscellany collected under loose titles, such as 'Cane Stalks and Chorouses [sic]', 'Leaves and Syrup Songs' and 'Leaf Traceries in Washington', to the complex patterning of the finished text (Scruggs and VanDemarr 1998, 119). As I have already noted, Frank likened his experience of reading *Cane* to 'adventuring through the pieces of a still unorganized mosaic' (Turner 1988, 159). In response, Toomer adopted an organic metaphor, explaining that '[t]he skeleton is knit by the dry cartilage of the two races' (McKay 1984, 52). For Toomer, the very form of his text is expressive of the foundational interdependence of the black and white races, which exists even before firm connective tissue has solidified into bone. Toomer's hostile attitude towards the anthologization of selected pieces from *Cane*, to which I will return later in the chapter, also stemmed from the inextricable link between his choice of form and his complication of racial labels.

The dust jacket of the original edition of *Cane* described it as 'a vaudeville out of the South' (McKay 1984, 83). In a publicity note produced in the 1930s, Toomer elaborated upon this description, bringing the implications of his heterogeneous form into focus:

> There can be no cumulative and consistent movement, and of course no central plot to such a book. It is sheer vaudeville. But if it be accepted as a unit of spiritual experience, then one can find in *Cane* a beginning, a progression, a complication, and an end. It is too complex a volume to find its parallel in the Negro musical comedies so popular on Broadway. *Cane* is black vaudeville. It is black super-vaudeville out of the South (Kerman and Eldridge 1987, 200).

Labelling *Cane* as 'super-vaudeville', Toomer marks it as a development from the vaudeville medley of apparently unrelated elements. Vaudeville dates back to the 1840s and comprises jokes, tall tales, song and dance routines and spoofs of elite culture that had their roots in southern plantation culture, P.T. Barnum's dime museums, southern American folklore and English pantomime (Douglas 1995, 75). It is a medium that combines ritualistic, repetitive routines with free improvisation upon high and low, written and vernacular culture. In keeping with such diversity, Toomer defines *Cane*'s form as a particularly 'complex' one that deploys rural African American sources but transplants them 'out of the South' into urban settings. He abandons realism, continuous narrative and plotting, but he stresses that there is a 'progression' to be teased out, if readers are willing to track down incomplete references, actively interpreting the text.

In a description that recalls Thomas P. Brockelman's theory that collage has the potential to challenge assumptions, Toomer suggests that 'complication' is crucial to the 'progression' of *Cane* (2001, 160). He begins the process of rethinking assumptions by refusing to associate particular cultural forms with specific racial groups. The term 'super-vaudeville', for instance, exceeds racial categorization. Toomer deliberately eschews a link with the mass consumption of 'Negro musical comedies' on Broadway as authentic 'Negro' expression. Moreover, his scrambling and stretching of vaudeville is not only inspired by African American vernacular culture; it is also a response to the aesthetic experimentation of avant-garde figures, such as Marsden Hartley and T.S. Eliot, who turned to popular culture in their search for alternative aesthetic templates. A comparison with e.e.cummings is particularly fruitful. In a review of *The Enormous Room* in *The Dial* in 1922, John Dos Passos presents vaudeville as the discourse through which cummings disgorges 'the underside of History with indelible vividness' (1963, 109). As in *Cane*, manipulation of a creatively stretched, multi-generic form enables the articulation of stories that remain concealed in conventional historical narratives.

Monumental History

In the second part of *Cane*, Toomer takes further his exploration of histories that have been marginalized in conventional accounts of national history, making particular reference to the 'whitewashed' monuments of Washington. To draw out the implications of Toomer's engagement with such conventional historical narratives, it is helpful to consider Pierre Nora's work on memory. In his collaborative seven volume study *Lieux de Mémoire*, Pierre Nora has described how group memory selects certain landmarks, such as places, dates and artworks, and invests them with political and symbolic significance, which inspires us to remember, to forget and even to fabricate myths of national identity. For Nora, the function of *lieux de mémoire* is 'to stop time, to block the work of forgetting, to establish a state of things, to immortalize death, to materialize the immaterial' (1994, 295-6). Through a series of representations of the Washington monuments, Toomer anticipates Nora's theory to show how American sites of hailed memory erase the realities of slavery and racial conflict. Making a direct correlation between seamless, coherent and integrated narrative wholes and politically dominant, whitened versions of American history, he explores the national histories articulated through Washington's monuments, and by extension, America's political system.

In 'Seventh Street', he describes the 'white and whitewashed wood of Washington' to expose slanted histories and to call into question the relationship between American civic pride and political democracy (*C* 39). Toomer's phrase 'white and whitewashed' recalls Christ's indictment of the Pharisees for their exclusiveness and hypocrisy. Jesus condemns the Pharisees as murderers of the Prophets' ancestors: '[w]oe unto you, scribes and Pharisees, hypocrites! for ye are like unto whited sepulchres, which indeed appear beautiful outward, but are within full of dead *men's* bones, and of all uncleanness' (Matthew 23.27) (Scruggs and VanDemarr 1998, 166). By aligning the whitewashed monuments with the Pharisees who 'shut up the kingdom of heaven against men', Toomer hints at an unspoken history of oppression, exclusion and exploitation (Matthew 23.13).

Through a cycle of portrayals of monuments, Toomer exposes the fissures and absences in whitewashed, monumental histories. In 'Rhobert', his mocking description of plans to erect a monument to the valiant Rhobert highlights the empty, even cynical, motives behind such memorials:

> Lets call him great when the water shall have been all drawn off. Lets build a monument and set it in the ooze where he goes down. A monument of hewn oak, carved in nigger-heads. Lets open our throats, brother, and sing 'Deep River' when he goes down (*C* 41).

Toomer describes the process of erecting official historical narratives. The details of Rhobert's life are subsumed and flattened into an overwhelming 'ooze' and the organic wholeness of a wooden monument. By making this process visible, Toomer marks the plan to erect a monument as a manipulative political decision to 'call' someone great after helplessly watching them die. Rhobert's personal history has become a narrative that is selected, manipulated and invented according to the needs of the moment: his past is, as Van Wyck Brooks argues in 'On Creating a Usable Past', 'an inexhaustible storehouse of apt attitudes and adaptable ideals' that can be cut and pasted into a continuous whole (Brooks 1968b, 223). This ritual exercise converts Rhobert's life into a model journey from the tribulations of earth to the freedom of heaven. Toomer alludes to the spiritual 'Deep River' to suggest ironically that Rhobert's life repeats the structures and injustices of slavery: he is completely powerless to speak about his inner life.

There is an even more specific historical revisioning going on here. The references to 'glory', a 'Red Cross man', Rhobert's canonization as a great man and his willingness to abandon his wife and child indicate that Toomer is concerned with the treatment of African American soldiers during World War I (*C* 40). Indeed, the description of the drowning Rhobert going down in the 'ooze' could be seen as a re-interpretation of Wilfred Owen's depiction of the 'drowning' soldier who 'plunges at [him], guttering, choking, drowning' in 'Dulce Et Decorum Est' (1983, 1037). If alluding to this poem, where the reader is a helpless, passive, guilty voyeur, strangely implicated in the soldier's death, Toomer adds a sting to his revisionist history. Read in this context, the description of the monument composed of 'nigger-heads' takes on a macabre twist. Toomer plays on the double meaning of the phrase, which is slang for cigarette ends, to suggest that African Americans are treated as the detritus of American society. Building upon his allusion to the 'dead *men's* bones' behind the façade of the pure white monuments in 'Seventh Street', he shows that white political supremacy is dependent upon the fruits of black labour, oppression and sacrifice. To borrow a phrase from *The Souls of Black Folk*, Toomer highlights a history of unacknowledged racial interdependence: white prosperity, peace and order are 'built upon a groan' (Du Bois 1996, 102).

In an essay on the significance of *Beloved*, Toni Morrison has lamented the absence of an official monument to the slaves in America:

> [t]here is no place you or I can go, to think about or not think about, to summon the presences of, or recollect the absences of slaves; nothing that reminds us of the ones who made the journey and of those who did not make it. There is no suitable memorial or plaque or wreath or wall or park or skyscraper lobby. There's no 300-foot tower. There's no small bench by the road. There is not even a tree scored, an initial that I can visit or you can visit in Charleston or Savannah or New York or Providence or, better still, on the banks of the Mississippi (1989, 4).

From the beginning of the building programme in Washington, the realities of slavery and racial conflict were deliberately erased from national, monumental histories. During the 1850s, Secretary of War Jefferson Davis worked hard to keep the liberty cap, an emblem commonly associated with abolitionism, from any decoration on the U.S. Capitol (Savage 1997, 41). In a similar way, the Lincoln Memorial, which was completed in 1922 while Toomer was writing *Cane*, removed Lincoln from the context of present, political concerns to a classical, idealized realm. The Republican-sponsored elite responsible for the memorial not only erased all mention of slavery from the central inscription behind the colossal Lincoln figure, but they also ignored countless protests from the general public that allusions to Greek culture were inappropriate since it was a slave-owning society (Savage 1994, 140).

In 'Avey', Toomer takes the image of the Capitol dome, which is included in Aaron Douglas's *Aspects of Negro Life: From Slavery Through Reconstruction* to express the promised transformation of the American polis by inclusion of African Americans (Figure 3), to highlight history that has slipped out of view in the stories that America tells itself. Toomer's highly figurative description of Avey sleeping in the shadow of the Capitol Dome articulates the suppressed history of slavery. In a flash of insight, the narrator recognizes that American official history is haunted by shame and indignity:

> I saw dawn steal over Washington. The Capitol dome looked like a gray ghost ship drifting in from sea. Avey's face was pale, and her eyes were heavy. She did not have the gray crimson-splashed beauty of the dawn. I hated to wake her. Orphan-woman ... (*C* 47)

Comparing the Capitol Dome to 'a gray ghost ship', Toomer invokes the opening of Herman Melville's *Benito Cereno* ('a gray ghost drifting in from sea') to suggest the horrors of the Middle Passage (Scruggs 1997, 75). This suggestive allusion to a history that leaves Avey tired, drained and orphaned shows that the legacy of slavery is hidden behind the façade of America's civic pride, embedded in its political system. The taint of slavery turns the mixed race Avey a ghostly white. This blanching could be seen as an incident of what Susan Gubar has called 'racechange', a moment of racial transfiguration when race boundaries are transgressed (1997, 5).[8] This transformation, which defies biracial categories, suggests that all Americans are marked by a history of violence, shame and theft. Indeed, the figurative association of whiteness with deadening resonates with a chain of representations of whites in *Cane*, in which the pain inflicted upon victims of racial violence scars both victim and victimizer. In 'Portrait in Georgia', for

---

8   Gubar provides a useful definition of 'racechange': '[t]he term is meant to suggest the traversing of race boundaries, racial imitation or impersonation, cross-racial mimicry or mutability, white posing as black or black passing as white, pan-racial mutuality' (1997, 5).

example, the burning of black flesh in a lynching converts into white ash, exposing the ultimate arbitrariness of racial categories, the ultimate interdependence of black and white. In this context, Toomer's depiction of the crimson-stained white edifice represents a historical burden of shame and guilt that stealthily haunts the American polis. Describing the 'gray' Capitol Dome, he highlights an unspoken, unacknowledged black history that colours, and complicates, the 'whitewash' of American democracy.

In an image suggestive of the collage cut-out, Toomer makes an explicit connection between tearing open whitewashed, overarching histories and exposing the realities of racial mixing and racial complexity in America. In 'Seventh Street', he dramatizes the violent action of shredding apart 'white and whitewashed wood of Washington' to reveal the miscegenation and cultural mixing that have been concealed by monumental histories:

> A crude-boned, soft-skinned wedge of nigger life breathing its loafer air, jazz songs and love, thrusting unconscious rhythms, black reddish blood into the white and whitewashed wood of Washington. Stale soggy wood of Washington. Wedges rust in soggy wood ... Split it! In two! Again! Shred it! (*C* 39)

The shredding and smashing of 'whitewashed' history reveals a liquefication and softening of racial barriers. Each time Toomer describes a distinct slice of racial life, such as the sexualized 'thrusting' '[w]edges' of 'nigger life' or the hard 'whitewashed' buildings, it collapses into softness, sogginess and, above all, the mixing of black blood and white wood in an uncontrollable bodily force that undermines racial separation. Toomer rips apart the façade of 'whitewashed' monuments to reveal the racial mixing and cultural interpenetration that exists behind it. Challenging racial segregation breathes energy and life into 'stale' forms that threaten to corrode free expression.

Voicing the realities of miscegenation and racial proximity was, as a number of critics have pointed out, an affront to the dominant racial ideology of the 1920s. In the early twentieth century, there was an increasingly rigid separation of the black and white races. As Joel Williamson has shown, the racial designations deployed in the U.S. census are a touchstone of this process (1995, 114). In 1890, enumerators were expected to take a quantitative approach, dividing individuals into 'blacks', 'mulattoes', 'quadroons' and 'octoroons' according to the proportion of black and white blood in their veins. 1920 was the last year when 'mulatto', the only remaining official term to describe racial mixture, was designated on the census (Nadell 2001, 158-9). This reflects a shift from recognition of biracial and interracial identity to the complete segregation of the population according to the one drop rule, which was accompanied by the rigid enforcement of racial difference through Jim Crow laws stipulating the physical separation of blacks and whites. Toomer was fully aware of the hardening of racial boundaries. In his essay 'Race Problems and Modern Society', he argues that 'racial animosity' was 'crystallizing' (179) and, in spite of a large body of scientific evidence proving the prevalence of racial mixing, 'there is the nation wide separation of the white and colored groups' (Toomer 1996c, 182).

For many white Americans in the early twentieth century, miscegenation was fraught with uneasiness and panic. In the wake of a resurgence of interest in eugenics, white commentators published inflammatory pamphlets condemning miscegenation as a 'crime' against humanity and God, a plague and an 'abomination' to be paralleled with prostitution and incest (Mencke 1979, 99-139). For example, in 1907, J.H. Currie, district attorney for Meridian, Mississippi, couched his plea for racial purity in apocalyptic terms:

> Our own people, our white men with their black concubines, are destroying the integrity of the Negro race, raising up a menace to the white race, lowering the standard of both races and preparing the way for riot, mob, criminal assaults, and finally, a death struggle for racial supremacy (Mencke 1979, 113).

Drawing upon a familiar equation of miscegenation with degeneration, Currie describes racial mixing as an indefensible, unnameable transgression aligned with criminality, riot and mob rule. "Mulattoes" are subversive of his racial ideology, which assumes the complete superiority of whites. For Currie, the prospect of an intermediate race provokes anxiety about the collapse of racial and political order. Bringing to mind Darwinism, he predicts a 'death struggle for racial supremacy', which is even more alarming because white men have instigated the crumbling of racial 'integrity'.

Miscegenation was also fraught with unease for African Americans. As Toomer explains in his essay 'Race Problems and Modern Society', racial boundaries were increasingly rigid, even as African Americans adopted professions that brought them closer to white Americans: 'just as certain as it is that this increasing correspondence of types makes the drawing of distinctions supposedly based on skin color or blood composition appear more and more ridiculous, so it is true that the lines are being drawn with more force between the colored and white groups. Negroes are themselves now drawing these lines. Interbreeding and intermarriage, for instance, are becoming as taboo among negroes as among whites' (1996c, 183). In this context, colour consciousness exacerbated tensions in the African American community and distinctions of colour created fissures between political groups. The pan-African nationalist Marcus Garvey, for instance, deliberately set his politics against what he referred to as Du Bois's 'bastard aristocracy', stigmatizing Du Bois's championing of the Talented Tenth in racial terms, as an affront to black nationalism (Gatewood 1990, 321).

Du Bois's discussion of miscegenation is also tinged with ambivalence. In *The Souls of Black Folk*, he grapples with the legacy of sexual exploitation of black women to face 'a dread that blackness has been inextricably contaminated by the unbearable shame of innocent suffering' (Gubar 1997, 105). For Du Bois, one of the most difficult burdens created by slavery was '[t]he red stain of bastardy, which two centuries of systematic legal defilement of Negro women had stamped upon his race, [which] meant not only the loss of ancient African chastity, but also the hereditary weight of a mass of corruption from white adulterers, threatening almost the obliteration of the Negro home' (1996, 9). Du Bois indicts white men for their corrupt 'defilement' of black women, which wilfully disregarded legal and familial codes. However, he is equally concerned that this 'stain', which he links to the site of slavery through a sequence of representations of the 'dull red hideousness of Georgia', may have corrupted black women and their families (1996, 90). For Du Bois, mulattoes carry the 'hereditary weight' of slavery in their physical make-up and bear the stamp of a shameful history.

Du Bois cannot detach this history of indignity from his discussions of miscegenation. For example, he laments that educated middle-class African Americans and whites are separated by the color line, 'while at the bottom of the social group, in the saloon, the gambling-hell, and the brothel, that same line wavers and disappears' (1996, 151). Du Bois associates racial mixing with degeneration, leisure, excess and what he regards as the lower class activities of prostitution, gambling and drinking. By contrast, he wishes for racial contact in the elevated realm of culture, dreaming of a quasi-religious, sublimated sphere where blacks and whites are 'co-worker[s] in the kingdom of culture' (1996, 5). His discussion of miscegenation is charged with anxiety about the need to avoid accusations of excess and unbridled sexuality.

Toomer's scrambling of familiar forms in *Cane* is integral to his attempt to prise apart the seams of whitewashed history to explore the difficult subjects of racial mixing and racial complexity, which troubled white Americans and African Americans alike. He develops an aesthetic technique of disjunction and violation to articulate a brutal history of concubinage and rape. In 'Kabnis', he grapples for a language through which to express the pain of confronting this difficult history. His stark description warps the standard tropes of romanticism:

> Lewis, seated now so that his eyes rest upon the old man, merges with his source and lets the pain and beauty of the South meet him there. White faces, pain-pollen, settle downward through a cane-sweet mist and touch the ovaries of yellow flowers. Cotton-bolls bloom, droop. Black roots twist in a parched red soil beneath a blazing sky. Magnolias, fragrant, a trifle futile, lovely, far off ...
> (*C* 106)

This encounter between Lewis and Father John, an embodiment of the slave past, is described as a moment when Lewis 'merges with his source' to confront his mixed race origins. Toomer graphically represents the violent, thrusting force of white men's sexual exploitation and rape of black women, illuminating a history that affected the racial composition of America, creating 'yellow flowers' or mixed race children, such as Carma with her 'yellow flower face' (*C* 10) and Kabnis's 'lemon face' (*C* 81). Toomer expresses the earth-shattering violence of a history that split the world into black and white, exploiter and exploited, the blank faces of the oppressors and the struggling, twisting enslaved. Received generic conventions, such as the poetic portrayal of overarching heaven, mist and sweet fragrances, are deformed by the brutal reality of rape. In this dark vision, sexual exploitation spills 'pain' everywhere, violating a sacred, fecund relation between heaven and earth, lover and loved: '[w]hite faces' distribute 'pain-pollen'. I interpret this phrase as a reference to the sexual coercion of female slaves. Southern laws did not recognize rape of black women as a crime and many women were sold into what was termed the 'fancy trade', in which they were trained for domestic service, but it was generally understood that they were purchased as prospective concubines (Williamson 1995, 69). The painful contradictions of this sexual exploitation, which crushes and stunts growth and yet creates new life, are vividly suggested through a tortured form that is derived from romantic tropes, but violently stretches them.

Nowhere is the inextricable link between Toomer's mixed form and his attempt to expose racial proximity better seen than in 'Kabnis'. The reality of a black mother nurturing a white child graphically bursts through the seams of a familiar lullaby:

> Some distance off, down in the valley, a band of pine-smoke, silvered gauze, drifts steadily. The half-moon is a white child that sleeps upon the tree-tops of the forest. White winds croon its sleep-song:

> rock a-by baby . .
> Black mother sways, holding a white child on her bosom.
> when the bough bends . .
> Her breath hums through pine-cones.
> cradle will fall . .
> Teat moon-children at your breasts,
> down will come baby . .
> Black mother (*C* 82).

Here, the tabooed topic of a black mother nurturing a white child breaks the integrated, familiar form of the lullaby from within. By grafting the lullaby onto images of black motherhood, Toomer voices a reality that exists between the lines of a 'whitewashed' form. He disrupts the idyllic unity of a famous English lullaby to illuminate the role of a black mammy who nurtures the white child with tender care, yet remains powerless to prevent the tragedy of the child's fall. He carefully pieces together a string of intertextual and intratextual images to highlight the pervasiveness of such racial proximity. By referring to 'moon-children', Toomer alludes to a poem in Du Bois's *Darkwater: Voices from within the Veil*, 'Children of the Moon', 'where the black children of Isis are hidden in caves, deprived of the sun, and protected by black mothers' (Scruggs and VanDemarr 1998, 276). This allusion points to a specific history, the 'damnation of women' by white men, 'spoilers of women, shameless breeders of bastards', which leaves black women powerless to protect their own children (Du Bois 1920, 53).

Toomer's figurative effects, the moonlight, the bands of colour and the pine-cones, also resonate with a mosaic of moments in *Cane* that depict black mothers with white children, white mothers with black children and interracial desire. '[R]ock a-by baby', for instance, invokes a crucial moment in 'Bona and Paul' when Paul's attempt to trace his origins culminates in the startling image of a Negress, who 'chants a lullaby beneath the mate-eyes of a southern planter' (*C* 71). This passage, which I have discussed as a kind of ghost narrative behind 'Carma', shatters the innocence of the lullaby, exposing the powerlessness of enslaved women.

Toomer represents a startling web of tangled racial lineages: black, white and yellow are tied together by what Harriet Jacobs called the 'tangled skeins' of 'the genealogies of slavery' (1997, 224). He explores the paradox of miscegenation in America: racial mixing was foundational to American history, in the institution of slavery, and yet shrouded in secrecy and denial. As Patricia J. Williams has noted, the image of the black Madonna with a white child has a radical political edge: she highlights '[t]he utter interdependence of such an image; the merging it implies; the giving up of boundary; the encompassing of other within self; the unbounded generosity and interconnectedness of such an image' (Gubar 1997, 228). Toomer's vision of black mother and white child pushes this radicalism a step further. He improvises upon an image from Van Wyck Brooks's 'America's Coming-of-Age' to intervene in a contemporary debate about the state of American culture. For Van Wyck Brooks, the image of the 'tree-top dream' represents irreconcilable poles of possibility in America's bifurcated culture: highbrow and lowbrow; literate and illiterate; theoretical and practical; intellect and action; spiritual and material (1968a, 81). Toomer gives this theory of binaries an unfamiliar spin, recasting it to highlight a history of racial interdependence.

For Toomer, the interpenetration of the black and white races is not only a result of miscegenation, the biological fact of racial mixing; the races are also locked together by the history of violence inflicted upon African Americans. In 'Portrait in Georgia', miscegenation and racial violence are inextricably linked:

> Hair – braided chestnut,
>   coiled like a lyncher's rope,
> Eyes – fagots,
>   Lips – old scars, or the first red blisters,
> Breath – the last sweet scent of cane,
> And her slim body, white as the ash
>   of black flesh after flame (*C* 27).

Toomer's deployment of a collage form, with its disparate fragments, is specifically tied to the terror of the social and political situation for African Americans in the South. By entitling this shocking representation of lynching 'Portrait in Georgia', he suggests that realistic representation or portraiture has been warped by the violent realities of race relations in the South. Toomer twists the conventions of the Petrarchan love sonnet, with its enumeration of body parts, into a fragmented form that disorientates readers. The stark violence of lynching bursts the form from within in a manner analogous with collage since it 'preserves on its surface the visible traces of the violence done to former units' (Adamowicz 1998, 194).

By overlaying images of a white woman, the charred flesh of a black victim and the equipment of lynching, Toomer defies the separation of black and white. The hurt inflicted on the burning victim also damages the victimizer: the white woman's body is marked with red blisters and scars, from the past and the present, which are suggestive of the diseased body politic of the South. Moreover, just as cubist collage can imply an underlying relation between irreducible fragments by strategic juxtaposition, Toomer establishes that the races are locked into what Eric J. Sundquist has described, in his analysis of *The Souls of Black Folk*, as 'a kind of anarchic symbiosis' (1993, 468). Black and white, male and female collapse into one another: Americans in Georgia are branded with the shame of racial violence, whether as a victim or a perpetrator.

Toomer and Boas: Towards a Definition of America

To some extent, my claim that Toomer warps received generic conventions to give voice to an unspoken history of racial mixing and racial violence in the South might be read as analogous to Houston A. Baker's account of the Harlem Renaissance as a distinctive kind of modernism that was necessarily subversive, deploying '*the mastery of form* and *the deformation of mastery*' (1987, 15). Baker describes formal innovation as a mode of resistance that has aesthetic, historical and political implications. However, when this approach is applied to Toomer, it threatens to disguise the complex intercultural and interracial quality of his aesthetic experimentation.[9] In other words, while Baker's emphasis on resistance illuminates the political dimensions of formal innovation, his approach obscures the common ground that Toomer shared with modernists like Franz Boas. On close inspection, it is clear that Toomer engages Boasian anthropology from an African American historical perspective. Such affiliations undermine Baker's attempt to identify a separate, distinctive African American modernism, particularly because Toomer's interest in mixed race histories gains some of its political punch from his sustained revisioning, or even collaging, of Boasian anthropology.

Toomer was a careful reader of Franz Boas and his students. 'Race Problems and Modern Society' (1929) and the unpublished essays 'The Negro Emergent' (1924) and 'The Crock of Problems' (1928) engage with the work of Boas, Melville Herskovits, Alfred Kroeber and Ales Hrdlicka. Boas's key work *The Mind of*

---

[9]   George Hutchinson's important study *The Harlem Renaissance in Black and White* (1995) pays close attention to the institutional framework that supported the Harlem Renaissance – publishing houses, magazines, the anthropology of Franz Boas and his students, pragmatism and cultural pluralism – to expose its interracial underpinnings.

Primitive Man, first published in 1911, makes a pivotal shift from the analysis of discrete racial types to the study of plural cultures. In contrast to the evolutionists who arranged cultures into 'a time series' demonstrating the progress of humanity from simple to complex civilization, he accounted for differences in populations by identifying historical processes of contact, migration, trade and exchange as the vehicle of cultural change (Boas 1938, 177). In this way, he launched a direct attack upon evolutionism to imagine 'cultural traits traversing racial classifications, and racial groups crossing cultural boundaries' (Hegeman 1999, 49). This shift of focus from race and evolutionism to culture enables Toomer to make a similar move from predetermined racial histories to a vision of a specifically American culture.

In 'Theater', he describes urban America as a crossover culture:

> Life of nigger alleys, of pool rooms and restaurants and near-beer saloons soaks into the walls of Howard Theater and sets them throbbing jazz songs. Black-skinned, they dance and shout above the tick and trill of white-walled buildings. At night, they open doors to people who come in to stamp their feet and shout. At night, road-shows volley songs into the mass-heart of black people. Songs soak the walls and seep out to the nigger life of alleys and near-beer saloons, of the Poodle Dog and Black Bear cabarets (*C* 50).

Toomer manipulates the aesthetic possibilities of Boas's investigation of racial mixing and cultural crossing to develop a utopian vision of cultural exchange. This anthropological attempt to document a culture describes a two-way process of contamination and interfusion, across the categories of black and white, high and low, inside and outside. Dynamic interchange locks the races into interdependence, as suggested by the circularity of the passage, which loops back into itself through repetition of the motif of 'alleys and near-beer saloons'. As in Boas's work, cultural contact acts as a catalyst for new forms and developments: the 'nigger life' of the city streets 'sets' the white walls of Howard Theater 'throbbing jazz songs'. Toomer describes the cultural activities of 'nigger life' – singing, dancing and shouting – that promise to revitalize the 'tick and trill' of tired white forms. A mishmash of elements comprises African American culture: jazz, folk forms, theatre, street culture and road-shows. These expressions of the 'mass-heart of black people', which recall Johann Gottfried Herder's notion of *Volksgeist*, 'soak' and 'seep' into white structures, imbuing them with a creative energy. This is suggestive of a new, crossover American culture, which 'open[s] doors to people who come in to stamp their feet and shout', a culture expressive of freedom as it spills beyond the confines of categories used to organize the world, such as black and white.

Toomer is not simply highlighting an aesthetic process whereby cross-cultural appropriations have a catalytic effect, making new art forms. As suggested by his listing of buildings from the northern cityscape, the creative interplay of black and white is tied to a historical process of adjustment: the migration of African Americans to the northern cities. The impact of urbanization upon African American migrants underlies Toomer's gesture towards the creation of a new culture. As he explains in an undated letter to Waldo Frank, the introduction of a larger African American population to America's modern, urban cities created beauty that could not be defined simply on racial lines: 'Seventh Street is the song of crude new life. Of a new people. Negro? Only in the *boldness* of its expression. In its healthy freedom. American. For the shows that please Seventh Street make their fortunes on Broadway' (Rusch 1993, 25). Toomer documents the emergence of a 'new' culture that is neither black nor white, but the result of intricate interplay between African American cultural styles and white American institutions.

In his forceful emphasis upon the newness of this urban culture, Toomer could be accused of neglecting a long history of intercultural contact spawning new cultural forms in America. For example, W.T. Lhamon and Eric Lott have revealed minstrelsy's syncretic character: even as minstrel players caricatured and counterfeited aspects of African American culture, they also revised and adapted it, adding 'home songs', the conventions of European pantomime and southwestern humour to the blend (Lhamon, 1998, 152; Lott 1993, 177-9). Accounts of the origins of jazz underline that intercultural exchange was not a new thing: it had been anticipated in the 'melding of white and black folk musics, African, European, and American influences' that led to the emergence of jazz in the South (White 2004, 197). That said, Toomer's description of a break from the past rather than a synthesis of old and new is an attempt to capture the vibrancy of a burgeoning, urban culture, which was being transformed by the huge influx of African American migrants (Lemann 1991, 16). Throughout the second section of *Cane*, Toomer indicates that both northern and southern cultures were transformed by the process of African American adaptation to the city environment. In particular, Toomer points to the development of unique cultural forms: he consistently presents jazz as an urban phenomenon, connecting it with city buildings that 'throb' with its energy and rhythm.

Toomer's vignettes of African American migrant life in the North often verge on the surreal: the '[e]ddying' blood and creative energy that overwhelms the 'whitewashed' order of 'Seventh Street' (*C* 39); Nora's dream 'cradled in dream-fluted cane' in 'Calling Jesus' (*C* 55); the elaborate courtship metaphor of '[d]ark swaying forms of Negroes' as 'street songs that woo virginal houses' in 'Box Seat' (*C* 56); and the 'Negress' who sits next to Dan Moore at the theatre in 'Box Seat', whose 'strong roots sink down and spread under the river and disappear in blood-lines that waver south' (*C* 62). As Farah Jasmine Griffin and James R. Grossman have shown, the geographical displacement of African Americans through the Great Migration introduces the history, culture, religion and blood-lines of the South to the North, transforming urban culture in the process (Grossman 1989; Griffin 1995).

Griffin emphasizes the strong sense of disorientation created as *Cane* moves from the South to the North: she argues that Toomer casts his readers as 'the migrants of this text', who are confronted with 'swiftness and technology' (65) that 'comes as a shock to our eyes, ears, and powers of comprehension' (1995, 66). In a manipulation of juxtaposition that is analogous to collage, Toomer creates a sharp break with his lyrical, poetic language in part one: the reader is faced with a jazz aesthetic of syncopated rhythms, 'harsh and quick verbs of movement' and formal fragmentation (Griffin 1995, 65). Furthermore, if Toomer's portrait of the South is underpinned by a concern with the history of slavery, the legacy of slavery also has the potential to disrupt or erupt in the northern metropolis, overturning any sense of security. For example, a startling description of the migrant 'Negress' in the audience in 'Box Seat' invokes the history of slaves sold down the Mississippi and the separation of families at the auction block, highlighting a past that remains tangible in the present and threatens to 'suck' the 'glossy health' from 'asphalt streets' (*C* 62). In distinction to Alain Locke's equation of the Great Migration with historical progress from backwardness to modernity, from serfdom to citizenship, 'from medieval America to modern', Toomer indicates that it is impossible to escape or leave behind the history of the 'medieval' South by migrating North (*N* 6).

Toomer's vision of history invading and unsettling the contemporary moment is developed most fully in 'Kabnis', the portrait of a secular urban intellectual who goes to teach in rural Georgia, as Toomer did in 1921. During his visit to the ancestral South, Kabnis has to confront his personal history. In particular, he has to come to terms with the realities of miscegenation. Lewis characterizes the difficulties of Kabnis's struggle with his mixed racial heritage, countering Kabnis's claim that there '[a]int much difference between black an blue':

> Enough to draw a denial from you. Cant hold them, can you? Master; slave.
> Soil; and the overarching heavens. Dusk; dawn. They fight and bastardize you.
> The sun tint of your cheeks, flame of the great season's multi-colored leaves,
> tarnished, burned. Split, shredded: easily burned. No use... (*C* 107)

Kabnis's sense of shame at his racial origins is compounded by 'denial' of his mixed race origins. He wrestles with the legacy of the slave past, particularly his position as a descendant of both slaver and enslaved. Caught between the history of victim and victimizer at a moment when racial boundaries were hardening, Kabnis's sense of self is 'bastardized', fragmented and in shreds. He is the product of a violation of family bonds and bears what Du Bois calls '[t]he red stain of bastardy' (1996, 9).

For Kabnis, facing up to his origins is fraught with uneasy tensions. On the one hand, an extraordinary energy, suggested through the violent imagery of shredding and burning, is generated by the thrusting differences that jostle and 'fight' within his body. As in 'Seventh Street', Toomer uses explosive ellipses to chop up conventional syntax, imitating a crackling creative energy with the potential to shatter biracial categories. With its dynamic, fluid vocabulary that undercuts strict racial categorization, the lyrical description of Kabnis's face, 'flame of the great season's multi-colored leaves', recalls Toomer's sustained project throughout

Cane to detail the beauty of bodies that transcend a black and white vision of the world.[10]

On the other hand, an acknowledgement of the brutal reality of slavery and his own mixed race status requires Kabnis to admit that his identity is embroiled in a destructive legacy of violence and violation. In the most literal terms, his body straddles the binaries of victim and victimizer, master and slave. By deploying motifs of heaven and earth, and soil and sky, Toomer invokes Lewis's vision of the 'pain and beauty of the South' which is born of an unsettling history of bondage, rape, exploitation and violence, to show that Kabnis is the product of a history that leaves individual lives and cultural expression 'tarnished' (*C* 107). Kabnis's burning sense of shame, which is represented by his blushing cheeks, harks back to the many 'face[s] of history' that haunt readers of *Cane*: Avey's blanched face under the shadow of the Capitol Building as the narrator recognizes the horrors of slavery; the decaying visage of 'Face'; and the charred flesh of the lynch victim in 'Portrait in Georgia'.[11] As Toomer suggests through Kabnis's fraught encounters with the taciturn Father John, the former slave who is 'symbol, flesh, and spirit of the past', this is a confusing, difficult past that lives on in the present (*C* 107).

Toomer's notion of history haunting the present suggests a further debt to Boas. For Boas, all cultures are the product of historical processes. As he writes in 'The Principles of Ethnological Classification', '[f]ormer events ... leave their stamp on the present character of a people' (Boas 1974b, 65). For Boas, historical 'events' are the shaping force of a culture's development. In contrast to the predetermined futures staked out by evolutionism, Boas argues that a culture is nothing more than the accretion of historical 'events' that leave their 'stamp' upon the culture and define its future. As in *Cane*, the cultural present is the product of its past and an indicator of the future.

In *Cane*, the process of confronting the ever-present ghosts of the past is shaped by an engagement with Boas's challenge to evolutionism. A reading of Toomer's essay 'The Negro Emergent' suggests that he revises anthropology to develop his own theory of historical development. The whole essay documents a shift in African American attitudes towards history. Toomer describes a process of breaking from complete preoccupation with racial oppression and 'a compound of beliefs, habits, attitudes, and emotional reactions superimposed upon him by external circumstance' (48): '[t]he Negro is emerging to a place where he can see just what these factors are, the extent to which he has merely reacted to their stimuli, the extent to which he has been controlled by them' (1996a, 51). He notices a shift from an evolutionist perspective, where African Americans were determined by history and 'external circumstance', to a point of awareness of the

---

[10]   In 'Blood-Burning Moon', for instance, Toomer describes Louisa in figurative terms that cannot be reduced to a specific skin colour: '[h]er skin was the color of oak leaves on young trees in fall' (*C* 28).

[11]   For a detailed discussion of the trope of the 'face of history' in *Cane*, see Charles Scruggs and Lee VanDemarr (1998, 189-95).

past. African Americans, he claims, have developed a detachment from 'image' or stereotype and can now determine their own notion of identity, discarding or absorbing external factors as they see fit (1996a, 50). Paying particular attention to the pernicious effects of denying mixed race histories, he advocates an honest acknowledgement of past events: 'since he himself has wished to force his slave root from his mind, and since his white root denies him, the Negro, psychologically and spiritually has been literally uprooted, or worse, with no roots at all' (1996a, 48). For Toomer, failure to face up to the realities of miscegenation has resulted in a sense of dislocation from history, and therefore a diminished sense of identity.

In a stylistic breakthrough that builds upon this revisioning of Boasian historicism, Kabnis's aesthetic utterances can be seen as an attempt to express this unspoken past by reclaiming mixed race 'roots'. Kabnis repeatedly refers to his orations as the expression of his 'soul', which he regards as the physical and cultural embodiment of miscegenation. As he tells Carrie K. in response to Father John's indictment of the white race for the 'sin' of making 'th Bible lie':

> It was only a preacher's sin they knew in those old days, an that wasnt sin at all. Mind me, th only sin is whats done against th soul. Th whole world is a conspiracy t sin, especially in America, an against me. I'm th victim of their sin. I'm what sin is. Does he look like me? Have you ever heard him say th things youve heard me say? (*C* 115)

Kabnis defines 'sin' in opposition to Father John's notion of religious betrayal, claiming that his mixed race heritage means that he physically embodies America's sins. Yet, in spite of his anger at racial hatred, Kabnis cannot name the fact of miscegenation except as a shameful 'sin': it remains transgressive, difficult to express. He is both the 'victim' of a 'conspiracy' that allowed the concubinage and rape of black women and now denies his legitimacy, and the descendant of such a union. As a result, he feels at odds with the 'whole world' and does not know where he belongs in American society. The questions he asks of Father John imply both a desire to belong to a community and a family, and a reluctant awareness of his difference. While he wants to integrate himself into biracial America, he also dreams 'of a new language to express his soul' (Hutchinson 1993, 242).

Kabnis's mixed race origins shape his stylistic choices as an artist or orator. His artistic forms, which mirror the broken forms of Toomer's collage aesthetic, are defined in distinction to the art of Fred Halsey, Sempter's wheelwright. Lewis describes Halsey as an artist who '[f]its here. Belongs here': his skills meet the needs of the community and his workshop acts as a public meeting place (*C* 99). Halsey's craftsmanship is part of a family tradition: it adheres to linear models of cultural influence and family inheritance. As his white customer, Mr Ramsay, puts it, the talent '[r]uns in th family' (*C* 100).

Kabnis argues that he cannot express his soul, the symbol of 'sin' or miscegenation, through cultural forms created by legitimate family tradition and inherited talent. When drunk, he tells Halsey:

An as f you, youre all right f choppin things from blocks of wood. I was good at that th day I ducked th cradle. An since then, I've been shapin words after a design that branded here. Know whats here? M soul … Been shapin words t fit m soul (*C* 109).

To express his soul, which represents 'the repressed soul of the nation itself', Kabnis needs a new cultural language (Hutchinson 1993, 242). He dismisses Halsey's artistry in the production of organic folk forms as an inappropriate aesthetic model. By describing Halsey's art of rural repetition as 'choppin things from blocks of wood', Kabnis alludes to the phrase 'a chip off the old block', locating traditional forms that are produced over and again within the context of family resemblance and acknowledged, legitimate inheritance. The wholesale imitation practised in organic folk forms leaves little room for expression of complicated familial relationships.

Kabnis's aesthetic draws upon different sources from the organic, circular forms of Halsey, who is '[a]n artist in [his] way' (*C* 93). He tells Carrie K.:

Great God Almighty, a soul like mine cant pin itself onto a wagon wheel an satisfy itself in spinnin round. Iron prongs an hickory sticks, an God knows what all … all right for Halsey … use him. Me? I get my life down in this scum-hole. Th old man an me – (*C* 114).

Kabnis insists that his 'soul' is at odds with traditional folk forms, which are locked into family and community tradition, and go round and round like a wheel. Traditional forms 'use' the inner resources of someone like Halsey, who is part of a family that can celebrate its longevity through an archive of photographs on the walls of the family home. However, rather like Toomer, the source for Kabnis's art is not raw, natural materials such as iron and hickory, but the history buried in Halsey's cellar, the 'scum-hole'. The stimulus for his broken, bastardized aesthetic is the history of racial conflict and exploitation, as symbolized by his incomplete, stunted and often aggressive conversations with the mumbling Father John in the cellar.

Toomer revises Boasian historicism to locate mixed race histories at the heart of the culture and cultural language of his contemporary America. There is also a political edge to Toomer's reworking of anthropology and, I would add, his choice of a collage form. In his essay 'Race Problems and Modern Society', he develops Boasian anthropology's mode of thinking culturally to critique American society and to envision a political future. He begins by analysing race in modern America. Drawing upon data from physical anthropology, especially Melville Herskovits's study of racial crossing in the African American population, Toomer illustrates the pervasiveness of racial mixing. As he explains, '[t]his mingling of bloods has been recognized and formulated as a maxim by anthropology' (1996c, 182). Even so, because of the American social system that keeps racial, national and cultural groups 'divided and repellent' (181), 'the consciousness of most so-called Americans lags far behind the organic process' (Toomer 1996c, 182).

It is here, in the gap between scientific fact and social custom, that Toomer finds a political use for anthropology: he deploys it to indict American race relations. In anthropology, the clash between sociological custom that insists upon separatism and the scientific reality of racial interpenetration creates a transitional and malleable discourse, tinged with possibility: ideas about race 'have at least in part broken from old forms [but] have not yet achieved stability in new forms' (Toomer 1996c, 169). Toomer contributes to this anthropological debate by challenging ingrained myths about the ideology of the American nation-state. Contrasting the lives of black and white Americans in thrall to 'their by now habitual rivalries, fears, egotisms, hatreds, and illusions' (185) with the facts of racial mixing unearthed by anthropology, he illustrates that Americans are trapped within racial ideology: 'from a racial point of view, and, to my mind, from several other points of view, America, which set out to be a land of the free, has become instead a social trap' (Toomer 1996c, 184). As in Boas's study of miscegenation, Toomer uses anthropological cultural description to fix the nation's gaze on uneasy realities that do not chime with the myths that the nation tells itself about democracy. He suggests that racial ideology enslaves Americans, restricting their freedom. By exposing the limits of democracy, he hopes to rethink American identity so that affiliation to the nation is privileged over race as a marker of identity. He highlights a need for political change to 'the major American customs and institutions' (1996c, 185).

In 'Kabnis', Toomer deploys anthropological discourse as a mode of critique to develop a striking, original political vision of America. Susan Hegeman has argued that Boas's most important breakthrough was his 'critique of progressivist visions of human difference', which opened the way for a 'spatial articulation of the culture concept' in investigations of American identity by modernists such as Waldo Frank, W.E.B. Du Bois, Randolph Bourne and Horace Kallen (1999, 12). Toomer's vision of the American nation in 'Kabnis', and indeed *Cane* itself, should be considered as a contribution to this debate:

> Th form thats burned int my soul is some twisted awful thing that crept in from a dream, a godam nightmare, an wont stay still unless I feed it. An it lives on words. Not beautiful words. God Almighty no. Misshapen, split-gut, tortured, twisted words. Layman was feedin it back there that day you thought I ran out fearin things. White folks feed it cause their looks are words. Niggers, black niggers feed it cause theyre evil an their looks are words. Yallar niggers feed it. This whole damn bloated purple country feeds it cause its goin down t hell in a holy avalanche of words. I want t feed th soul–I know what that is; th preachers don't–but I've got t feed it. I wish t God some lynchin white man ud stick his knife through it an pin it to a tree. An pin it to a tree (*C* 110).

Toomer marks his description of Kabnis's soul as an intervention in the contemporary debate about the ethnic composition of America, which is neatly summarized by

Randolph Bourne's question, '[w]hat shall we do with our America?' (Bourne 1996, 106). In 'Trans-National America' (1916), Bourne articulates a striking conception of the nation as a federation of cultures: 'America is coming to be, not a nationality but a trans-nationality, a weaving back and forth, with the other lands, of many threads of all sizes and colors. Any movement which attempts to thwart this weaving, or to dye the fabric any one color, or disentangle the threads of the strands, is false to this cosmopolitan vision' (1996, 106). For Bourne, the logic of assimilation runs counter to the spirit of American democracy: his warning against dyeing the fabric of the nation a single colour speaks of the dangers of cultural dominance, and also suggests an uneasiness about miscegenation. By contrast, he develops a vision of the American nation in which different cultural, racial and national groups maintain their distinctiveness in 'spatially arrayed' ethnic units, creating strings of attachment across the world (Hegeman 1999, 58). This spatial construction of identity recalls Locke's graphical representation of the segments that constitute the American nation in *The New Negro*.

In Kabnis's concept of his soul, Toomer specifically alludes to Bourne's striking imagery of coloured threads to develop his own, historically informed, version of the American nation. In contrast to Bourne's neat patches of colour, he describes how America's history of racial hatred has created a 'damn bloated purple country', which bruises and contaminates its citizens, including Kabnis, who is profoundly scarred by the past. The significance of the colour purple is two-fold. Toomer signals the centrality of miscegenation to the nation by selecting a pigment that can only be created by mixing colours. His vision of the nation as a bruised, damaged form also acknowledges the violence and violations of the 'godam nightmare' of American history, which have been omitted from Bourne's abstract vision.

For Toomer, American culture is the product of its violent history, which remains tangible and frightening in the present. Kabnis has swallowed the 'words' of racial hatred so that it is parasitic upon his soul. His present 'nightmare' is shaped by the legacy of racial violence, which has knocked poetry, the language of his natural bent, out of shape. When Kabnis wishes for lynching as an escape from suffering, he likens his soul to the brutal story of Mame Lamkins, who tried to protect her husband from a lynch mob. In the violent incident, which the preacher Layman related to Kabnis earlier in the sketch, the pregnant Mame Lamkins was murdered and her unborn child ripped from her womb and pinned to a tree, as a troubling trophy of the violation of family and life. This account of a nation brutalized by racial conflict is not fictional in origin. Toomer reproduces the stark realism of the 1919 NAACP publication *Thirty Years of Lynching in the United States, 1889-1918*, which included a detailed account of the murder of the pregnant Mary Turner. The earnestness of Toomer's attempt to turn the nation's gaze upon its violent history and to confront the past is evident in his repetition, with minor alterations, of NAACP investigator Walter White's account of Mary Turner's death, which became 'an archetypal instance of Southern barbarism' in African American publications such as *The Crisis* and 'the liberal-to-left press' (Foley 1998, 187).

In his stark portrayal of a nation damaged and bastardized by its violent past, Toomer shows that a long history of racial hatred has bred a culture of fear and hatred, which paralyses individuals such as Kabnis, who feel consumed by racial conflict. Toomer's use of the word 'bloated', for instance, directs attention back to Layman and Halsey's discussion of violence in the South, in which they relate the story of Mame Lamkins and the multiple killings of black labourers on a 'Death Farm' in Jasper County (Foley 1998, 188-9). As they talk, a brick is thrown through the window bearing the message '[y]ou northern nigger, its time fer y t leave. Git along now' (*C* 90). Toomer describes Kabnis's response: '[f]ear flows inside him. It fills him up. He bloats' (*C* 91). By repeating the word 'bloat' in Kabnis's concept of his soul, Toomer creates a thread of connection between these two scenes to suggest that violence and fear 'feed' the American soul, preventing the development of healthy appetites and preoccupations.

Such repetition could be read as an example of Toomer's jazz aesthetic, his use of call and response patterning. However, I would also like to preserve the sense that this intratextual reference also operates as a kind of collage, not least because the metaphor of collage serves to underline a sense of violent disjunction that makes readers 'think' about unsettling contemporary realities. Racial conflict has triggered a 'holy avalanche' of violence: uncontrollable hatred has taken over. In this context, Stephen Dedalus's modernist hope to 'forge in the smithy of my soul the uncreated conscience of my race', which haunts the passage as a kind of aesthetic template for the poet Kabnis, is crushed by the stark reality of racial violence (1960, 257).

Conclusion

Toomer's now legendary opposition to Alain Locke's inclusion of selected pieces from the book in *The New Negro* highlights the importance of the politics of form to *Cane*. In an account of his dealings with Countee Cullen, Alain Locke and James Weldon Johnson, Toomer argues that the nuances of *Cane*, which he describes as 'an organism', were lost when it was 'dismembered, torn to bits and scattered about in the pages of anthologies' (Rusch 1993, 102). He felt cheated because anthologists could obscure the meanings created by his careful juxtapositions and patterns of repetition to frame their selections in a manner that 'trumpet[ed]' and 'over-play[ed] … the Negro' (Rusch 1993, 102).

As Toomer points out, Locke directs interpretation of *Cane* in *The New Negro* anthology for his own purposes, framing his selections in the essay 'Negro Youth Speaks'. Confirming his theory that folk material should be transformed into high art, Locke implies that Toomer's transfiguration of the folk spirit is the most important aspect of his representation of life in the South. Privileging aesthetic achievements over the treatment of historical or political realities, Locke presents *Cane* as an example of the 'tendency to evolve from the racial substance something technically distinctive, something that as an idiom of style may become a contribution to the general resources of art' (*N* 51). This emphasis upon stylistic innovation obscures Toomer's crucial contribution to present political concerns, such as the early twentieth-century political debate about American cultural identity, which preoccupied cultural critics with whom he had close links in New York, such as Waldo Frank and Gorham Munson, as well as anthropologists like Edward Sapir and Franz Boas.

Turning an uneasy, reflexive gaze onto American culture, *Cane* articulates a shocking vision of the 'godam nightmare' of America, a nation bastardized by its shameful slave past, a past of racial hatred, sexual exploitation and inequality (*C* 110). This exposure of the violence and horror that underlie American history is Toomer's most striking difference from Alain Locke's editorial framing of *The New Negro*. Locke's New Negro is an American ideal and the anthology maps out a future of political emancipation and cultural freedom; while, in *Cane*, Toomer remains pessimistic about American democracy, holding back from the projection of a future African American identity. Such uncertainty, of course, finds expression in Toomer's collage aesthetic since his violently fragmented forms remain haunted by a fantasy of unity and integration.

Chapter 4
'Think[ing] in Hieroglyphics': Zora Neale Hurston's Cross-Cultural Aesthetic

In her important essay 'Characteristics of Negro Expression', written for inclusion in Nancy Cunard's *Negro* anthology of 1934, Hurston outlines distinctive features of African American expression – 'asymmetry' (834), '[t]he will to adorn' (831), 'angularity' (834) and the 'art' of '[m]imicry' – to develop her own conflicted version of the Harlem Renaissance collage aesthetic (1995b, 838). Hurston's examination of cross-cultural impulses at play in African American culture directs us towards paradoxes that lie at the crux of her work, paradoxes that have provoked an extraordinary array of critical responses.

Interest in Zora Neale Hurston's work was rekindled in the 1970s by Alice Walker's womanist retrieval of her forgotten, discredited novels and ethnographies. Walker's project of communal recovery, which is represented symbolically by her homage to, and acknowledgement of, Hurston's unmarked grave, is a search for an artistic foremother, an aesthetic model, 'a golden key to a storehouse of varied treasure' (1983a, 12). Walker's essays on Hurston – 'Saving the Life that is Your Own: The Importance of Models in the Artist's Life' (1976), 'Zora Neale Hurston: A Cautionary Tale and a Partisan View' (1979) and 'Looking for Zora' (1975) – are moving personal accounts of her encounter with Hurston's writings, which mythologize the earlier writer's life, articulating an artistic model of 'undaunted pursuit of adventure, passionate emotional and sexual experience, and … love of freedom' (1983b, 91). Walker presents Hurston as an exceptional figure, who is ahead of her contemporary moment; for Walker, Hurston's 'sense of black people as complete, complex, *undiminished* human beings' and her serious study of African American folklore is more in keeping with the Black pride movement of the 1960s than the 1920s and 1930s (1983b, 85). Indeed, she claims that 'Zora's pride in black people was so pronounced in the ersatz black twenties that it made other blacks suspicious and perhaps uncomfortable (after all, *they* were still infatuated with things European)' (1983b, 85).

This veneration of Hurston as an exceptional individual, detached from her cultural context, has cast a long shadow on Hurston studies. Hurston has become such a loaded symbol for black feminists, from bell hooks, Nellie McKay and Mary Helen Washington to Deborah McDowell and Cheryl Wall, that her work has often been considered in isolation from historical trends and cultural developments, with *Their Eyes Were Watching God* featuring as an '"Ur-Text" in the tradition of black women's writing' (Wall 1995b, 160). Moreover, Walker's polarization of Hurston's "authentic" African American utterances with her contemporaries' 'infatuated' imitation of European fads obscures the irony that Hurston herself had affinities with 'things European' (1983b, 85). As we shall see, creative re-interpretation of Euro-American culture is fundamental to Hurston's cross-cultural aesthetic.

Since Walker's initial feminist recovery of Hurston, her work has been fought over by a motley band of critics, from the traditionalist Harold Bloom, modernist scholar Michael North and Marxist critic William J. Maxwell to white feminists like Barbara Johnson, and anthropologists such as Deborah Gordon. The almost excessive attention to Hurston's output, which Ann duCille has termed 'Hurstonism', has worried critics like Hazel Carby and Michele Wallace, who wonder what is at stake in such a reception (duCille 1993, 11). Carby, for instance, explains Hurston's popularity in political terms, claiming that her 'representation of African-American culture as primarily rural and oral' allows readers to retreat into a pastoral idyll, avoiding engagement with racism and inequality in contemporary American society (1994, 31). In the last few years, Hurston's reception has become a serious topic of study in its own right. Genevieve West's meticulously researched monograph *Zora Neale Hurston and American Literary Culture* (2005), for example, interprets Hurston's fluctuating reputation against the backdrop of 'changes in American culture and literary studies', including the Black Arts movement and second-wave feminism (2005, 5). Pairing detailed analysis of Lippincott's (and later Scribner's) sensationalist marketing of Hurston's writings with close reading of contemporary critical reviews, West provides a paper trail showing that this initial 'framing of blackness' gave rise to a set of critical preoccupations that have governed her reception ever since (Edwards 2003, 49).[1]

In the main, critics have concentrated their attention upon Hurston's use of oral traditions: the folkways and linguistic structures of African American voice. Karla F.C. Holloway (1987) has categorized the linguistic registers of Hurston's fiction, examining how she incorporates a vital oral culture into the literary domain. This attempt to capture oral patterns and rhythms on the page is also the focus of Henry Louis Gates's hugely influential *The Signifying Monkey* (1988), in which he argues for acknowledgement of a separate, distinctive tradition of African American letters in the United States, notable for its deployment of vernacular styles. Gates pays detailed attention to Hurston's manipulation of voice in *Their Eyes Were Watching*

---

[1]   To take only one example from this richly detailed study, West convincingly demonstrates that Lippincott's marketing of *Mules and Men* accounts, at least in part, for Hurston's mixed reception among both anthropologists and Harlem Renaissance writers. The status of *Mules and Men* as 'a serious anthropological study that would appeal to folklorists' (79) was compromised by sensationalist claims about Hurston's personal knowledge of 'weird hoodoo practices' (West 2005, 77). West also argues that 'repeated comparisons to Harris's Uncle Remus tales' troubled African American readers who associated these tales with negative stereotypes (2005, 84).

God, exploring her mediation between a lyrical, metaphorical oral tradition on the one hand and Standard English on the other. For Gates, this supple rendering of the black speaking voice in a written form is an accomplished example of what he terms 'the speakerly text' (1988a, 170).

More recent analysis represents a departure from both feminist-inspired study and Gates's project of canon formation: it attempts to locate Hurston in her cultural context, complicating assumptions about her feminist, rural and political position. William J. Maxwell, for instance, revisits the familiar polarization of Hurston and Richard Wright, demonstrating that both writers draw upon northern (and, at least in part, European-inspired) intellectual models – Boasian anthropology, and sociology and Communism respectively – to rediscover and remember the South in a fictional form (1997, 87). This historicist trend, which is also noticeable in essays by David Kadlec (2000b) and Philip Joseph (2002), comes to fruition is in Carla Kaplan's comprehensive collection of Hurston's letters, which is interspersed with historical commentary for each decade of her 'life in letters' (2002).

My own approach to Hurston's diverse body of work in the following chapters combines historical contextualization with a detailed focus upon aesthetic forms and strategies. Rather than reaffirming Walker's image of Hurston as a custodian of an "authentic" African American culture, I pose questions about her complex engagement with European, American and African cultures. To this end, I am centrally concerned with Hurston's anthropological description of African American culture as a thing of reconstructed fragments, a collage.

Given the lyrical, apparently seamless quality of Hurston's most celebrated fiction, it might seem to be pushing the point to insist upon an analogy with visual collage. A closer look, however, reveals Hurston's preoccupation with impulses toward fragmentation and integration in African American culture. Not only does her influential account of African American cultural distinctiveness in 'Characteristics of Negro Expression' pivot upon a practice of appropriation and reformulation that can be likened to collage. She also employs selection, appropriation and rearrangement as structural principles in her ethnography *Mules and Men*, a composite text that comprises songs and stories told by named informants.

My aim in this chapter, however, is not simply to identify another version of the Harlem Renaissance collage aesthetic. Rather, I scrutinize Hurston's pronouncements on African American cultural development, especially her contention that 'the Negro thinks in hieroglyphics' (1995b, 831), seizing upon tensions that animate her collage theory and practice. There is, for instance, an intriguing inconsistency between Hurston's celebration of cultural styles that traverse the colour line, and her insistence upon organic cultural wholes. While Hurston remains alert to the radical possibilities of collage form, its potential to disrupt notions of cultural provenance and ownership, she often reinstates a binary logic that assumes individuals can be defined according to rigid categories of identity such as black and white, insider and outsider. The concept of collage, with its potential to stage contradictions and to resolve them, provides a flexible framework for examining such formulations of cultural identity. When producing a collage, artists can either accentuate jarring discordance between elements taken from pre-existing works, or they can smooth over such discontinuities, placing emphasis upon the creation of a new, integrated whole. Reading Hurston with reference to these possibilities not only prompts us to resist the temptation to resolve contradictions; it also forces us to pay attention to the cultural fragments that lie underneath her apparently seamless narratives. In short, I am arguing for a reading practice analogous to the double take, that crucial instant of recognition when we realize that a collage is at once a collection of disparate parts and an integrated whole.

Collage as Culture Pattern: '[t]he will to adorn'

Like Toomer, Zora Neale Hurston was a leading pioneer of the Harlem Renaissance tendency to represent African American culture in a collage-like pattern. In her only exclusively interpretive anthropological essay, 'Characteristics of Negro Expression', Hurston explains the significance of this cross-cultural impulse to African American expression. She argues that an aesthetic urge for cutting and pasting, for gathering together cultural odds and ends, is a characteristic of African American expression, which can be diametrically opposed to the integrated wholeness that white artists aspire towards in their art (1995b, 836). Hurston coins a neat phrase for this desire for beauty: '[t]he will to adorn' (1995b, 831).

As well as identifying the African American's infinite capacity to '[make] over a great part of the tongue to his liking' through improvisation upon white modes of expression, she illustrates '[t]he will to adorn' graphically through description of a typical African American home (1995b, 831). According to Hurston, African American homes tend to be 'over-stuffed', with a glut of coloured calendars, Sunday supplements, wallpapers, doilies, lithographs, lace and crêpe paper cluttering the walls (1995b, 833). And this deeply ingrained 'desire for beauty' (833) features in other cultural forms: black music and dance comprise improvisatory sections, or 'the rhythm of segments' (835), while African American sermons transform a variety of sources into 'true works of art' through ingenious revisioning in 'the frenzy of creation' (1995b, 834).

A long line of critics, from Richard Wright to Paul Gilroy, have interpreted Hurston's delineation of specifically African American characteristics as an essentially conservative gesture (Gilroy 1993, 91). In her influential essay 'The Politics of Fiction, Anthropology, and the Folk', for instance, Hazel Carby argues that Hurston's writings function outside 'the culture and history of contestation', articulating instead 'a representation of "Negroness" as an unchanging, essential entity, an essence so distilled it is an aesthetic position of blackness' (1994, 32).

Yet, Hurston's description of 'cultural identity not as something that one *has* by virtue of group affiliation, but something one *does*' also seems to disrupt strict racial and cultural compartmentalization (Elliott 2002, 168). African American originality, she tells us, lies in an endless capacity to recast white civilization. Hence, in African American folklore, 'nothing is too old or too new, domestic or foreign, high or low, for his use' (1995b, 836). Rather than developing an essentialist idea of blackness, Hurston affirms African American originality, describing a process of transformative cultural exchange. And it is this emphasis upon 'cross-cultural appropriations [that] have a catalytic effect on creating new art forms' (136) that has prompted Sieglinde Lemke to hail Hurston as an astute cultural commentator who was among the first to recognize the intercultural quality of modernist aesthetic experimentation (Lemke 1998, 136).

Hurston's singular representation of African American culture is fleshed out in a discussion of language. 'Characteristics of Negro Expression' opens with extended analysis of the differences between what Hurston terms 'primitive' and 'highly developed' language use (1995b, 830). To illustrate this distinction, she develops an analogy between language and systems of monetary exchange. Claiming that '[l]anguage is like money', Hurston identifies three kinds of language: she compares descriptive, 'primitive' language with barter of actual goods; more abstract communication is equated with 'legal tender'; and elevated literary registers are likened to 'cheques' because any straightforward relationship between meaning and 'action' has been interrupted (1995b, 830). Making an unexplained leap that is characteristic of an essay full of odd shifts and juxtapositions, Hurston uses this analogy to clinch her argument that 'the white man thinks in a written language and the Negro thinks in hieroglyphics' (1995b, 831). With this move, Hurston aligns African American oral traditions with the visual designs used by the ancient Egyptians to represent objects, sounds and sights. To some extent, Hurston's visual motif is reminiscent of collage, or at least stylistic incongruity, because hieroglyphics are at once pictographic and alphabetic. Moreover, these visual images represent a departure from an enduring European obsession with deciphering hieroglyphics, an interpretive action implicated in an assertion of colonial power. By contrast, Hurston moves towards a mode of expression which retains visual, dynamic qualities, refusing to close down into a single, authoritative meaning.

As many readers have noted, Hurston's celebration of African American hieroglyphics is a highly ambivalent act, which 'attempts simultaneously to deploy and rehabilitate the category of the primitive and its corollary, the imitative, as artistic resources' (Jacobs 2001, 121). On the one hand, Hurston overturns contemporary notions of aesthetic value, celebrating the vividness of African American 'primitive' (831) expression over and above '[t]he stark, trimmed phrases of the Occident' (1995b, 833). On the other, delineation of a 'primitive' culture in relation to a concept of 'development' runs the risk of reinscribing evolutionary theory, which tended to chart an advance from simple to complex forms in order to bolster racial hierarchies. In this sense, Hurston 'displays essentialist ideas of her time while illustrating the contradictions implicit in racialist conceptions of culture' (Hill 1996, 2).

The closer one looks at Hurston's modernist African American hieroglyphic the more conflicted her understanding of cross-cultural impulses in African American culture appears to be. For a start, Hurston's model implies a layering of word and image, a mode of communication that is at once uncomplicated picture writing and a sophisticated language that cannot be accurately deciphered without specialist cultural knowledge.

In terms of Hurston's delineation of African survivals in African American culture, this ambivalence really does count since she invokes a continuing debate about the racial make-up of Egyptians (Johnson 1997, 20). Martin Bernal has shown that before 1945 'the extent to which the Ancient Egyptians were civilized was seen as the measure of their "whiteness"' (2001, 23). For example, in the 1910-11 edition of the *Encyclopedia Britannica*, the Egyptologist Francis Llewellyn Griffth stated that evidence provided by Egyptian mummies proved that Egyptians were 'of Caucasian type' (Bernal 2001, 403). At the same time, African American writers, such as Pauline Hopkins and W.E.B. Du Bois, confirmed the African origin of Egyptian peoples, adding to a tradition that stemmed back as far as Herodotus. In *Darkwater: Voices from within the Veil* (1920), for instance, Du Bois's pan-African sweep in 'Riddle of the Sphinx' encompasses West Africa, Egypt and America, with an extended analogy between European exploitation of African land and the double colonization of African and African American women lying at the heart of the poem. Given the frequent incorporation of Egyptian motifs and themes into Harlem Renaissance art that sought to foster racial pride, it makes sense to interpret Hurston's allusion to hieroglyphics as an affirmation of the 'cultural and historical depth' of black culture (Jacobs 2001, 122).[2]

Nevertheless, hieroglyphics carry other, competing associations, which serve to complicate this picture of an organic pan-African culture. There has been a recent critical turn towards analysis of an intriguing inconsistency in Hurston's thinking between her 'very exacting folk standard of cultural authenticity', which included warnings against 'what she interpreted as insidious assimilationism and destructive hybridization', and her bedrock assumption that cultural exchange is a catalyst for aesthetic innovation (Anderson 2001, 205). Hurston's image of the hieroglyphic embodies these (and other) tensions. Reference to Egyptian culture certainly implies an abiding interest in cultural continuities across the black diaspora, but hieroglyphics also suggest collaging of African, African American and European cultural elements, not least because Boasian anthropologists routinely connected the achievements of Egyptian civilization with its mixed racial and cultural heritage, talking of a dynamism born of intercultural exchange.[3] Furthermore, mention of hieroglyphics invokes a long history of European colonial exploitation,

---

[2]   See Michel Feith, 'The Syncopated African: Constructions of Origins in the Harlem Renaissance' for a more sustained discussion of Egyptian motifs and themes in Harlem Renaissance art (2001, 54-7).

[3]   See Boas's 'The Real Race Problem', in which he blasts the myth of racial purity. Egyptian culture features in a list of ancient cultures positioned 'on the borderland of the

in which Egyptologists raided tombs and archaeological sites, removing valuable cultural artifacts to European museums. As Edward Said has pointed out, the race to decipher hieroglyphics played a significant role in such cultural appropriation since, in the words of the nineteenth-century French scholar and traveller Jean-Jacques Ampère, 'empty or lifeless' forms 'had to be made to speak' (1993, 142). And of course, direct, simple and striking visual expression was also central to several significant strands in Euro-American modernism, including imagism. Why the hieroglyphic is so important to any attempt to position Hurston's writings in relation to Euro-American modernism is something to which I shall return.

Much of the energy of 'Characteristics of Negro Expression' derives from Hurston's awareness of the radical possibilities of cross-cultural expression, its potential to unsettle a binary logic of racial difference. At the same time, Hurston retreats from such untidy, non-dialogic openness when she insists such expression is distinctively African American. For all its intercultural resonances, Hurston's theory of 'thinking in hieroglyphics' is underpinned by a celebration of cultural distinctiveness. Notice, for instance, that she speaks of appropriation, a model of exchange that preserves distinct cultural entities, rather than transformative hybridity.

Reference to James Clifford's championing of a collage sensibility in *The Predicament of Culture* helps explain the significance of this strategy. Making reference to surrealist incongruity, Clifford calls for an anthropological method in which '[t]he cuts and sutures of the research process are left visible; there is no smoothing over or blending of the work's raw data into a homogeneous representation' (Clifford 1988, 146). While there are clear correspondences here with the jarring discordances of *Cane*, Hurston is more interested in documenting a process of cultural development whereby "foreign" elements are incorporated into a pre-existing cultural whole without altering its underlying structure. This impulse towards synthesis bears comparison with Clifford's account of anthropological interpretations that smooth over '[t]he surrealist moment in ethnography' (146), establishing logical grounds for difference and similarity that blend 'the work's raw data into a homogeneous representation' (1988, 146).

Taking Clifford's formulation as its point of departure, this chapter considers what is at stake in Hurston's blending of diverse cultural fragments into an integrated whole, an impulse that finds expression in 'Characteristics of Negro Expression' and *Mules and Men*. In *The Predicament of Culture*, Clifford implies that smoothing over jagged edges is necessarily a conservative gesture. Yet, there are no hard and fast rules when it comes to the relationship between a formal staging of incongruity and political radicalism in Harlem Renaissance literature. The integrative impulse in much of Hurston's anthropological writing suggests something more complicated. On the one hand, she seems to hanker after a utopian world beyond race, a newly energized American culture born of productive

---

Negro races', which developed 'peculiar and interesting culture[s] of their own' as a result of historical patterns of interracial contact (1910, 24).

intercultural exchange. On the other, binaries between insider and outsider, black and white resurface at those moments when she opens out cultural identity beyond the confines of a separatist tradition. Such moves towards strategic essentialism do not only indicate Hurston's willingness to play off conflicting ideas; they also mark out her writings as the product of a cultural moment when assertions of hybridity could all too easily be misinterpreted as a capitulation to Euro-American cultural values.

Hurston and Boas: Collage as Culture Concept

In 'Characteristics of Negro Expression', Hurston describes African American culture in spatial terms, as a creative collage made up of diverse sources. Hurston's argument that blending of disparate sources to create something new is distinctive to African American culture shares much with Boas, with whom she studied in the 1920s, but her work does not slot neatly into a Boasian model. Consequently, any consideration of Hurston's theorization of African American culture must examine her close affiliation with Boasian tenets without underestimating the extent to which she recast, or collaged, Boas's ideas for her own ends.

Accounts of Hurston's contact with Boas are now fairly common, but it is worth sketching out the broad contours of their relationship. Hurston's interest in anthropology as an academic discipline began with her enrolment for a B.A. degree at Barnard College from 1925 to 1928, where she took a course with the Boasian anthropologist Gladys Reichard (Hurston 1995d, 683). Fired up with enthusiasm for examining African American culture within a social scientific framework, Hurston took courses with Boas and Ruth Benedict, and 'thereby gave up [her] dream of leaning over a desk and explaining Addison and Steele to the sprouting generations' (Hurston 1995d, 683).

From the outset, Boas took a keen interest in her work. In 1926, he appointed her as a research assistant to Melville Herskovits, who was collecting exhaustive data on African Americans' biological make-up for *The American Negro: A Study in Racial Crossing*. Dispatched to Harlem with a set of callipers, Hurston gathered statistical information in an effort to overturn enduring ideas about African American physical inferiority. Boas later filed an application for research funding on Hurston's behalf so that she could collect songs, customs, tales, superstitions and jokes in the South in 1927, following completion of her undergraduate coursework (Hemenway 1980, 84).

Hurston regarded Boas, who she praised in *Dust Tracks on a Road* for 'his genius for pure objectivity' and 'his insatiable hunger for knowledge', as a mentor long after her official affiliation with Barnard had ceased (1995d, 687). When collecting material in the South in 1928, for example, she broke the terms of her contract with her wealthy, white patron, Charlotte Osgood Mason, by consulting Boas about specific topics, such as the origins of fire-worship, and more general questions about how best to write up her extensive material (Hemenway 1980,

124; Kaplan 2002, 135). Always alert to economic realities, she recognized that an endorsement from Boas would help to decide the fate of *Mules and Men* in the marketplace. In a somewhat anxious letter dated 20 August 1934, Hurston asked Boas to write a preface for her ethnography, as he had done for Margaret Mead's *Coming of Age in Samoa*, in spite of 'the between-story conversation and business' and 'unscientific matter' which she had included at the request of her publisher (Hemenway 1980, 163).[4]

Hurston's relationship with Boas has provoked considerable debate, with critical assessments of her writing often turning upon an evaluation of her investment in, or subversion of, anthropological discourse. For many critics, anthropological inquiry inevitably established limiting parameters for an African American woman writer. Houston A. Baker sets the tone for such accounts, describing Hurston's uneasy relationship with Boas as a corollary to her creative subversion of his scientific assumptions (1993, 95-7). Even Hazel Carby, whose indictment of Hurston's romantic construction of 'the folk' is fundamentally at odds with Baker's position, assumes that social scientific documentation of a culture curtailed artistic freedom. Shifting attention to Hurston's definition of a culture concept opens up an alternative assessment of this question, which sees Boasian anthropology as a malleable, transitional discourse, ripe for revision.[5]

In this vein, Boas was certainly a significant influence upon her methodology and cultural politics. The intercultural collage aesthetic that Hurston describes in 'Characteristics of Negro Expression', with its central claim that a vibrant American culture is born of energizing cultural contact between African Americans and white Americans, derives straight from Boas's early work. Moving outwards from the specific instance of Paul Whiteman's 1924 concert of symphonic jazz, with its celebrated performance of George Gershwin's 'Rhapsody in Blue', Hurston valorizes adaptation as a fundamental component of African American expression:

> Everyone is familiar with the Negro's modification of the whites' musical instruments, so that his interpretation has been adopted by the white man himself

---

[4]   Hurston moved further away from the academic discipline later in her career. In 1934, she worked with Boas to design a PhD programme appropriate to her interests, but later abandoned the course due to financial concerns and frustration with intensive library work (Mickell 1999, 61). Nevertheless, anthropological inquiry remained a shaping influence on her writing. She collected folklore for the Library of Congress with Alan Lomax in the South in 1934 and she studied the rituals of the Sanctified Church in and around Beaufort, South Carolina under the direction of Margaret Mead and Jane Belo in May 1940 (Basalla 1997, 16).

[5]   My interest in the aesthetic possibilities opened up by Hurston's immersion in Boasian anthropology builds upon a recent critical trend that acknowledges Hurston's simultaneous affiliation to, and departure from, Boasian thought. See Manganaro (2002), Jacobs (2001), Kadlec (2000b).

and then re-interpreted. In so many words, Paul Whiteman is giving an imitation of a Negro orchestra making use of white-invented musical instruments in a Negro way. Thus has arisen a new art in the civilised world, and thus has our so-called civilisation come. The exchange and re-exchange of ideas between groups (1995b, 838).

If Boas's theory that intercultural contact galvanizes cultural development forms part of a general argument for the 'interrelation of the races of man' in *The Mind of Primitive Man*, Hurston narrows attention to a specific culture at a particular historical moment, examining tangled lines of influence in her contemporary America (Boas 1938, 169). Highlighting that 'new art' is produced through interaction between supposedly discrete groups, she develops an inclusive vision, which recognizes that African Americans have transformed many aspects of the national culture, including music, language, foodways and dance. Consequently, Hurston challenges any effort to compartmentalize racial expression, undermining the logic of a historical association between black culture and subservient imitation in Euro-American thought, which stems back to Immanuel Kant and David Hume (Gates 1988a, 113; Gubar 1997, 53-94).

In describing a dynamic process of interpretation and re-interpretation that traverses the colour line, Hurston lines up her anthropological description with Boas's spatial articulation of the culture concept. As in Boas's work, formulating a theory of culture is a method of critique, which offers a new way of thinking about cultural difference. Crucially, Hurston offers a sharp reassessment of American culture, finding African American influence at every turn. As Cheryl Wall explains, she eschews direct political comment; instead, '[t]he arena for struggle and resistance that Hurston defines is cultural' (Wall 2005a, 216).

Nowhere are these concerns more apparent than when Hurston, in her essay 'How It Feels to be Colored Me', recasts Boas's collage-like cosmopolitan vision at the end of *The Mind of Primitive Man*. Bringing his book to a close, Boas urges his contemporaries to 'treasure and cultivate the variety of forms that human thought and activity has taken, and abhor, as leading to complete stagnation, all attempts to impress one pattern of thought upon whole nations or even upon the whole world' (1938, 272). In a crucial shift of emphasis, Hurston tilts away from abstract generalization towards a personal, even idiosyncratic, concept of identity that remains firmly rooted in the material world:

> [I]n the main, I feel like a bag of miscellany propped against a wall. Against a wall in company with other bags, white, red and yellow. Pour out the contents, and there is discovered a jumble of small things priceless and worthless. A first-water diamond, an empty spool, bits of broken glass, lengths of string, a key to a door long since crumbled away, a rusty knife-blade, old shoes saved for a road that never was and never will be, a nail bent under the weight of things too heavy for any nail, a dried flower or two, still a little fragrant. In your hand is the brown bag. On the ground before you is the jumble it held – so much like the jumble in

the bags, could they be emptied, that all might be dumped in a single heap and the bags refilled without altering the content of any greatly. A bit of colored glass more or less would not matter. Perhaps that is how the Great Stuffer of Bags filled them in the first place – who knows? (Hurston 1995a, 829).

This well-known passage represents Hurston's most striking use of collage-like logic, giving shape as it does to a theory of cultural development, which accords with broader anthropological interest in the relationship between cultural whole and fragment, community and individual. Presenting actual detritus and bric-à-brac from history as a kind of three-dimensional collage of apparently random objects, Hurston describes the make-up of each individual as a motley collection of 'priceless and worthless' things accumulated through circumstance. Describing individuals as a miscellany of orts and scraps, she challenges any notion of significant racial difference or superior content, disturbing what, in *Dust Tracks*, she calls 'the pigeon-hole way of life' (1995d, 581).

Following Boas, Hurston negates biological determinism by showing that it is impossible to trace a single genealogical root or 'ancestral family' (1966, 54). Instead, our fragmented selves are products of history or, as Boas would put it, '[f]ormer events … leave their stamp on the present character of a people' (1974b, 65). Coloured bags, which appear to represent various races, may tidy up (or conceal) the 'jumble' but Hurston exposes the reality of America's tangled ancestry and heterogeneous culture. In the midst of a whole spectrum of differences between individuals, the shards of coloured glass that are suggestive of racial pigmentation diminish in significance; in fact, emptying the bags and refilling them with other objects would have little noticeable effect.

That said, these individual items of historical jumble are arguably part of a more serious questioning of evolutionist efforts to articulate a single, unified narrative of human development. On close inspection, every object in Hurston's apparently random list frustrates formulation of a coherent, complete narrative of historical development. For one thing, only certain items, such as fragrant dried flowers, are preserved and then incorporated into our sense of the past. Consequently, any quest for origins is stalled by an incomplete record, which tantalizes us with a 'key' of knowledge but ultimately withholds its secrets. Next, the value assigned to particular artifacts is contingent upon contemporary assumptions, as indicated by shoes that direct assiduous researchers towards a road that never even existed. Taken as a whole, these objects endorse Boas's hesitancy about making overarching cultural generalizations, a commitment nicely illustrated by his life-long collection of a 'five-foot shelf' of Kwakiutl ethnography. Laying stress upon inevitable gaps in historical narrative, Hurston affirms Boas's insight that 'all patterns of thought … are contingent upon the dense contextual web called culture' (Elliott 2002, 8).

Despite such affiliations, it is difficult to understate the complexity of Hurston's engagement with Boasian anthropology. David Kadlec is quick to point out that Hurston 'quietly resisted' some of the ways anthropology was being 'institutionalized', even though many hallmarks of her work (her detailed study of a specific culture; the focus upon interplay between diverse cultural groups; and her interest in linguistics) are Boasian (2000b, 477). One of her most significant departures from Boas is her refusal to subscribe to his assimilationist views, which were widely disseminated in populist works such as 'The Problem of the American Negro' (1921) and *Anthropology and Modern Life* (1929). Hurston's understanding of cultural exchange in 'Characteristics of Negro Expression', which pivots on dynamic interplay between distinctive traditions that remain unassimilated, disputes Boas's model:

> So if we look at it squarely, the Negro is a very original being. While he lives and moves in the midst of a white civilisation, everything that he touches is re-interpreted for his own use. He has modified the language, mode of food preparation, practice of medicine, and most certainly the religion of his new country, just as he has adapted to suit himself the Sheik hair-cut made famous by Rudolph Valentino (Hurston 1995b, 838).

There is a significant debt to Boas here. As in the passage I quoted earlier, a notion of cultural contact as the motor of cultural change undergirds Hurston's celebration of African American creativity. Yet, in Hurston's hands, cross-cultural exchange does not result in a lessening of cultural distinctiveness. Instead, revision becomes the 'cardinal principle of African American vernacular culture' (Wall 2005a, 214).

In a recent essay, Lori Jirousek has argued that a Boasian concept of cultural hybridity underpins Hurston's anthropology, giving her diverse *oeuvre* political coherence since she consistently draws attention to 'the shared hybrid culture in which African Americans participate' (2004, 425). Nevertheless, I would contend that Hurston's frequent deployment of destabilizing, distancing irony complicates this political strategy. In the passage quoted above, for example, it is difficult to know whether we are supposed to take Hurston seriously, given that she clinches her argument with the bathetic example of a Rudolph Valentino haircut. How are we to read this? Is Hurston criticizing the pervasiveness of white culture and African American emulation of that culture? Or is she celebrating African Americans' capacity to recast and subvert white 'civilisation'?

For many critics, such ambivalence is a calculated strategy, a deliberate attempt to elude the grip of scientific discourse.[6] Hurston's comic tone certainly undercuts her serious, scientific voice, destabilizing the serious project of white anthropology in the process. Furthermore, her written style enacts the very capacity for originality that she claims for African American culture as a whole, revelling

---

[6]   See Beth Harrison (1996, 89-97), Graciela Hernández (1995, 160-61), Houston A. Baker, Jr. (1991, 95-7), Susan Edwards Meisenhelder (1999, 15-18). The classic analysis of the political intention that underpins Hurston's 'divided voice' is, of course, Henry Louis Gates, Jr.'s *The Signifying Monkey* (1988a, 193).

as it does in mimicry as 'an art in itself' (1995b, 838).[7] What emerges is a highly unstable discourse that maintains two distinct voices: a scientific, reasoning voice and an ironic signifying voice. These voices never blend, but remain suspended in creative, unpredictable play.

But to insist that such ambivalence always functions as a political strategy does less than justice to the complexity of Hurston's revision, or even collaging, of Boasian anthropology. For one thing, Hurston's inconsistency is, at least in part, a consequence of constraints under which her writing was produced. Dependent upon the support of various mentors and patrons, she struggled to meet 'the scholarly demands of Boas, Mason, and Locke, a diverse triad of social managers of African-Americans' who advocated collection of folklore for very different reasons (Gordon 1990, 161). To highlight only the most obvious contrast, Charlotte Osgood Mason encouraged 'the collecting, amassing, and documenting of African-American exotica for consumption as "art"', while Boas was primarily concerned with documenting folklore as part of a broader historicized whole, namely culture (Gordon 1990, 160). Given these diverging expectations, it is hardly surprising that Hurston adopts a contradictory stance (Hemenway 1980, 163-4, 278).[8]

Keeping these institutional pressures in mind, it is also worth pointing out that a blanket interpretation of inconsistency as a political strategy masks a revealing tension between antihierarchical thought and a 'reliance on racial, cultural, and aesthetic hierarchies' that runs through Hurston's writings (Jacobs 2001, 123). Building upon a compelling account of ideological cross-currents that complicate Boas's anti-racist thought, Karen Jacobs identifies comparable contradictions in Hurston's *oeuvre*, contradictions that stem from her 'very reliance on the sort of cultural evolutionary theory Boas worked to discredit, a theory that sought to distinguish "primitive" from "highly developed" languages in the first place' (Jacobs 2001, 123). In the light of Jacobs's insights, it is difficult to see Hurston's odd stylistic juxtapositions in her anthropological essays as wholly purposeful. 'How it Feels to be Colored Me', for instance, begins to look like a patchwork of contradictory ideas about race and origin: colour as a curse; race as a social construct; primitivism; transcendent individualism; and the 'bag of miscellany' passage that I have already discussed.

---

[7]   See Keith Walters for a more detailed discussion of Hurston's incorporation of African American styles into her ethnography (Walters 1999, 343-71).

[8]   Hurston's publisher required alterations to *Mules and Men*, including the incorporation of a substantial section on hoodoo, so that it would appeal to the general reader. Later in her career, Hurston's opinions on international politics were excised from *Dust Tracks* because her analysis was considered too anti-American to be published after Pearl Harbor (Hemenway 1980, 163-4, 278).

A Vernacular Aesthetic?

Speaking of the stylistic and thematic incongruity that is such a striking feature of Hurston's anthropological writings, Marc Manganaro makes the compelling point that 'these kinds of discursive shifts of register – from textual narrative tellings to professional discursive asides – are characteristically ethnographic' (2002, 184). Even so, it is important to recognize that Hurston's formal innovation also draws inspiration from African American vernacular forms. Indeed, such productive juxtapositions underline the aptness of my metaphor of collage, which encourages us to hold onto the diverse sources that underpin Hurston's writings.

One way of accounting for the odd tonal juxtapositions in 'Characteristics of Negro Expression' is to interpret the essay as an enactment of the vernacular aesthetic she seeks to document. Among other things, Hurston emphasizes that African American culture is always dramatic, always in motion: folklore, for instance, 'is not a thing of the past. It is still in the making' (1995b, 836). Such a formulation draws attention to the creative act of cultural collage, in which performers collect scraps, making them into new wholes. This means that representations of African American culture, in concert halls and on Broadway, have often failed to capture its mobile fluidity. Clearly, Hurston positions her own work as a more accurate alternative, partly because she attempts to reproduce such dynamism, registering cultural fluidity.

By way of illustration, it is worth quoting Hurston's account of black music: '[t]he presence of rhythm and lack of symmetry are paradoxical, but there they are. … There is always rhythm, but it is the rhythm of segments. Each unit has a rhythm of its own, but when the whole is assembled it is lacking in symmetry' (1995b, 835). Taken as a whole, the essay gives full form to this idea that African American culture is a 'thing of shreds and patches' that does not quite cohere into a seamless whole (Lowie 1949, 428). Specific qualities of the culture – 'the will to adorn', 'mimicry', 'angularity', 'asymmetry', 'drama' – are treated separately in brief, snappily titled sections, often accompanied by descriptions of striking visual images that encapsulate particular aspects of black culture (a dancer in warrior pose, an 'overstuffed' African American home and so on). Each segment functions as a coherent mini-essay, with a 'rhythm' of its own; but the parts do not harmonize into an integrated cultural whole. Instead, there is an unpredictable play of voices, with folktales and expressions jostling for attention with interpretive commentary. Furthermore, contradictory stances adopted in various 'segments' of the essay embody a tension between cultural fragmentation and integration, which bears witness to the difficulties of capturing African American culture in its dynamics.

Analysis of the essay's formal features focuses attention on a second principle that is crucial to Hurston's collage aesthetic, namely active interpretation. Critics have often remarked that African American vernacular forms require 'active [audience] participation', not least because of expected patterns of call and response (Smitherman 1977, 108). Hurston endorses this claim, identifying participatory interpretation as a fundamental component of black cultural expression. Take, for instance, her description of African American dance: '[i]t is compelling insinuation. That is the very reason the spectator is held so rapt. He is participating in the performance himself – carrying out the suggestions of the performer' (1995b, 835). Indirectness and dynamic suggestion, qualities fundamental to many cultural forms mentioned in the essay, foster an intimate, if complex, relationship between performer and audience. In a formulation that echoes her notoriously ambiguous description of African American 'feather-bed resistance' in *Mules and Men*, in which Hurston implies that outsiders will never understand 'The Negro' no matter what scientific method they employ, there is at once a sense of close connection between performer and dancer here and a feeling of distance, a suspicion that something is being withheld (*MM* 2).[9] Indeed, the apparent brevity, simplicity and directness of the dancer's poses are complicated by the strategy of manipulation, or at least doubleness, implied in such phrases as 'compelling insinuation'.

It is worth pausing here for a moment to note that Hurston's obsession with the question of intercultural encounter, or more specifically how cultural outsiders interpret African American culture, comes with an emphasis upon cultural distinctiveness. Ultimately, she appears to be uncomfortable with the utopian undertow of her universalism, not least because it threatens to silence the realities of racism. Consequently, close involvement with the performance does not necessarily guarantee privileged understanding of these cultural forms, in spite of appearances to the contrary. Sketching out an ambiguous relationship between performer and spectator, Hurston instead depicts a shifting, often elaborate dance that skips from intimacy to distance. And any sense that active interpretation of African American culture will enable white viewers and readers to transcend damaging cultural stereotypes is undermined when Hurston launches into a discussion of the ways in which prejudices determine audience interpretation. The dancer merely flexes one knee, pulls a face and straightens his arms, '[t]hat is all. But the spectator himself adds the picture of ferocious assault, hears the drums and finds himself keeping time with the music and tensing himself for the struggle' (1995b, 835). Such a reading is informed by a discourse of primitivism that serves to limit the suggestiveness of African American dancing.[10] Hurston certainly endorses the importance of active interpretation of African American cultural forms, but she never loses sight of the fact that readers' cultural and social assumptions play a large part in shaping their aesthetic responses.

---

[9]   References to *Mules and Men* are abbreviated to *MM*.

[10]   It is difficult to read this discussion of the pervasive influence of primitivism without referring to Hurston's later essay 'What White Publishers Won't Print' (1950), in which she argues that a deep-seated tradition of stereotyping limits white American perceptions of African Americans. Belief that '[u]nder a superficial layer of western culture, the jungle drums throb in our veins' not only limits cultural understanding, but it also acts as an obstacle to any sense of commonality among different ethnic groups (1995f, 953).

Not only does Hurston theorize interactions between performer and audience in her essay on vernacular culture; she also positions readers of her essay as active participants in the formulation of her argument. As Cheryl Wall notes, 'Characteristics' employs a variety of rhetorical techniques – metaphor and simile, direct and indirect mode of address, examples that are left to speak for themselves without explanations or mediating frameworks – to draw readers in: 'the essay asks its readers to puzzle out its argument and to confirm the validity of its claims' (Wall 2005b, n. p.).

Some of these concerns with interpretation are explored through Hurston's concept of African American hieroglyphics. To some extent, the idea of a language in which 'everything [is] illustrated' is suggestive of predominantly oral culture (1995b, 830). In line with Walter Ong's theory that '[o]ral cultures tend to use concepts in situational, operational frames of reference that are minimally abstract' (1982, 49), Hurston lays stress on 'empathetic and participatory way[s] of knowing rather than the distanced objectivity found in literate cultures' (Fulton 2006, 27).

At the same time, her formulation of the hieroglyphic speaks to an issue that has been central to my exploration of the collage aesthetic: the reader's active role as interpreter of an indirect, oblique form. Most of the word-pictures mentioned in 'Characteristics of Negro Expression' immerse readers in a specifically African American cultural world. Hurston's extensive list of metaphors and similes, double descriptives and verbal nouns, for instance, alludes to lynching, African American cuisine and 'flambeaux' cafes. Such hieroglyphics apparently close up the distance between anthropologist and reader, insider and outsider, drawing a predominantly white audience into an African American frame of cultural reference. In other words, the kind of figurative language Hurston describes, with its qualities of brevity, simplicity and directness, apparently aids intercultural understanding; readers are not detached onlookers, but participant observers who are introduced to the patterns of a particular culture.

Given that Hurston explicitly addresses the relationship between interpreter and performer in 'Characteristics of Negro Expression', it is worth spelling out what such a formulation of distance and proximity means for our understanding of the collage aesthetic. Hurston's idea of the interpreter as a participant, captivated by African American cultural performance because of its openness and suggestiveness, differs from Jean Toomer's positioning of readers in relation to *Cane*'s collage form. The patterns of fragmentation and juxtaposition that are so carefully orchestrated in *Cane* give the reader an active role as a researcher, or bearer of knowledge. Toomer's tissue of quotations from sources as diverse as Emerson, Coleridge, the Bible, Du Bois, African American worksongs and Hawthorne, invites readers to identify allusions, figuring out the significance of his juxtaposition of discordant elements. Even as they are brought face to face with the realities of racial violence in the South, interpreters are also required to step back to survey the text as a whole, piecing together its highly allusive meaning.

By contrast, Hurston positions readers in close proximity to her literary collage. As her description of 'close fitting' language implies, she provides detailed contextual information that might be unfamiliar to those outside the community (1995b, 830). In 'Spirituals and Neo-Spirituals', for instance, Hurston explains expectations that undergird African American religious expression: '[b]eneath the seeming informality of religious worship there is a set formality. Sermons, prayers, moans and testimonies have their definite forms. The individual may hang as many new ornaments upon the traditional form as he likes, but the audience would be disagreeably surprised if the form were abandoned' (1995c, 873). In short, she offers an alternative perspective to the dominant anthropological view that Claude Lévi-Strauss has termed 'The View from Afar' (1985). Moving beyond the 'seeming informality' that a cultural outsider might observe, she explains governing cultural principles that remain invisible to casual observers.

What is at stake in these qualitative differences becomes clear if we pursue a comparison with visual art. Reading *Cane* is analogous to viewing a Picasso collage from afar: above all, viewers notice jarring juxtaposition of high art with strange and unfamiliar objects, debris from the everyday world. However, as in Picasso's collages, there is thematic consistency whereby certain ideas and shapes reappear in various formats, 'challeng[ing] us to imagine images that can never be organically whole, which shimmer forever as fragments, but which evoke and suggest a series of nameable wholes' (Staller 2001, 228). Consequently, analysis of Toomer's sophisticated patterning of fragments and genres holds a mirror to American cultural identity, revealing a racial complexity that is often repressed in 'monumental' national histories.

Interpreting Hurston's work is perhaps more akin to viewing a Joseph Cornell box. An American avant-garde artist who developed an idiosyncratic style, Cornell began producing what he called 'shadow boxes' in the 1930s. He filled beautifully crafted wooden boxes with an extraordinary variety of found objects, including marbles, newspaper, feathers, sand, bits of cloth and stuffed birds. Each box was covered with glass so that it became 'an exceptionally convincing way of focusing an image and presenting it as both real and private: plainly in view, but protected from the embrowning air of real life by its glass pane' (Hughes 1991, 257). Although many of Cornell's boxes are thematically integrated, an unusual relationship is established between the viewer and image because we are invited to linger on each object in turn. Speaking of Cornell's *L'Egypte de Mlle Cléo de Mérode* (1940), 'a votive cosmetic box' fitted with many small phials that contained 'sand, wheat, curls of paper labelled "Serpents of the Nile," pearls, the Sphinx, and so on', Robert Hughes explains that Cornell was not concerned with 'Surrealist incongruity'; rather, he encouraged a subtle appreciation of the world's rich variety through careful examination of the shape and texture of individual objects (1991, 257).

Hurston's close-up technique, which invites readers to visualize intimate details of each cultural fragment that she isolates, is analogous to peering closely at the objects in a Cornell box. She immerses readers in specific cultural forms so that they come to appreciate the collage-like variety of African American culture *from within*. Taken together, such cultural fragments formulate a complex cultural whole. Yet, as in Cornell's magical collections of souvenirs, Hurston ultimately leaves us guessing about her intentions; African American cultural forms are left to speak for themselves without a consistent mediating framework.

Consider an example. In describing specifically African American speech acts in *Dust Tracks on a Road*, Hurston establishes a shifting web of allegiances between herself as anthropologist, her informants and readers to test the limits of intercultural understanding:

> 'Dat's Big Sweet,' my landlady told me. 'She got her foot up on somebody. Ain't she specifying?'
>
> She was really giving the particulars. She was giving a 'reading,' a word borrowed from the fortune-tellers. She was giving her opponent lurid data and bringing him up to date on his ancestry, his looks, smell, gait, clothes, and his route through Hell in the hereafter. My landlady went outside where nearly everybody else of the four or five hundred people on the 'job' were to listen to the reading. Big Sweet broke the news to him, in one of her mildest bulletins that his pa was a double-humpted camel and his ma a grass-gut cow, but even so, he tore her wide open in the act of getting born, and so on and so forth. He was a bitch's baby out of a buzzard egg.
>
> My landlady explained to me what was meant by 'putting your foot up' on a person. If you are sufficiently armed – enough to stand off a panzer division – and know what to do with your weapons after you get 'em, it is all right to go to the house of your enemy, put one foot up on his steps, rest one elbow on your knee and play in the family (1995d, 696).

Here, readers are positioned as witnesses, who are gradually inducted into the codes of 'specifying' by a cultural insider. In this case, Hurston's landlady adopts the anthropologist's role, explaining culturally specific practices such as 'specifying' and 'got her foot on somebody'. This seems to distance Hurston from the community she is describing, not least because mention of rented accommodation emphasizes her temporary, transitory status. As observers, Hurston and her readers are given a kind of how-to guide to the ritual of 'specifying' and this knowledge allows them to cross the threshold from cultural outsider to insider. By the end of the passage, readers have become potential participants, who are addressed directly as 'you'. In this way, Hurston appears to develop a performative theory of language that is communal without being exclusive.

As in her ambiguous account of African American dance in 'Characteristics of Negro Expression', Hurston's narrative position is more complex than it appears at first glance. She does not simply substitute the landlady's voice for her own, performing an act of ventriloquism. Instead, curious effects are evoked as Hurston slips in and out of the roles of passive observer, patiently waiting for explanation from her informant, and authoritative scientist, who betrays an insider's knowledge when explaining the origins of the word '"reading"'. Hurston's final rhetorical flourish, which testifies to her dexterity with metaphorical language, positions her squarely as a full participant, a wordsmith who could hold her own in any contest with Big Sweet. In sum, Hurston demonstrates verbal agility, manipulating and mediating various styles. While she shows a deep understanding of what Marcyliena Morgan calls 'directed discourse', or unambiguous defamation of character, she deliberately refrains from direct participation in such rituals (1998, 263).

Hurston vacillates between speaking for and as a participant, from the role of insider and outsider, holder of knowledge and eager pupil. These contradictory poses make it difficult to pin down her voice, or to gain a sense of her opinion of the events. Instead, Hurston remains herself unreadable in a particular way: her narrative voice is dispersed as she negotiates the tensions of joining in and explaining cultural performances. She shares narrative authority with both Big Sweet and her landlady in such a way that her own voice begins to slip away. Taken together with her sustained interest in interpreters, these silences direct us towards a revealing tension in Hurston's anthropological writings. On the one hand, she strains to open out cultural identity beyond the confines of separatism, reaching towards a utopian humanism in which culture carries the potential to bridge racial differences. On the other hand, such optimism is cut short by a sharp awareness of misrecognitions and misreadings that characterize intercultural encounters in a racist society. In this context, Hurston reinscribes what Edward Said has termed 'identitarian consciousness' whereby individuals are defined according to categories of identity such as black and white, Western and Oriental (Said 1993, 330). Even when she describes her own experiences as an anthropologist, a distinction is maintained between insiders and outsiders. At one moment, she either inhabits the pose of anthropologist or informant; there is little room for connection between the two.

Thinking 'in hieroglyphics': African American Modernist Expression

Keeping this ambiguity in mind, I now want to consider how Hurston's theory of thinking 'in hieroglyphics' can be read as another version of the Harlem Renaissance collage aesthetic. Hurston describes African American speech as a series of images that must be interpreted in turn and then pieced together to create a whole. Unlike collage, such expression is linear, but it shares collage's capacity to generate meaning through juxtaposition of distinct images.

When teasing out the significance of these 'hieroglyphics', interpreters must take an active role, fleshing out suggestions and synthesizing fragments. To underline this point, Hurston draws particular attention to 'hieroglyphics' that perform a word's meaning, depicting the very object or action being described. Clearly, vivid 'picture[s]' or 'action' words, such as '"chop-axe"', draw readers or listeners into the speaker's world (1995b, 830). Moreover, 'hieroglyphics' immerse interpreters in a specifically African American culture. When Hurston provides a list of metaphors, similes, 'double descriptives' and 'verbal nouns', it becomes clear that such phrases depend upon culturally specific references to black cuisine, music and material culture (1995b, 832).

It would be a mistake, however, to assume that 'hieroglyphics' offer a transparent window on African American culture. In Hurston's formulation, African American culture never settles into a static whole; it is always 'in the making' (1995b, 836). Consequently, 'hieroglyphics' retain a visual quality and dynamic energy that remains beyond words, defying any notion of a definitive interpretation. Given the long history of cultural imperialism that has characterized Egyptology, this refusal to 'translate' visual symbols into a written script carries political significance. Such openness represents a departure from European Egyptologists' treatment of hieroglyphics as a code to be cracked, which would lay bare Egyptian culture for consumption by white Europeans.

The motif of hieroglyphics also brings us to the controversial question of Hurston's engagement with Euro-American modernism. In this context, 'Characteristics of Negro Expression' offers a kind of interpretive template for reading the patterning of stylistic and thematic allusions in Hurston's work. In claiming that 'the Negro thinks in hieroglyphics', Hurston registers an abiding interest in cultural continuities across the black diaspora (1995b, 831). At the same time, her theory is highly suggestive of a collaging of African, African American and European cultural segments. Focusing on tensions that arise as she draws upon both vernacular forms and modernistic experimentation sheds light on the complexity of Hurston's collage aesthetic. When Hurston states that 'the white man thinks in a written language and the Negro thinks in hieroglyphics' (1995b, 831), she reveals her simultaneous investment in a specifically African American cultural tradition and her engagement with modernistic styles that criss-crossed the Atlantic. Given these tangled affiliations, it is important to map points of contact between the Harlem Renaissance and modernism without underestimating complexities that underlie such intercultural encounter.

Since much of my analysis hinges on an account of cultural cross-currents that vivify Hurston's concept of hieroglyphics, it is worth quoting the relevant passage from 'Characteristics of Negro Expression' at length:

> Frequently the Negro, even with detached words in his vocabulary – not evolved in him but transplanted on his tongue by contact – must add action to it to make it do. So we have "chop-axe," "sitting-chair," "cook-pot" and the like because the speaker has in his mind the picture of the object in use. Action. Everything illustrated. So we can say the white man thinks in a written language and the Negro thinks in hieroglyphics (Hurston 1995b, 830-31).

As I mentioned above, Hurston identifies a rich oral culture that is firmly rooted in the everyday, material world. At the same time, her emphasis on direct, highly visual communication parallels the aesthetic programmes embraced by Euro-American modernists. Karen Jacobs connects Hurston's hieroglyphics with Pound's

Chinese ideograms in the *Cantos* and H.D.'s palimpsests and hieroglyphics, identifying a shared interest in a kind of picture writing that lays emphasis on visual presentation rather than explanation (2001, 123). In distinction to these writers, Hurston's reference to African culture is an affirmation of her cultural heritage. Nevertheless, she echoes 'the combination of directness, simplicity and exoticism at which [avant-garde imagists] aimed' as they drew inspiration from non-European cultural forms perceived to be exotic – haiku, Indian poetry and song, and Irish folklore to name but a few (Carr 2000, 81).

In balancing 'the visual and dynamic immediacy of "primitive" word pictures against the abstract remove of "more civilized" "cheque words"', Hurston falls into 'an uneasy alignment with a range of canonical European American writers' (Kadlec 2000a, 308). Yet such correspondences are always tinged with ambivalence. For one thing, Hurston's celebration of 'the will to adorn', glorying as it does in gaudiness and excess, is fundamentally at odds with an understated, pared down imagist aesthetic. Next, although she comes perilously close to stereotype in her emphasis upon African American spontaneity and sensuality, Hurston interrogates the automatic equation of primitivism with otherness and exoticism. She instead locates primitivism squarely inside U.S. borders, drawing attention to African American vernacular culture in universal rather than particular terms. Notice, for instance, the emphasis placed on activities like cooking, which imply a certain level of commonality between cultures.

If modernists like Pound turned to non-European forms in search of alternative modes of representation, Hurston finds a formal template for simple, direct expression in familiar, often domestic, places. To put it another way, the concept of hieroglyphics captures what Karen Jacobs, in a perceptive account of Hurston's reliance upon racial and cultural hierarchies, calls the 'overall instability in her thought', her 'internal conflicts and divisions' (Jacobs 2001, 123-4). Even though Hurston seems to reiterate a troubling binary opposition between "primitive" and "civilized" cultures, her refusal to draw a sharp dividing line between such cultures would seem to correspond with broader trends in Euro-American modernist poetry. In her important essay 'Modernism and Empire', Helen Carr identifies 'a new perception of the world which lay behind the imagist aesthetic; a world which was fragmented, heterogeneous' (2000, 87). For Carr, the formal experimentation that is so often named as modernism's identifying feature stemmed from engagement with non-European cultures, an interest that was not unrelated to the increasingly cosmopolitan composition of Europe's metropolitan cities. In this context, Carr names collage, with its 'qualities of fragmentation and juxtaposition' (87) as the 'characteristic' modernist form. Taking Ezra Pound's interest in haiku and Chinese ideograms as the basis for a compelling case study, she astutely observes that '[t]he collages of modernism came out of a hybrid, multiracial world' (Carr 2000, 87). Hurston's concept of hieroglyphics, with its emphasis upon cultural hybridity, can be interpreted as a version of modernist collage, but the political implications of her formulation diverge from Euro-American concerns. Indeed, for Hurston, hieroglyphics encapsulate African American identity, registering a particular kind of cultural hybridity that derives from ruptures and discontinuities in African American history.

Hurston's engagement with, and departure from, avant-garde aesthetic experimentation has sparked considerable, if unsustained, critical interest in recent years. Much less attention has been focused on the ways in which her anthropological writings intersect with a specifically American discourse about cultural identity, a discourse in which ancient Egypt became an important trope for imagining American identity. Marc Manganaro and Michael A. Elliott have paved the way for such analysis, paying detailed attention to Hurston's formulation of a culture concept within the context of a broader cross-disciplinary 'intellectual conversation that invented culture as a separate patterned whole' (Manganaro 2002, 37). Without losing sight of the transatlantic character of these debates, it is worth remembering that, in 1930s America, '"[c]ultural" rhetoric was deployed to talk not only about what it meant to experience a uniquely "American" way of life, but to address such problems as immigration and assimilation; the personal experiences of group belonging and alienation; and questions of what constituted the best, or purest, expressions of a group of people, be they the "folk," the nation, or a region in the nation' (Hegeman 1999, 5).

In developing her concept of 'thinking in hieroglyphics', Hurston gives form to a definition of culture that goes against the grain of much early twentieth-century American thinking about racial assimilation. In the wake of Robert Park's sociological model, which was influential in propagating the view that assimilation was an inevitable process, many historians and sociologists subscribed to an acculturalist notion of racial development. In *The Negro Family in the United States*, for instance, E. Franklin Frazier averred that African Americans, who had been 'so nearly completely stripped of [their] social heritage' by the dislocation of slavery, were gradually being absorbed into white American cultural patterns (1966, 15). Ulrich B. Phillips made a comparable argument to different political effect in his history of the Old South when he wrote in 1929 that African Americans 'were as completely broken from their tribal stems as if they had been brought from the planet Mars' (1948, 160). The ubiquity of such claims in early twentieth-century America helps account for Hurston's urgent insistence upon African American cultural distinctiveness.

Challenging the acceptance of inevitable Euro-American cultural dominance that seems implicit in such models, Hurston describes a dynamic process whereby cultural contact generates new, hybrid forms that incorporate African, African American and European elements. In this sense, she follows Boas's manipulation of anthropology to 'unravel the processes that are going on under our eyes', articulating her own slant on race in America (Boas 1940, 285). Nevertheless, my concern here is not simply to establish Hurston's participation in a broader debate about what constituted American culture. Attention to the connections between constructions of national identity and representations of ancient Egypt, especially the trope of hieroglyphics, sheds light on some of the ways in which Hurston's thinking converges with, and departs from, certain strands of Euro-

American modernism. To grasp the significance of representations of Egypt to such discourses, it is helpful to sketch the historical coordinates of an enduring American fascination with Egypt.

Given that Hurston began her academic career as a literature student at a time when American literature was being institutionalized in colleges and universities, it is tempting to speculate that she was aware of the symbolic resonance of hieroglyphics in American Renaissance literature (Graff 1987, 211-16). John T. Irwin has convincingly demonstrated that hieroglyphics play a prominent role in Ralph Waldo Emerson's 'History' and 'The Poet', Henry David Thoreau's *Walden*, Herman Melville's *Mardi* and *Moby-Dick*, Edgar Allan Poe's *Eureka* and Nathaniel Hawthorne's *The Scarlet Letter*. For these writers, the process of decipherment, which fascinated Americans in the wake of François Champollion's interpretation of the Rosetta Stone and his subsequent breakthrough in reading hieroglyphics in the 1820s, strongly resonated with a quest for origins, not only the origins of writing, but also questions of race and nation.

In a celebrated passage from Walt Whitman's 'Song of Myself', for instance, a child inquires '*[w]hat is the grass?*' After volunteering several answers, the poet settles on the idea of 'a uniform hieroglyphic', open to multiple interpretations (1994a, 2051-2). Significantly, it is through this image, which carries associations with spiritual roots, that Whitman articulates an inclusive vision of America, embracing the varied heritage of African Americans, Native Americans, French Canadians and other racial groups. Thoreau's re-imagining of American identity in *Walden* also turns on the concept of hieroglyphics. Challenging a model of national identity rooted in commerce and trade, he seeks new interpretations of the landscape and, by extension, the nation: '[t]he Maker of this earth but patented a leaf. What Champollion will decipher this hieroglyphic for us, that we may turn over a new leaf at last?' (Irwin 1980, 19). In short, Thoreau equates the detailed historical knowledge required to decipher hieroglyphics with an urgent need to reinterpret America's past, a process of self-examination that heralds alternative conceptions of national identity.

Of more immediate relevance to Hurston's concept of hieroglyphics is an early twentieth-century fascination with visual immediacy and photographic precision among writers who were firmly committed to representing the particulars of American experience. One of the things that unites such diverse writers as Willa Cather, William Carlos Williams and Vachel Lindsay is a shared effort to find a space in between the written word and the visual image, a style often characterized as a paradoxical blend of the ultra-modern and the "primitive".[11]

Drawing inspiration from cubism, William Carlos Williams created poems that might be interpreted as hieroglyphics, not least because of their photographic

---

[11] In *The Art of the Moving Picture* (1915), a pioneering analysis of film, Vachel Lindsay uses the word 'hieroglyphics' to describe the new medium of film (1970, 21). Deploying a vocabulary derived from contemporary race science, he aligns this modern medium with a primitive mode of thinking in pictures (1970, 22).

stillness. In 'The Red Wheelbarrow', for example, Williams eschews metaphor for direct, sharp delineation of a particular moment without offering any kind of interpretive framework. A comparable commitment to visual immediacy governs Willa Cather's celebrated description, in *My Ántonia*, of a plough suddenly illuminated by the sun. Cather describes this startling image as 'a picture writing on the sun' (140), inviting readers to decode its significance as if it were a hieroglyphic. Taken together, such examples imply a link between literary hieroglyphics and the formulation of a specifically American (national and regional) cultural consciousness. Indeed, Egmont Arens made this connection concrete in a discussion of Alfred Stieglitz's photography, which, he argued, pioneered a new, distinctively American way of seeing the world, 'the hieroglyphics of a new speech between those of us who find all the spoken languages too clumsy' (Dijkstra 1969, 160).

This sense that Hurston's theory of hieroglyphics contributes to a broader debate among anthropologists and cultural critics concerning what constituted American culture is confirmed by reference to Vachel Lindsay, a neglected but popular writer who immersed himself in ancient Egyptian culture. In addition to a sharp analysis of silent films, in which he likened the new medium to 'hieroglyphics', Lindsay's amateurish fascination with hieroglyphics inspired him to create hybrid poetic forms, which crossed disciplinary lines, maintaining a strong commitment to the written word and the visual image. Lindsay's poetic hieroglyphics, a term he used 'freely and almost synonymously with any form of symbol or statement' (258), did not entail imitation of Egyptian expression; instead, he wanted to develop a 'picture writing of his own' (Massa 1970, 256).

There are several striking correspondences with Hurston's concept of hieroglyphics here. For one thing, Lindsay's hieroglyphics combine compression, or at least isolation of a single image, with excessive decoration. In line with Hurston's emphasis upon 'the will to adorn', Lindsay's visual hieroglyphics in *Going-to-the-Sun* (1923), a book of illustrated verse, are romantic and ornate. In this sense, Lindsay occupies a complex position in relation to imagism: while he is committed to a visual aesthetic, his romantic, abundant sensibility remains at odds with spare imagist poetics.

Secondly, in a move that anticipates Hurston's celebration of African American vernacular expression, Lindsay's hieroglyphics are firmly rooted in popular culture. In *The Art of the Moving Picture* (1915), for instance, he uses the term hieroglyphics to register a shift of emphasis in American culture from text to image. 'American civilization grows more hieroglyphic every day' (1970, 21), he announces, recording a growing dominance of visual media such as photography, advertising billboards and cartoons. These new media necessitate a fresh approach to interpretation, which lays emphasis upon a viewer's immediate, even intuitive, grasp of an object's significance in the 'real' world, rather than cerebral interpretation of an abstract image. Of course, this connection between hieroglyphics and popular culture was beyond doubt by the time Hurston wrote 'Characteristics of Negro Expression'. Hieroglyphics were a popular motif in the wake of Howard Carter's discovery of Tutankhamen's tomb in 1922, which stimulated a fad for all things Egyptian. It is difficult to overestimate the pervasiveness of Egyptomania: women were wearing 'Cleopatra' earrings, biscuit tins were produced in the shape of Egyptian vases, Egyptian architectural styles became popular and there were a string of spin-off films, including Cecil B. De Mille's *Cleopatra* (1934) (Curl 1994, 211-17).

What emerges most strongly from *The Art of the Moving Picture* is Lindsay's conviction that 'hieroglyphics' promised a specifically American aesthetic template, a radical departure from European cultural influences. In accordance with a wider modernist turn to non-European forms, Lindsay draws on a mystical, exotic narrative of 'Egyptian wizardry' and magic in order to 'learn ... how best to express and satisfy the spirit-hungers that are peculiarly American' (288). As Ann Massa explains, 'hieroglyphics, though derivative, offered an art form uncommon in the West, which would set America apart from Europe' (1970, 257).

Even though Hurston shares Lindsay's interest in a distinctive American aesthetic, it is important to acknowledge substantial differences between these two writers. For Lindsay, Egyptian culture is simply a rich seam to mine for new forms, styles and themes; but Hurston's allusions to ancient Egypt are bound up with a delineation of African American cultural identity, a topic of considerable controversy in the early twentieth century. As Martin Bernal has shown, nineteenth- and twentieth-century scientists constructed an Aryan model of ancient history, clinging to the assumption that whiteness was a prerequisite for cultural achievement. Insisting that the ancient Egyptians were white, they forced a wedge between African and Egyptian culture, a distinction that has long been used to maintain racist suppositions of black inferiority (Bernal 1991, 245). In this context, Hurston's alternative, pan-African understanding of hieroglyphics, with its emphasis upon African, African American and European elements, carries political weight.[12]

With this in mind, it is clear that Hurston's concept of hieroglyphics must also be examined in the context of Harlem Renaissance representations of Egypt. Attention to African American historiography, art and popular culture reveals that representations of ancient Egypt served as a linchpin for discussions of cultural identity, particularly African retentions. As Michel Feith points out, 'the image of Egyptian heritage at work in the Harlem Renaissance – and later – is clearly a fabrication; it participates in the creation of a New Negro ethos' (2001, 57). Since

---

[12]   Hurston's emphasis upon diffusionism bears affinities with E.A. Wallis Budge's call, in his hieroglyphic dictionary of 1920, for detailed analysis of cross-cultural exchanges that gave rise to hieroglyphics. Departing from Karl Otfried Müller's influential model, which limited itself to comparison with Semitic languages, Budge makes room for borrowing from African and Hamitic languages (Bernal 1991, 31). In other words, Budge's dictionary registers diverse linguistic influences upon the Egyptians: he places his translations of hieroglyphics alongside the Coptic, Syriac, Hebrew alphabets and the Ethiopic and Aramaic syllabary, inviting readers to adopt a comparative framework.

the majority of slaves imported to America came from West Africa, allusions to Egyptian imperial grandeur had more to do with fashioning a 'politics of pride' and contemporary Pan-Africanism than a scientific tracking of specific survivals (Feith 2001, 57).

What was at stake in ubiquitous references to African achievements during the Harlem Renaissance becomes clear if we turn to revisionist histories, such as Pauline Hopkins's *A Primer of Facts Pertaining to the Early Greatness of the African Race and the Possibility of Restoration by its Descendants* (1905). An obsession with historical themes should not be mistaken for a retreat from present social and political issues; rather, writers and artists looked to the past with an eye to present political concerns. In line with Boas's mobilization of historical evidence to overturn prejudice about African culture, Hopkins deploys empirical data to support her claims for Egyptian and Ethiopian cultural achievements. As the subtitle tells us, Hopkins's arguments piggyback on the institutional authority of established academic disciplines: the analysis is '[c]ompiled and [a]rranged from the [w]orks of the best known [e]thnologists and [h]istorians' such as Martin R. Delany (1905, n. p.).

In this context, hieroglyphics play a prominent role in the construction of Africa as a symbol of pride and accomplishment. Establishing a nourishing narrative of pan-African cultural continuity, Hopkins charts connections between Ethiopia and Egypt, 'the only two African civilizations comparable to that of the United States, as far as power, influence, and architectural grandeur are concerned' (Feith 2001, 57). She assembles evidence demonstrating that these two empires shared 'not only the same kind of statutes, but also the same characters and hieroglyphics were used … since it is generally allowed that those were the repositories of Egyptian wisdom and literature' (1905, 12). In short, Hopkins creates a composite image of black identity, undercutting a damaging tendency to equate Africa with backwardness. For Hopkins, such historical recovery should pave the way for a better future: she advocates acceptance of this Pan-African heritage among African Americans as the first step towards a healthier self-image, with an eventual promise of improved social and political status (1905, 20).[13]

It is difficult to miss a parallel interest in Egyptian motifs and hieroglyphics as a trope for cultural interfusion in Harlem Renaissance visual art. In *The Ascent of Ethiopia* (1932), Loïs Mailou Jones adopts a similar approach to Hopkins: she seems to elevate Ethiopia through association with Egyptian civilization. Echoing Hurston's theorization of an African American aesthetic of appropriation and revision, Jones implies that a layering of cultural influences generates new styles and forms. There is a historical narrative of ascent from slavery to artistic self-expression in art, drama and music in modern America. However, Jones also

---

[13]   There are striking parallels with Boas's commencement address at Atlanta University in 1906, in which he told assembled students that 'clear insight into the capabilities of your own race' in the ancient world should encourage them to struggle for a gradual change to the social, political and economic order (Boas 1974g, 311).

flattens out distinctions between the past and the present, creating an enduring pan-African image of pride, a synthesis of old and new. Aspects of ancient Egyptian culture undergo a process of transformation in the ultra-modern cityscape, a transformation vividly captured in the bold splashes of colour that animate the painting.

Aaron Douglas's *Building More Stately Mansions* (1944) is also underpinned by an inclusive vision of African American cultural heritage, making space as it does for Egyptian architecture, a Buddhist pagoda, a Roman portico and a modern American cityscape (Feith 2001, 56). Yet there are contradictory affiliations at work here, contradictions that resonate with Hurston's investment in essentialism and cultural interfusion in 'Characteristics of Negro Expression'. On the one hand, Douglas seems to accept the logic of what Jan Morris has termed 'stones of empire', imperial buildings that serve a political purpose by reminding subjects of the wealth and power of their oppressors.[14] Judging from the grand scale of his painting, it seems appropriate to interpret Douglas's imposing monuments as an index of African (and by extension African American) cultural achievement, a shorthand for imperial confidence and power. On the other hand, Douglas alludes to an alternative assessment of Egyptian culture found in the African American spirituals, a tradition that conflates Ole Pharaoh's exploitation of the Hebrews in the Book of Exodus with white planters' enslavement of African Americans. Such associations allow Douglas to critique American imperialism. He establishes an analogy between black slave labour in America and exploitation of non-European workers by European colonizers, a parallel underlined through recognizable motifs of imperial ambition such as the globe in the right hand corner of the painting. Juxtaposition of architectural wonders with images of African and African American labourers shifts attention from the monuments towards those who created them, an alteration of perspective that heralds a 'more stately' democratic political order.

Comparable tensions surface in representations of Egyptian culture in African American popular culture. For Michael North, the sudden proliferation of Egyptian imagery in Euro-American culture that followed Howard Carter's discovery of Tutankhamen's tomb is an archetypal modernist story, not least because it 'expresses some fundamental association between modern media and the past' (1999, 27). One aspect of Egyptomania that escapes North's attention is Egyptian imagery in advertisements aimed at a black audience. There is a revealing tension in such adverts between a pan-African politics of pride and an appeal to market forces, an astute manipulation of contemporary Egyptomania. In his 1925 campaign for 'Madagasco', a hair straightener 'of no regrets', the pan-African sweep of Charles C. Dawson's design is, to some extent, compromised by a pragmatic appeal to Egyptian fashions (Powell 1997, 63). Paradoxically, hair straightener, a beauty product that adheres to white standards of beauty, is presented as a route to African

---

[14]   I borrow this phrase from Jan Morris, *Stones of Empire: The Buildings of the Raj* (1983).

American distinctiveness and a uniquely Africanized style, 'that native black Madagasco effect' (Powell 1997, 63). Such advertisements register the profound ambivalence surrounding ancient Egypt in early twentieth-century culture, an uncertainty that resonates with Hurston's concept of hieroglyphics.

Attention to the motif of hieroglyphics in modernist visual art, literature and popular culture identifies this overdetermined figure as trope for representing American *and* African American identity. To understand what lies behind Hurston's theory, it is crucial to acknowledge that she draws inspiration from international modernism as well as African American vernacular forms. Yet, there is an unresolved tension in Hurston's concept of hieroglyphics: while she lays claim to African American cultural distinctiveness (tracking cultural continuities across the African diaspora), her theory of hieroglyphics is nourished by mutual cross-cultural influences. A closer look at the diverse cultural fragments that Hurston smoothes over to construct a monolithic black culture reveals unexpected connections and affiliations.

Collage as Textual Form: *Mules and Men*

Analysis of the concept of hieroglyphics demonstrates that Hurston developed a critical vocabulary to think through intercultural synthesis and fragmentation in African American culture. But my notion of the collage aesthetic does not only refer to such cultural description. As in *Cane*, collage, with its ambiguous potential for disjunction and cohesion, is the primary structural principle of Hurston's ethnography. With this in mind, I now turn to the most striking example of a collage form in Hurston's *oeuvre*: the ethnography *Mules and Men*. Based on material collected from black communities in the South from 1927 to 1929, *Mules and Men* is a text composed of fragments, a miscellany of stories, songs, customs, conjure and rituals, which falls into two distinct parts.

The first section is a collection of songs, sermons and folktales, including stories about creation, the church, the origins of race and gender roles to name only a few. As commentators have often noted, a distinctive feature of *Mules and Men* is its overarching chronological narrative, which dramatizes Hurston's quest for material, establishing a recurring pattern of arrival, immersion in the social rituals of a community, and departure. This sense of motion, of perpetual travel, is paralleled in the unsettled, if not inconsistent, character of Zora herself. At times, Hurston's 'ethnographer persona' is highly visible; we become aware of the ethnographer's role as a catalyst who encourages informants to tell 'lies' with a ready supply of buttermilk and gingerbread. At other times, Zora disappears almost entirely from the narrative and informants are left to speak for themselves with little in the way of authorial intervention. As Michael A. Elliott explains, 'Hurston's ethnographer persona is least present in those scenes where her informants are most useful to her *as* an ethnographer: during the fishing trip, for example, when her companions tell story after story involving the major figures of their folkloric traditions' (2002, 174).

In a shift of emphasis that adds to this uneven quality, part two focuses on hoodoo in Louisiana, offering an account of 'a suppressed religion' from an insider's perspective (Hurston *MM* 183). Continuing the pattern of arrival, immersion and departure established in section one, Hurston describes her experiences as an initiate of various hoodoo doctors: Eulalia, 'who specialized in Man-and-woman cases'; Marie Leveau's disciple Luke Turner; the 'swamper' Dr Duke, who collects his own roots and herbs; and the powerful Frizzly-Rooster (*MM* 187). Throughout this section, Boasian cultural description, with its emphasis upon extensive detail, provides a context for the raw ethnographic data – including recipes for various hoodoo rituals such as how 'to make a man come home' – that is recorded in these pages (*MM* 276). Much of the substance of these chapters is derived from 'Hoodoo in America', an essay written for *The Journal of American Folk-Lore* (1931), but Hurston dispenses with the interpolating analytical voice that is prominent in the earlier text.[15] Since it is relatively easy to track down these sources, it becomes clear that *Mules and Men* is shaped by Hurston's collage technique, her insertion of pre-existing fragments into a new context.

Such narrative techniques – the absence of a consistent analytical framework, the insertion of 'between-story conversation' and the inclusion of a variety of genres and forms – serve to maximize the ragged, uneven shape of Hurston's narrative form (Kaplan 2002, 308). Moreover, as Martha Jane Nadell points out in her sophisticated account of 'interartistic' Harlem Renaissance texts, Hurston's generically hybrid form, which blends fiction and anthropology, is complicated further by the inclusion of ten illustrations by the Mexican caricaturist and anthropologist Miguel Covarrubias (Nadell 2004, 101-12). These images occupy a prominent position in the text (they are usually integrated into the tale to which they refer or placed on the opposite page), but they 'subtly shift [the] focus' of Hurston's narrative even as they follow its 'general contours' (Nadell 2004, 104). The illustrations do much more than simply give visual form to the content of individual stories: they add another layer of tension to an already crowded narrative, putting conflicting styles of representing black folk culture – anthropology and primitivist caricature among them – into conversation. Covarrubias's drawings, with their sharp modernist silhouettes, move away from the photographic realism

---

[15] Lippincott required substantial changes to the manuscript as a condition of publication. In addition to the 'between-story conversation' that Hurston inserted to make the collection more readable, part two was added to satisfy Lippincott's request for a longer manuscript (Kaplan 2002, 308). As Genevieve West points out, this fact tended to undermine Hurston's credibility as a social scientist among reviewers. The reader in *North American Review*, for instance, interprets the material on hoodoo as a publicity stunt: 'I have the teasing conviction that [hoodoo] has always been, and always will be overemphasized because of those who like its appeal to the romantically macabre' (West 2005, 83).

with which twentieth-century ethnography began, towards primitivism and aestheticism.

It is worth remembering, for example, that the second section of *Mules and Men* is framed by a nude drawing of Hurston lying face down on a snake skin. Breaking the chronological flow of the narrative, this sketch, which depicts Hurston as a passive subject who cannot even meet the viewer's gaze, chimes with Lippincott's dubious marketing of the volume, characterized as it was by a tendency to sensationalize what was described on the dust jacket as 'the weird hoodoo practices carried on by negroes in the South today' (West 2005, 77). In distinction to Hurston's neutral documentary description of her initiation, Covarrubias's picture deploys primitivist motifs that make Hurston an anthropological subject rather than an observer. As Nadell notes, 'Covarrubias' technique of using black and white to create palpable volume forces attention on her body. This drawing thus seems more about Hurston as a female body than it does about the hoodoo ritual in which she participated' (2004, 110). In other words, dialogue between text and image triggers a series of questions about Hurston's position as ethnographer, especially the extent to which her reception will be determined by a racialized and gendered gaze.[16]

Given that *Mules and Men* 'generates more questions than answers' (Nadell 2004, 112), it comes as no surprise that it provoked a mixed response from the outset. According to Genevieve West, the lukewarm reception among African American reviewers was guided, at least in part, by a tendency in white publications to equate *Mules and Men* with Joel Chandler Harris's Uncle Remus tales, a 'comparison [that] put Hurston and her work in an unfavorable light, suggesting that readers associate Hurston and the collection with oversimplified stereotypes of African Americans in pastoral southern settings' (West 2005, 84). Sterling A. Brown's 1936 review, for example, indicts Hurston for failing to document the social and political inequalities of contemporary rural life: '[t]he picture is too pastoral, with only a bit of grumbling about hard work, or a few slave anecdotes that turn the tables on old master' (Sollors 1990, 37). A comparable logic underpins Alain Locke's review for *Opportunity* in the same year, in which he praises Hurston's grasp of 'race native material and local color', but judges the whole volume 'too Arcadian' (Sollors 1990, 61). Like Brown, Locke aligns focus on the rural folk with nostalgia and political escapism at a time when the critical tide was turning in favour of social realism.

On a separate front, Hurston has received criticism for what I am calling collage form, her unorthodox ethnographic methodology, her fragmentary, even random, patterning of material, in which folktales are presented without sustained

---

[16]   Among her fellow Boasians, Hurston was perceived as 'both a subject and an object of her discipline' (171). Meville Herskovits, for instance, wrote a letter in 1927 which described her as '"more White than Negro in her ancestry", but that her "manner of speech, her expressions, – in short, her motor behaviour" were "what would be termed typically Negro"' (Elliott 2002, 171).

scientific analysis. As Marc Manganaro comments, '[t]he chief objection was that the book was not a finished product in fellow Boasian [Ruth] Benedict's well-wrought-urn kind of way. Its two-part division into Florida tale-telling and New Orleans hoodoo, when read in terms of anthropological conceptions of culture of the day (Benedict's configurational theory among them), comes off as confusion, as ragged juxtaposition, justified by the slim reed, dangerously travelogue-like, that Hurston had been there, that New Orleans was where she went after Florida' (Manganaro 2002, 178).

With several notable exceptions, including Marc Manganaro, Michael A. Elliott and Martha Nadell, critics have tended to smooth over such dissonance, transforming *Mules and Men* into a coherent text with a clear political message. To take a representative example, Lori Jirousek tidies up odd juxtapositions and unexplained shifts of tone, claiming that Hurston's entire *oeuvre* is underpinned by an identifiable political project 'to move America beyond a preoccupation with the "race problem" and to promote a harmonious cultural hybridity in its place' (Jirousek 2004, 426).

Mules and Men is anything but harmonious. For a start, the folktales create an effect of polyphony: many informants speak, and they often disagree with one another (and Hurston) about such matters as religion, gender, sexuality and the value of black folklore. As Michael A. Elliot demonstrates, African American culture does not seem to be a static whole, but rather an arena of conflict where values are constantly under discussion (Elliott 2002, 177). Even so, Hurston does not follow Toomer's lead, staging violent disjunctions to unsettle readers' assumptions. Instead, she gives prominence to the new whole created by her collage form, identifying a unifying African American aesthetic that gives coherence to her ragged, uneven ethnography. In this sense, *Mules and Men* gives form to Hurston's theory in 'Characteristics of Negro Expression' that subversive revision is a governing principle in African American folk culture. With this move, she finds a kind of coherence in incoherence. Although she is unable to smooth away all the tensions inherent to collage form, her emphasis upon an aesthetic of cutting and pasting that never compromises upon cultural consistency recalls Boas's description of cultures as 'a development from diverse sources which are gradually worked into a single cultural unit' (Boas 1940, 217).

Some of the tensions between integration and fragmentation in *Mules and Men* stem from Hurston's complex engagement with, or even collaging of, Boasian pronouncements on cultural development. In accordance with her theorization of African American culture in 'Characteristics of Negro Expression', Hurston's formal choices bear the signs and strains of her commitment to both Boasian anthropology and African American vernacular forms.

To a large extent, *Mules and Men* is underpinned by Boasian assumptions. On one level, the collection is a compendium of carefully recorded southern folk culture. This commitment to salvaging culture conforms to Boas's priorities: he published a huge number of original texts during his lifetime, often without providing any commentary on them at all. Ironically, Hurston's emphasis upon the specific contexts in which stories are told – her careful dramatization of local environments and settings – is also an extension of Boasian logic. Although Boas seldom offers this kind of explanatory context in his own ethnography, Hurston's attention to modes of telling and styles of performance accords with his often repeated argument that the full meaning of individual artifacts in museum collections could only be understood in the midst of '"a complete collection of a single tribe"' (Elliott 2002, 2). In this sense, the unstable tone of Hurston's volume, which oscillates between specific cultural examples – songs and stories – and contextual background, owes much to Boas. Even so, because of its dramatization of folk performance *Mules and Men* inhabits a different textual space from such works as *Chinook Texts* (1894) and *The Ethnology of the Kwakiutl* (1921). While folktales were assigned 'the status of scientific specimens rather than artistic creations' in Boas's ethnography, the swift changes of pace and tone that characterize *Mules and Men* showcase African American folk stories as imaginative, artistic creations (Elliott 2002, 10).

As in 'Characteristics of Negro Expression', Hurston's involvement with Boas's theories is more complex when it comes to the question of cultural hybridity. A series of '[f]raming gestures' establish cultural diffusion as a central theme for the volume (Edwards 2003, 38). Hurston's introduction places emphasis upon historical processes of contact, migration, trade and exchange in African American culture. And this approach is linked to Boas from the outset since Hurston records a conversation with her mentor in which they discussed her chosen topic: '"Florida", she tells him, 'is a place that draws people – white people from all over the world, and Negroes from every Southern state surely and some from the North and West." So I knew that it was possible for me to get a cross section of the Negro South in the one state' (*MM* 1). Far from returning to Eatonville in search of a culture unaltered by interracial contact, Hurston seeks a melting pot of diverse influences, a culture where 'even the Bible was made over to suit our vivid imagination' (*MM* 3). Echoing the 'complex layering of frames' that characterizes 'generically hybrid, subtly prefaced books by Du Bois, Johnson, and others' (Edwards 2003, 43), Boas also stresses cultural hybridity in his preface when he mentions 'the peculiar amalgamation of African and European tradition which is so important for understanding historically the character of American Negro life, with its strong African background in the West Indies' (*MM* xiii-xiv).

Yet, in spite of this overarching frame, Hurston's treatment of hybridity throughout the volume is marked by ambivalence. Given the tension between synthesis and fragmentation that runs through Hurston's treatment of hybridity, the metaphor of collage captures some of the contradictions in her attitude to anthropology. Witness, for instance, her commentary on Eatonville tale-telling early in Chapter 2:

> But they told stories enough for a volume by itself. Some of the stories were the familiar drummer-type of tale about two Irishmen, Pat and Mike, or two Jews as the case might be. Some were the European folk-tales undiluted, like Jack and

the Beanstalk. Others had slight local variations, but Negro imagination is so facile that there was little need for outside help. An't Hagar's son, like Joseph, put on his many-colored coat an paraded before his brethren and every man there was a Joseph (*MM* 19-20).

Coming on the heels of an account of a Wood Bridge toe party, this paragraph registers a sharp change from Zora's role as full participant in the community to Hurston's position as a detached scientific observer who comments with authority on cultural patterns. Given Hurston's emphasis upon appropriation and adaptation, she appears to be in step with Boasian hybridity. However, as in 'Characteristics of Negro Expression', Hurston ends up performing an elaborate balancing act, pairing hybridity with an assertion of cultural distinctiveness. The paragraph gradually tilts away from Standard English towards dialect, underlining a continuing commitment to an organic vernacular culture.

Ambivalence towards cultural exchange is captured in the image of Joseph's coat itself, which is at once a symbol for artistic hybridity and an emblem of the unique 'gaudy' African American aesthetic celebrated by Hurston in 'Characteristics'.[17] In terms of my formulation of the collage aesthetic, much hangs upon this assertive celebration of the essential coherence, if not exclusivity, of African American culture, a coherence vividly captured in the image of Joseph's coat. While Toomer's magpie's nest of allusions in *Cane* compels readers towards recognition of the interracial quality of America's pluralist culture, Hurston insists that cross-cultural interplay never disrupts the authenticity of African American forms. In short, Hurston places considerable emphasis upon the creative power of the African American collage-maker, who can unify diverse materials into a rich, colourful (and seamless) whole.

Interestingly, Hurston reinscribes a narrative of cultural distinctiveness when speaking about diffusion, which carries the potential to unsettle any notion of a closed cultural tradition. A comparable desire to draw attention to racial binaries is evident in Hurston's engagement with Boas's ideas in *Mules and Men*. Questions of racial identity, for example, are fundamental to Hurston's ambiguous position in relation to Boas's assessment of the anthropologist's role. A recurring motif in Boas's work is his idealization of the anthropologist, who, he claims, can transcend his or her own culture to obtain a uniquely objective view of the world. As he puts it in 'The Aims of Ethnology', anthropology 'alone opens to us the possibility of judging our own culture objectively, in that it permits us to strip off

---

[17] Countee Cullen also deployed the image of Joseph's coat to encapsulate the synthesis of cultural influences that characterize African American culture. In 1925, he argued that all art is appropriated from various sources, that there was 'no "simon pure" thing' (Douglas 1995, 341). Instead, he adopted a chromatic symbol for his art: Joseph's coat 'with its "many colors, all of which contributed to its beauty" and its "mischief working" powers' (Douglas 1995, 341). Reference to 'beauty' and 'mischief' indicates that a collage-like form constituted an attempt to push aesthetic boundaries and a political strategy for subversion.

the presumably self-evident manner of thinking and feeling which determines even the fundamental part of our culture. Only in this way can our intellect, instructed and formed under the influences of our culture, attain a correct judgment of this same culture' (Boas 1974c, 71). For Boas, anthropology facilitates what Susan Hegeman has called 'estranged perception': immersion in another culture provokes a searching reappraisal of one's own cultural outlook (Hegeman 1999, 4).

One problem with this model for Hurston is that Boas presumes a distance between the anthropologist and the culture under scrutiny. Hurston directly addresses her position as an anthropologist who views her own culture through the framework of social science in an often-quoted passage from the introduction:

> I was glad when somebody told me, 'You may go and collect Negro folklore.'
>
> In a way it would not be a new experience for me. When I pitched headforemost into the world I landed in the crib of negroism. From the earliest rocking of my cradle, I had known about the capers Brer Rabbit is apt to cut and what the Squinch Owl says from the house top. But it was fitting me like a tight chemise. I couldn't see it for wearing it. It was only when I was off in college, away from my native surroundings, that I could see myself like someone else and stand off and look at my garment. Then I had to have the spy-glass of Anthropology to look through at that (*MM* 1).

Hurston's exposure of both the possibilities and limitations of participant observation complicates Boas's model of cultural detachment. Admittedly, Hurston's description of her progress from naïve participant, who cannot even see the culture she inhabits, to adept social scientist seems to endorse Boasian methods. Yet Hurston's ambivalent appreciation and resentment of the way anthropology transforms what she has always 'known' into commodified scientific knowledge destabilizes any uncomplicated celebration of the anthropologist's privileged role.

More specifically, Hurston's emphasis upon the visual inserts her comments into a broader debate about anthropological ways of seeing. *Patterns of Culture* is of particular relevance here since Ruth Benedict remarks that '[n]o man ever looks at the world with pristine eyes'; rather he 'sees it edited by a definite set of customs and institutions and ways of thinking' (1935, 2). Nevertheless, Benedict's argument culminates in the claim that anthropologists 'can see objectively the socially conditioned behaviour of other peoples' (1935, 8).

In developing the metaphor of 'the spy-glass of Anthropology', Hurston scrutinizes Benedict's theory of circumscribed yet objective vision, pointing to the pitfalls of both scientific objectivity and an unexamined insider's view. As a cultural insider, she simply inhabited her culture as a familiar, close-fitting garment. But her role as an anthropologist is similarly circumscribed: not only is her view of the world peculiarly disembodied but she is also completely dependent upon 'the spy-glass of Anthropology', a technological tool that mediates her perspective. In voicing this critique, Hurston implies an alternative view that straddles both perspectives, a method that frames cultural material in Boasian terms without losing sight of the particularity of African American experience. Indeed, a sense that African American culture defies easy summary is captured in Hurston's image of the 'tight chemise', an 'unambiguously female garment' that 'both reveals the form and conceals the surface of the black body beneath' (Jacobs 2001, 111). In this image, Hurston shatters the Boasian assumption that cultural meanings are transparent to professional social scientists. Giving a new twist to Boas's metaphor of 'strip[ping] off' cultural assumptions, she implies that the depths of African American culture will remain a tantalizing puzzle to outsiders (Boas 1974c, 71).

The resurfacing of sharp lines of cultural difference at this point in the narrative is significant. As in 'Characteristics of Negro Expression', engagement with modernist thought, in this case Franz Boas's anthropology, does not lead to an emphasis upon plurality or hybridity; rather, cultural diffusion triggers profound anxiety about the need to establish dividing lines between cultural insiders and outsiders. In the main body of the text, Hurston dramatizes contradictions that stem from her position as a social scientist (trained in a discipline that prizes detachment and objectivity) researching the culture in which she was raised. When she enters the community of Polk County, for example, which is famous for its rich folkloric heritage, she is immediately an object of suspicion because of the obvious signs of her economic and cultural difference: her Chevrolet and her '$12.74 dress from Macy's' (*MM* 63). Throughout this section, Hurston makes her reader privy to tactical manoeuvres she uses to gain the community's trust. She overcomes resistance by participating in a performance of the John Henry song cycle: '[b]y the time that the song was over, before Joe Willard lifted me down from the table I knew that I was in the inner circle. I had first to convince the "job" that I was not an enemy in the person of the law; and, second, I had to prove that I was their kind. "John Henry" got me over my second hurdle' (*MM* 65).

Hurston's racial identity does not guarantee access to the 'true inner life' of African Americans in the way that Boas claims in his preface (*MM* xiii). Instead, posturing is required to convince the folk to recognize her status as an insider: readers are aware that she has only just learnt extra verses to 'JOHN HENRY, the king of railroad track-laying songs' in her native Eatonville (*MM* 55). Faced with such opposition, Hurston occupies a precarious position in relation to the communities she studies, a position that depends upon a delicate balancing of knowledge and performance, a complex blend that throws received notions of cultural authenticity into question. Such uncertainty impacts upon the reading spaces, or interpretive modes, opened up by the narrative. Point of view is hardly a settled matter: as in Joseph Cornell's 'shadow boxes', readers wheel between extreme close-up and distanced observation.

Any reader of *Mules and Men* cannot fail to notice the contradictory poses that Hurston inhabits as the narrative progresses. In the 'Hoodoo' section, the gap between Hurston and her audience widens as she steeps herself in the world of hoodoo as a participant observer. Rather than positioning herself as an authoritative guide to Southern traditions, she becomes an informant, adopting '[t]he profound silence of the initiated' until her ability to communicate collapses under the weight of terror she feels at the Black Cat Bone ritual (*MM* 185). When she attempts to explain how she feels, she can only manage a rather desperate 'I don't know. I don't know' (*MM* 221). Consequently, Hurston strikes a different note from the confident, confiding voice that characterizes her accounts of negotiations in the field in Polk County. It seems that her status as an insider or an informant makes it impossible to communicate her experiences to the reader. Once again, she is wearing her culture 'like a tight chemise' and she can neither see it nor describe it (*MM* 1).

At the end of *Mules and Men*, Hurston adds another complicating layer to her sustained examination of the anthropologist's role. Suddenly, with no explanation, Hurston tells her own tale for the first time, launching into the story of Sis Cat, who is duped out of dinner after responding to a lecture on table manners delivered by a rat that she has caught to eat. The next time a rat tries to trick her into opening her mouth, she eats her food and only then washes her face. Hurston suggests an analogy with the enterprise of collecting folklore and finding an appropriate format to serve up such tales to the public: 'I'm sitting here like Sis Cat, washing my face and usin' my manners' (*MM* 246). As Barbara Johnson has noted in her often-quoted analysis of Hurston's shifting modes of address, the unexplained tale leaves us asking 'who, in the final analysis, has swallowed what. The reader? Mrs. Mason? Franz Boas? Hurston herself?' (1993, 139). For Johnson, multiple levels of signifying make it impossible to capture a single, authentic authorial voice in the ethnography.

An alternative to this view is to ask what has escaped from Hurston's narrative. What is missing? Who or what is the rat? Significantly, in this final passage, Hurston's authoritative, scientific voice has been completely subsumed by that of an informant irredeemably located in her own culture. Far from using 'the spy-glass of Anthropology' to maintain an omniscient view of her subjects, Hurston closes up the distance between herself and the folk; she speaks as an informant. In this context, it is worth taking time to identify Hurston's glancing allusions to other stories in the collection. Mention of table manners recalls Mr Allen's strict instructions of how to eat fish, instructions that illustrate how customs are passed on from one generation to the next (*MM* 135). Another intertext is Mack Ford's account of the origins of the phrase 'unh hunh' (*MM* 160-61). Like Sis Cat, the devil is tricked into opening his mouth when a man asks what he is doing, thereby allowing the angels he has stolen from heaven to escape. From then on, he uses the phrase 'uh hunh' so that he can keep his mouth firmly closed.

Even a cursory examination of these intratextual connections tells us something about the significance of Hurston's collage technique in *Mules and Men*. It is clear that Hurston's patterning of material amounts to a formulation of a culture concept. As Marc Manganaro explains, 'Hurston, it could be said, does not make explicit the definition of culture in tatters but in fact in *Mules and Men* gives it full form, gives it embodiment' (2002, 199). In this sense, Hurston's method of referring back to images and concepts from earlier in the text is reminiscent of Toomer's aesthetic of assemblage in *Cane*, but these allusions are of a different order to his jarring juxtaposition of diverse cultural referents. Rather than provoking disorientation, what emerges is a sense of cultural continuity or coherence, an awareness of underlying patterns that connect the diverse, even fragmentary cultural examples that are so prominent in *Mules and Men*. The implication seems to be that there is a kind of cultural unity to rural folk culture despite appearances to the contrary. In other words, through her selection and arrangement of examples Hurston gives shape to a definition of African American culture in which multiple cultural examples – songs, stories and rituals – do not quite harmonize into an integrated whole, but there is nonetheless a sense of cohesion, or at least dynamic interplay between parts.

In Hurston's formulation, African American culture is made up of many fragments, or many colours, to return to the metaphor of Joseph's coat. Repetition of particular images or ideas, such as the stories about silence mentioned above, is suggestive of Hurston's taste for what Alice Gambrell has called 'versioning' (1997, 14), an aesthetic method whereby Hurston revised existing fragments of her published writing for incorporation into new contexts. In Hurston's hands, such revision and reformulation often implies coherence rather than discontinuity. She directs readers' attention away from the rupture implicit in such a method, emphasizing relationships between fragments, and between part and whole.

Given this, it is important that *Mules and Men* demands active interpretation. To grasp the full significance of individual stories, readers must immerse themselves in the volume, making connections and comparisons between tales. Specific cultural examples should be read in the context of the entire collection, which in itself becomes an argument for analysis of individual stories and songs in relation to a complex cultural whole. Furthermore, Hurston demonstrates that anthropology's scientific 'spy-glass' must be combined with an emotional engagement with, or immersion in, African American folk culture. As in Joseph Cornell's 'shadow boxes', readers come to appreciate African American culture's collage-like variety *from within*, as they become familiar with its underlying patterns and structures.

Hurston's network of allusions in the Sis Cat tale tacitly reinforces this emphasis upon cultural context. Read in isolation, the story is just another example of an aesthetic of lying. Within the context of the book, Hurston's tale identifies creative revision as a structuring principle in African American culture. There is a narrative logic in *Mules and Men*, she implies, if readers are willing to immerse themselves in African American folk culture, making connections between fragments and actively interpreting the text. Even so, it would be a mistake to claim that everything slots neatly into place. For one thing, Hurston's slippery tale, with its intriguing elision of anthropologist and informant, suggests there is always something missing from any cultural representation: either the rat, or informant, escapes or the anthropologist has to withhold information to protect (or maintain a grip on) their subject. In other words, Hurston highlights the expediency of remaining silent at certain moments, thus overwriting the authority of the supposedly all-seeing anthropologist. To the last, she introduces unexpected contradictions into her account of African American culture, identifying 'Characteristics of Negro Expression' by one turn and questioning the value of such generalizations at the next.

Conclusion

If Toomer accentuates violent discontinuities in *Cane*, Hurston's collage theory and practice foregrounds integrative representation. Although her writing is enriched by allusions to African, American and European culture, she attempts, with varying degrees of success, to smooth over the ruptures implicit in such a method. Indeed, creative revision becomes, in 'Characteristics of Negro Expression', an aesthetic impulse that gives coherence to African American cultural expression. Even so, attention to Hurston's collage aesthetic, which makes room for synthesis and fragmentation within a single text, brings into focus certain tensions that animate her anthropological project. Hurston's interest in, and practice of, cultural recycling is underpinned by recognition of the subversive potential of a cross-cultural aesthetic in the context of Jim Crow. Yet, such cultural hybridity is always fraught with an anxiety that prompts her to reinscribe fundamentally static binaries of identity. It might be tempting to interpret this attachment to narratives of cultural authenticity as a missed opportunity, not least because Hurston tends to downplay the complexity of the African American community in her eagerness to celebrate a monolithic black culture. In the final analysis, such contradictory poses must be read in their historical context; they resonate with broader debates among Harlem Renaissance thinkers about nationalism and internationalism, hybridity and essentialism.

Chapter 5

Reading Zora Neale Hurston's Textual Synthesis in *Jonah's Gourd Vine* and *Moses, Man of the Mountain*

In 'Spirituals and Neo-Spirituals', an essay written for inclusion in Nancy Cunard's *Negro* anthology, Hurston offers a parable to illustrate differences between African American and European styles of singing and preaching:

> A white man built a house. So he got it built and he told the man: 'Plaster it good so that nobody can see the beams and uprights.' So he did. Then he had it papered with beautiful paper, and painted the outside. And a Negro built him a house. So when he got the beams and all in, he carved beautiful grotesques over all the sills and stanchions, and beams and rafters. So both went to live in their houses and were happy (Hurston 1995c, 872).

With a nod to Boasian cultural relativism, Hurston identifies a collage-like pattern at the heart of African American culture, affirming her argument in 'Characteristics of Negro Expression'. For Hurston, the African American's artistic impulse is primarily decorative, to individualize and pattern a private space. By contrast, the white man's urge to produce clear lines and smooth surfaces is a public gesture of authority, which masks processes of construction. He even employs a labourer to complete the work.

Hurston positions 'her formulation about black vernacular music against the symmetrical rhythms and linear organization associated with Western classical music' (211), emphasizing a complex interweaving of 'parts and voices without submerging their disparate elements into a seamlessly unified product' (Allen Anderson 2001, 198). But this argument for African American cultural independence is not as straightforward as it appears. For one thing, in the broader context of her essay, Hurston assiduously avoids a static notion of authentic African American expression: theorizing identity by way of form enables an articulation of cultural identity as a process rather than a fixed entity. Challenging Du Bois's interpretation of the 'sorrow songs' in *The Souls of Black Folk*, she argues that 'each singing of the piece is a new creation' (1995c, 870). Given that Hurston defines spirituals as an endless series of improvisations, there can be no such thing as authentic expression: '[t]here never has been a presentation of genuine Negro spirituals to any audience anywhere' (1995c, 870). Consequently, she represents

African American culture while simultaneously asserting that any attempt to depict these forms is inadequate since they are constantly in motion.

Paul Allen Anderson takes this point further, noticing 'a revealing tension between Hurston's sense of originality as revisionary imitation and the more demanding standard of folk authenticity in her critique of the "neo-spirituals"' (2001, 200). In attending to such contradictions, Anderson contributes to a growing body of criticism that moves beyond a celebratory feminist framework, focusing instead on the ways in which 'Hurston also spoke to other discourses, occupying and opening distinctive ideological points of friction' (Warnes 2006, 375). Like Andrew Warnes, Delia Caparoso Konzett and Lynda Marion Hill, Anderson implies that it is at those moments when coherence is under strain that Hurston's work is most revealing. As Delia Caparoso Konzett explains, '[Hurston's work] is not merely symptomatic of a nation's pathological ideology of race displaced onto black culture, but it also stages and exposes its inconsistencies' (Konzett 2002b, 133).[1]

In line with these critics, I am centrally concerned with the elaborate balancing act Hurston performs as she strives to celebrate the distinctiveness of African American cultural forms, demonstrating an 'obvious weakness for racial essentialization' (Warnes 2006, 368), while also guarding against the pitfalls of 'race consciousness'. Opening up new areas for discussion, I pay special attention to formal patterning in Hurston's early folklore novel *Jonah's Gourd Vine* (1934) and her puzzling, even eccentric, revision of the Moses story in *Moses, Man of the Mountain* (1939) to extend these critical conversations.

Both novels employ an aesthetic of appropriation and revision; they recast biblical stories in an African American context, adding supplementary material from folklore, sermons and recent history. Analysis of patterns of juxtaposition and synthesis in the pages of these texts not only reveals Hurston's deliberate staging of contradictions and conjunctions; it also lays bare tensions that remain unacknowledged by the author. In *Jonah's Gourd Vine*, Hurston presents her novel as being representative of a specifically African American aesthetic, a style with its roots in a unified, nourishing black culture that spans the African diaspora. Attending to Hurston's formal techniques, however, demonstrates her openness to the formal experimentation of international modernism, with its jagged lines of intercultural influence. In *Moses, Man of the Mountain*, questions about hybridity and cultural distinctiveness take on greater urgency as Hurston addresses present political concerns. In this context, her manipulation of collage techniques, such as citation and grafting, to disrupt notions of cultural ownership is tinged with unease.

---

[1]   In the wake of the women's and Black Arts movements, early criticism tended to emphasize Hurston's depiction of an autonomous, organic folk culture. More recent commentators have focused upon inconsistencies that characterize Hurston's diverse *oeuvre*. Lynda Marion Hill, for instance, contends that Hurston 'displays essentialist ideas of her time while illustrating the contradictions implicit in racialist conceptions of culture' (Hill 1996, 2).

Jonah's Gourd Vine: A Novel Taken from ''tween de lids uh de Bible'

It is difficult to miss the composite form of *Jonah's Gourd Vine*. The loose plot, which relates the rise and fall of the preacher John Pearson, is often interrupted by collage-like fragments that are the very stuff of the novel. First, *Jonah's Gourd Vine* is packed with folk material that Hurston collected during her field trips, including songs, games and rituals. Anthropological vignettes frequently divert the narrative as Hurston halts the plot to discuss African American cultural forms. In her extended portrait of song-making and dancing at a barbecue on Pearson's farm, for instance, she illustrates her anthropological theory, elaborated most fully in 'Characteristics of Negro Expression', that African American culture comprises various components (*J* 60).[2] Secondly, the novel pivots on episodes concerning religious expression: John's prayer 'You are de same God' (*J* 145); his speech about being called to preach; a sketch of John's first sermon; a brief account of his 'Dry Bones' sermon; and, finally, the complete text of John's last sermon at Zion Hope. In keeping with Hurston's careful documentation of African American cultural forms, John's words derive from a sermon given by C.C. Lovelace at Eau Gallie in Florida on 3 May 1929, with minimal alterations (Hurston 1976, 239-44). Yet, as she explains in the glossary, when the preacher 'warms up' and stops trying 'to achieve what to him is grammatical correctness', Hurston adapts her fieldnotes, putting his speech into verse, complete with the '"ha"' that 'marks a breath' (*J* 316). She retains Lovelace's words, but recasts them in a literary form, conveying the sermon's poetic qualities. Finally, Hurston incorporates recent historical events into her narrative, including a fragmented, modernistic account of the Great Migration.

A number of commentators have asserted that Hurston's use of folkloric sources allows her to affirm essential racial difference. According to Anthony Wilson, *Jonah's Gourd Vine* eschews politics by staking its claim to cultural authenticity: he describes Hurston as 'a proponent of an almost primitivistic "pure art" of the folk against the politicized "propaganda" of Locke, DuBois and the New Negro' (Wilson 2003, 65-6). Eric Sundquist, whose deft reading of the novel foregrounds the 'exposed architectonics' (81) of its 'jagged' sermonic form (53), presses home Hurston's 'indulgent celebration of folk culture as the only undiluted voice of black America' (1983, 54). With this move, he interprets *Jonah's Gourd Vine* as an attempt to '[reconstruct] the notion of the novel in an African-American context' (Sundquist 1983, 53). For these critics, *Jonah's Gourd Vine*'s fragmentary form draws inspiration from specifically African American sources. Taking her text from ''tween de lids uh de Bible' (*J* 95), Hurston adapts African American sermonizing techniques to fiction. Finding precedent for her piecemeal structure in a sermon form that eschews the didacticism of the 'lecture' (250) for creative 'plunder' from the Bible (*J* 247), she flaunts her debts to nonliterary sources.

---

[2]   References to *Jonah's Gourd Vine* are abbreviated to *J*.

Such attempts to incorporate *Jonah's Gourd Vine* into an exclusively African American cultural tradition seem appropriate given Hurston's intentions for the novel. The original dedication for *Jonah's Gourd Vine* read: '[t]o the first and only real Negro poets in America – the preachers, who bring barbaric splendor of word and song into the very camp of the mockers. Go Gator, and muddy the water' (Lowe 1994, 90). Coupling a comic folkloric sign-off with a straightforward dedication, Hurston presents her novel as a celebration of the artistry, or 'barbaric splendor', of African American sermons. In a letter to James Weldon Johnson on 16 April 1934, she evinces a similar concern when she identifies Johnson's cycle of poems *God's Trombones: Seven Negro Sermons in Verse*, which recreates the content, language and style of the sermon poetically, and her own fictional account of John Pearson, 'a Negro, preacher who is neither funny nor an imitation Puritan ram-rod in pants. Just the human being and poet that he must be to succeed in a Negro pulpit', as the only literary works that capture the 'art' of black preaching (Kaplan 2002, 298).

There is undoubtedly a connection between Hurston's formal choices and the stylistic features of the folk sermon. Take, for instance, the apparently digressive description of the preacher at Lucy and John's choir practice:

> 'Ah takes mah tex' and Ah takes mah time.' He pursed up his wrinkled black face and glared all over the church. No one accepting the challenge he went on – 'Ah takes mah tex' 'tween de lids uh de Bible,' and slammed it shut. Another challenging glare about the room. Same results. 'Don't you take and meddle wid *whar* Ah takes mah tex'. Long ez Ah gives yuh de word uh Gawd, 'tain't none uh yo' business whar Ah gits it from' (*J* 95).

Hurston describes a specifically African American mode of religious expression with its own codes and rules. In accordance with Gary Layne Hatch's claim that '[t]he appeals to reason in Black folk sermons are embedded in the narratives, examples, comparisons, and biblical references chosen by the preacher' (1996, 228), Hurston's preacher refuses to offer a transparent, portable message. Instead, his sermon moves 'horizontally from one specific instance to the next' without offering an overarching interpretive framework (Hatch 1996, 239). Like the narrator of *Jonah's Gourd Vine*, who ranges from anthropology to fiction, he refuses to hurry the plot, taking his time to explore various biblical themes. Arguing that the congregation should not 'meddle' with where his text is from, he values nuanced reworking of scriptural allusions.

Rewriting the Jonah Story

Guided by this explanation, it is significant that *Jonah's Gourd Vine* elaborately rewrites a particular biblical text. In the story of Jonah's gourd vine, Jonah gets angry with God for showing mercy to the sinful people of Nineveh. He goes outside the city to observe the people's fate, and God prepares a gourd that shades him from the sun. The following morning, God sends a worm that makes the plant wither and die. Consequently, Jonah gets so hot that he blasphemously wishes for death. God tells him that if he laments the loss of the gourd, he should also be willing to show mercy to the people of Nineveh (Jonah 4.5-11).

Hurston takes this little known story as the text for an improvisatory performance that adapts sermonizing techniques to fiction. Through her fluid revision of the tale, she implies that sacred texts should not be rigidly embalmed because of an obsession with authenticity; they should be open to reinterpretation. In this sense, Hurston's treatment of biblical texts accords with Cheryl Wall's recent theory of 'worrying the line', in which she contends that 'nonliterary texts, such as blues, sermons, and recipes for conjure, insert themselves in African American tradition and worry this literary line' (Wall 2005a, 11).

Accounts of Hurston's reworking of the Jonah story are now fairly commonplace, even though critics find it difficult to agree on the significance of such revisions. To take only one example, John Lowe sees John's sexuality as the worm and Lucy as the comforting vine (Lowe 1994, 94) while Susan Meisenhelder interprets the novel as a feminist revision of a patriarchal text. It is less often remembered that Hurston's chosen text foregrounds certain features of the folk sermon, especially its investment in provisional meanings. In *A Biblical Text and its Afterlives: The Survival of Jonah in Western Culture*, Yvonne Sherwood notes that mainstream interpretations of the Jonah story, from Martin Luther and John Calvin to Victorian treatises responding to Darwinism and Herman Melville's *Moby-Dick*, rarely pay attention to the gourd vine incident because of its 'awkward surpluses' (2001, 268). Not only does Jonah twice blasphemously plead for death so that he can escape an apparently unjust world, but the biblical account also raises concern that God does not look after the faithful. If God is merciful, why does he treat Jonah so cruelly, sending the gourd and then smiting it? God's bizarre explanation for the vindictive plant-worm, relying as it does upon a body count of the people and livestock of Nineveh, also makes it difficult to pin down the story's moral message.

Perhaps it is precisely this ambiguity that appeals to Hurston. As a consequence of the '*equity* and *legitimacy* given to Jonah's voice' in his frank exchanges with God (Sherwood 2001, 273), the story suggests alternatives for dealing with transgression without privileging a particular solution. God shows mercy, but his motives appear suspect, tainted by an investment in commercial values. Moreover, Jonah questions theories of grace to such a degree that an abstract principle of mercy becomes untenable (Jonah 4.2).

In her depiction of John as a fallible leader, whose sexual philandering results in his eventual ostracism from the church, Hurston maximizes narrative ambiguity, exploring various attitudes towards his religious leadership. Some members of the church establishment, such as Reverend Harris, are uncomfortable with John's role as an exemplary figure. For Harris, the gourd vine is an appropriate metaphor for the talented yet flawed preacher who seems immune to plots to effect his downfall:

'Ah'd cut down dat Jonah's gourd vine in uh minute, if Ah had all de say-so' (*J* 230). By contrast, John's long-suffering wife, Lucy, always shows forgiveness.

Questions are raised about John's position as a preacher, but they ultimately remain unanswered. Towards the end of the novel, in a shift that reflects Jonah's lesson about the need for humility, John accepts his fallibility and abandons preaching. Realizing that he has been 'borne up on a silken coverlet of friendship', he experiences an epiphany comparable to Jonah's recognition of his absolute vulnerability to God's power (*J* 267). When congregational support is withdrawn, he becomes a scapegoat figure, blamed whenever anyone is 'in hard luck' or 'in debt' (293): '[h]e felt inside as if he had been taking calomel. The world had suddenly turned cold. It was not new and shiny and full of laughter. Mouldy, maggoty, full of suck-holes – one had to watch out for one's feet' (*J* 268). Hurston's substantial revision of the image of the plant-worm that smites Jonah's gourd invokes two further biblical tropes, the tree of life and the serpent, to illustrate John's feeling of weakness. In the past, John felt sheltered by his community, but, like Jonah, he now prays blasphemously for death, for release from 'dis sin-sick world' where '[n]obody pushed him uphill, but everybody was willing to lend a hand to the downward shove' (*J* 268). Yet, by juxtaposing John's humiliation with the community's enthusiastic response to his final sermon, in which poetic energy unites the congregation in 'frenzy', Hurston raises doubts about the instructiveness of such moral judgements (*J* 281).

Broadly speaking, *Jonah's Gourd Vine* engages the sermon as a specifically African American mode of religious expression, but emphasis on viable multiplicity and adaptation warns against any attempt to conceptualize cultural tradition in absolute terms. Hurston's novel is enriched by references taken freely from ''tween de lids uh de Bible' and secular texts. Rather like the unnamed preacher, she juxtaposes multiple sources without indicating where she 'gits it from' (*J* 95). That said, it would be a mistake to argue that these impulses always neatly resolve. Indeed, I part with Philip Joseph when he claims that Hurston sustains a consistent 'emphasis on imaginative mobility in the world while attacking entrenched parochialism and assertions of cultural purity' (Joseph 2002, 476). Instead, 'an understanding of African American identity as something that has itself been "collaged" by the vicissitudes of modern history' often becomes the platform for an assertion of cultural uniqueness in Hurston's work (Mercer 2005, 125). In line with early twentieth-century anthropological studies by Franz Boas and Melville Herskovits that emphasized the distinctive hybridity of African American racial identity, Hurston rather paradoxically affirms black originality by describing a process of cultural exchange.[3] Furthermore, emphasis upon an underlying cultural

---

[3]   In terms of Harlem Renaissance writers, the most influential articulation of this argument among Boasian anthropologists was Melville Herskovits's *The American Negro: A Study of Racial Crossing* (1928). Employing quantitative techniques derived from physical anthropology, Herskovits concluded that racial mixing in America had resulted in the formation of a new racial type: '[a]s has been shown, there are in his ancestry all of the

logic that remains unaltered by intercultural contact chimes with Boas's spatial model of cultural development, in which 'diverse sources' gradually blend into an integrated whole (Boas 1940, 217).

Attention to the set piece that represents the culmination of Hurston's fictional adaptation of the sermon form endorses such a reading of the novel. John's final sermon at Zion Hope, a transcription of an address given by C.C. Lovelace, is underpinned by an expansive biblical framework: he refers to Zachariah 13.6, where Jesus talks of the wounds he received in 'the house of [his] friends', and Isaiah 53.7, which describes Jesus as 'a lamb to the slaughter', wounded for our transgressions. However, rather than limiting himself to these cited religious texts, John's sermon is in fact a tissue of allusions to various Bible stories and vignettes, including the Creation (both in its biblical and folktale permutations), the Passion, the story of Christ calming the storm at Galilee (Mark 4.37-9), the Last Supper, Judgement Day (Rev. 20, Matt. 24, Joel 2, Acts 2), Ezekiel and the wheel, the description of the wounds of Christ in John 19 and God's Covenant. In short, it is a composite form.

By foregrounding C.C. Lovelace's technique of textual synthesis, Hurston reveals a poetic, allusive structure, in which the origin of individual pieces is secondary to their combined effect. For Hurston, blending diverse sources to forge a new cultural style is a distinctive feature of African American culture. 'Characteristics of Negro Expression', for instance, celebrates African American 'adaptability', arguing that 'nothing is too old or too new, domestic or foreign, high or low, for his use' (Hurston 1995b, 836). Yet, as David Kadlec reminds us, emphasis upon cultural expression that is always 'in the making' complicates Hurston's insistence upon cultural distinctiveness; it implies that African American culture is 'vibrant not because it [is] authentic or indigenous to any people or place', but because it is constantly evolving (Kadlec 2000b, 482).

The sermon's fusion of text, music and the vernacular showcases an aesthetic of reformulation:

---

principal racial elements of which humanity is composed – White, Negro, and Mongoloid. And from this mixture there is being welded, and is already discernible, a definite physical type which may be called the American Negro. It is not like any type from which it has come; it is not White; it is not Negro; it is not Mongoloid. It is all of them, and none of them' (1985, 19). In June 1928, Du Bois reviewed Herskovits's study in *The Crisis* alongside Claude McKay's *Home to Harlem* and Nella Larsen's *Quicksand*, but he made a significant shift of emphasis from physical anthropology, or race, towards an examination of cultural and social identity. Speaking of a 'singular group stability' that is not just biological, Du Bois commented that 'one feels that this group stability has been even more largely a matter of social and rational accomplishment than of mere physical descent' (Du Bois, 1928, 202).

> I heard de whistle of de damnation train
> Dat pulled out from Garden of Eden loaded wid cargo goin' to hell
> Ran at break-neck speed all de way thru de law
> All de way thru de prophetic age
> All de way thru de reign of kings and judges –
> Plowed her way thru de Jurdan
> And on her way to Calvary, when she blew for de switch
> Jesus stood out on her track like a rough-backed mountain
> And she threw her cow-catcher in His side and His blood ditched de train
> He died for our sins (*J* 280).

With its potted history of the Bible, this passage draws upon spirituals equating progress to heaven with a train journey, such as 'Get on Board, Little Children', 'If I Got my Ticket, Can I Ride', 'Dis Train' and 'Little Black Train'; spirituals that represent the wounds of Christ like 'See How They Done My Lord'; and what James Weldon Johnson, in *God's Trombones*, refers to as 'the "Train Sermon", in which both God and the devil were pictured as running trains, one loaded with saints, that pulled up in heaven, and the other with sinners, that dumped its load in hell' (Johnson 1961, 1). In accordance with Geneva Smitherman's claim that '[t]he orchestration of the sermon requires that Biblical persona be brought to life and the events recast in a present-day context', John gives such biblical imagery a new twist (1977, 151). Echoing the inventive adaptation of stock symbols that is central to the blues (Levine 1977, 160; Davis 1999, 66-90), he crafts an immediate version of Jesus' sacrifice, which is firmly rooted in the everyday, material world.

Eric Sundquist claims that 'the sermon's precise sources are purposefully obscured by the syntactical slippage and fusion of idea with incantatory sound' (Sundquist 1983, 83); but I would argue that Hurston maintains a sense that the sermon is a collage of references derived from various sources, not least because this serves to underline John's ability to improvise, turning a familiar story inside out to create something unexpected. John proves himself adept in the 'analogical reasoning' (239) that is fundamental to folk sermons, 'a type of "poetic" logic' (228), in which 'the logical progression moves horizontally from one specific instance to the next' (239) rather than making a case explicitly 'as a thesis with support or as claims backed by reasons and evidence' (Hatch 1996, 228). As in a jazz performance, there is a sense of upstaging the original – particularly in the startling image of the cowcatcher, a modern, technological spin on the crucifixion story – which focuses attention on creative reconfiguration of familiar cultural narratives.[4]

---

[4]   Lawrence Levine identifies the elasticity of religious imagery as a feature of both African American sermons and the blues. In particular, he notes that the Great Migration gave rise to inventive adaptations of the blues image of the train (1977, 160).

Modernist Echoes: African Themes in *Jonah's Gourd Vine*

For the most part, Hurston manipulates collage form to give shape to a definition of African American culture whereby 'diverse sources … are gradually worked into a single cultural unit' (Boas 1940, 217). Nowhere is this more apparent than at the close of the novel when Hurston describes the sermon at John's funeral, 'a barbaric requiem poem':

> On the pale white horse of Death. On the cold icy hands of Death. On the golden streets of glory. Of Amen Avenue. Of Halleluyah Street. On the delight of God when such as John appeared among the singers about His throne (*J* 311).

It is difficult to read this quotation without noticing Hurston's 'camouflaged use' of other writings, especially her incorporation of biblical diction and concepts into the text (Lowe 1994, 37). Merging imagery from the Book of Revelations, such as the 'horse of Death' and Jesus' throne, with shorthand references to the tuned streets in 'Amen Avenue' (a stock image in folkloric representations of heaven) reduces the sermon to a sequence of vivid snapshots that lay bare its collage patterning.[5] Hurston's fragmentary style stems from her immersion in African American cultural forms that involve 'active [audience] participation' (Smitherman 1977, 108). The reference to tuned streets, for instance, remains unglossed and readers must recall an earlier allusion to 'Amen Street' in John's final sermon at Zion Hope, piecing together the implications of Hurston's 'compelling insinuation' (Hurston 1995b, 835). Such writing demands a kind of participatory interpretation that Toni Morrison has characterized as 'holes and spaces [through which] the reader can come into it' (Tate 1994, 164). As witnesses to intense emotional events, readers are propelled towards awareness of multiple profane and sacred sources that are moulded into new forms in African American religious expression.

Yet, Hurston's reworking of the sermon form is animated by tensions that slip out of view when her interest in cross-cultural influences is overlooked. For a start, it would be a mistake to see the novel as a straightforward 'translation' of 'authentic' African American oral forms onto the written page. Hurston's formal and thematic choices were, of course, shaped by ideological considerations. Above all, she contests notions of aesthetic value circulating among white Americans and middle-class African Americans. As Genevieve West points out, Hurston's meticulous anthropological documentation must be interpreted against the backdrop of stereotypical portrayals of African American religion in popular texts such as Marc Connelly's play *The Green Pastures* (1930), with its condescending

---

[5]   In her portrait of African American folk visions of heaven for the Federal Writers' Project, Hurston writes: '[a]ll of the streets are a pleasure to walk on, but Hallelujah Avenue and Amen Street are "tuned" streets. They play tunes when they are walked upon. They do not play any particular or set tunes. They play whatever tunes the feet of the walker play as he struts' (Hurston 1999, 109).

portrait of a black Sunday school class's failure to understand a biblical lesson (West 2005, 58). Furthermore, as Hurston explains to Lewis Garnett in a letter dated 12 May 1934, *Jonah's Gourd Vine* recuperates a form 'utterly scorned by the "Niggerati"' (Kaplan 202, 304).

Of more immediate relevance to my formulation of the collage aesthetic is Hurston's sustained engagement with modernistic formal experimentation. In spite of Hurston's avowed emphasis upon cultural distinctiveness, it is clear that she draws inspiration from African American vernacular forms *and* modernist techniques, reworking modernist tropes from a particular cultural perspective. Hurston's manipulation of visual fragments that remain distinct resonates with a wider modernist interest in taking concrete objects as the starting point for a new, predominantly visual, aesthetic, a trend registered in such slogans as William Carlos Williams's '[n]o ideas but in things' and Ezra Pound's assertion that '[t]he natural object is always the *adequate* symbol' (Kadlec 2000a, 223). It is also worth mentioning Marianne Moore, who was well known for her poetic collages, with their 'tight juxtaposition of short quoted passages' from natural history, travel guides, magazine advertisements and scientific tracts (Kadlec 2000a, 167). Mixing sources derived from high and low art forms, Moore's free verse collages of the 1920s owe much to cubist techniques that 'set edges and fragments into arrangements that sharpened particular qualities by foregrounding distinctness rather than blending parts into a whole' (Kadlec 2000a, 165).

In suggesting that Hurston's formal techniques are comparable with such textual practices, it is not my intention to establish a direct line of influence from Euro-American modernism. Rather, I wonder if analysis of such intersections might expose an engagement with 'a discourse on the image' that 'was certainly available to [Hurston] and to the Harlem Renaissance milieu of which she was a part' (Jacobs 2001, 122). In accordance with her argument in 'Characteristics of Negro Expression', Hurston presents the improvisatory qualities of *Jonah's Gourd Vine* as part of an organic, even monolithic, cultural tradition. In doing so, she tidies up complex patterns of intercultural exchange so that her concept of authentic African American culture remains unchallenged. Nevertheless, Hurston's blending of vernacular cultural expression with modernistic preoccupations produces several revealing contradictions.

Some of these tensions stem from Hurston's thematic exploration of African cultural retentions. John's requiem, for instance, ends with an invocation to the African drum 'O-goe-doe, the voice of Death – that promises nothing, that speaks with tears only, and of the past' (*J* 312). African influences over the sermon form are 'loudly trumpeted' throughout *Jonah's Gourd Vine* (Warnes 2006, 376), beginning with Hurston's first account of John's preaching: '[h]e rolled his African drum up to the altar, and called his Congo Gods by Christian names' (*J* 145-6). Such an account of wholesale African cultural survivals prefigures Melville Herskovits's influential theory that in spite of striking differences between African languages and cultures, there were enough deep-seated commonalities to ensure cultural retentions in 'a generalized form' (Lawal 2002, 43). Downplaying the violent catastrophe of the Middle Passage, Hurston describes an authentic, seamless Black Atlantic culture. Hurston's emphasis upon the vitality of African culture as transplanted to the American context must be aligned with a broader Harlem Renaissance effort to combat prevalent racist depictions of Africa as a place outside history and development.[6]

At the same time, African cultural retentions, in *Jonah's Gourd Vine*, are veiled in an ambiguity that reaches beyond words, towards feelings that can only be expressed through a kind of visual shorthand. Comparison with Hurston's later representation of Nanny in *Their Eyes Were Watching God* illuminates this gesture towards the inexpressible: 'Old Nanny sat there rocking Janie like an infant and thinking back and back. Mind-pictures brought feelings, and feelings dragged out dramas from the hollows of her heart' (*TE* 32). Nanny's '[m]ind-pictures', which are suggestive of Hurston's hieroglyphics in 'Characteristics of Negro Expression', allow for representation of feelings that usually remain beyond the grasp of words. Through this visual mode of expression, Hurston unearths buried layers of history and repressed memories, bypassing conscious thought to expose the empty 'hollows of her heart'. In an understated way, she acknowledges the trauma of slavery.

On one level, such 'hieroglyphics' affirm black culture through an Egyptian figure suggestive of complexity and poetic economy as well as 'historical depth' (Jacobs 2001, 122). Even so, Hurston ends up reiterating certain primitivist tropes, especially in her emphasis upon African mystery and silence. Africa, for Hurston, is primarily a symbolic place, figured in general rather than specific terms as a privileged site of cultural origin. While Hurston's emphasis upon African cultural retentions represents a significant departure from the shallow exoticism that often characterized European engagement with African art, *Jonah's Gourd Vine*, with its investment in a heavily mythologized Africa, remains marked, to some degree, by a transatlantic discourse about Africa that inspired formal experimentation among figures as diverse as Pablo Picasso, Alain Locke and Josephine Baker.

African American Modernism and Collage of the Image

Hurston consistently frames her novel with reference to the aesthetic codes and practices of an organic African American folk tradition. In this context, it is significant that she incorporates a theme of audience engagement into *Jonah's Gourd Vine*, providing readers with a loose interpretive template. The novel is scattered with vignettes that document the African American congregation's

---

[6]   In his 1915 study *The Negro*, for instance, Du Bois assembled considerable archaeological and historical evidence to challenge Hegel's view that Africa was 'no historical part of the world'. He also 'wanted to face the ignorant racism of eminent politicians and spokepersons at home', who claimed that all African cultural achievements owed something to European influence (Lorini 2001, 171).

responses to various sermons. This serves to authenticate a particular version of the sermon, positioning the novel squarely inside a specifically African American cultural tradition. For instance, the need to construct a sermon from a tissue of biblical citations is underlined by Sister Hall's 'gloat[ing]' reaction to John's 'Dry Bones' sermon. She says, '[d]at's uh preachin' piece uh plunder', praising John's dexterous manipulation of allusions stolen without acknowledgment from the Bible (*J* 247). Faced with the self-professed 'race man' Reverend Felton Cozy, Sister Boger and Sister Pindar quickly agree: 'Ah ain't heard whut de tex' wuz' (*J* 248).

For these interpreters, Cozy's performance fails because of its lack of biblical allusiveness. Rather than involving his audience in an experiential journey, Cozy's 'sermon' is a closed text, a list of facts that 'solves the race problem' without making reference to a source text (*J* 248). He plods through his evidence methodically until he reaches his final point, 'twelfth and lastly' (*J* 249). Since Cozy's speech is not underpinned by a deep knowledge of the 'word of God' Hurston's ideal readers, the African American congregation, dismiss it as a 'lecture' rather than a 'sermon' (*J* 250). Throughout the novel, Hurston treads a delicate line between insisting upon the openness of black discourse and arguing for preservation of an authentic culture, but the implicit assumption here is that Cozy's performance panders to white American values.[7]

Notwithstanding Hurston's careful framing of her novel, correspondences between such orchestration of biblical quotations and modernist juxtaposition of disparate fragments suggest a double context for her stylistic choices. Such affinities complicate Hurston's narrative of cultural authenticity, revealing a collage-like structure, which draws inspiration from African American vernacular culture and modernistic experimentation. Reference to Eisenstein's filmic montage, for instance, in which 'he spliced together individual shots with no transitional material, creating disjunctions in the finished text', sheds light on the significance of stylistic incongruity in *Jonah's Gourd Vine* (Carroll 2005, 27). According to Eisenstein, montage facilitated an oblique method of communication, in which fragments were placed side by side to reveal 'a third something', created by juxtaposition of disparate pieces (Carroll 2005, 28).

As Anne Elizabeth Carroll has convincingly demonstrated, theories about the political and aesthetic effects of stylistic incongruity illuminate the politics of form in Harlem Renaissance texts (2005, 27-9). These insights can be brought to bear on a pivotal, if rarely discussed, moment in *Jonah's Gourd Vine* when Hurston writes with an eye to contemporary events, offering a sharp assessment of the Great Migration. At this juncture, a discursive shift of register is echoed

---

[7]   This association between 'the white man's prayer' and 'the lecture' is explicit in Hurston's essay 'The Sanctified Church': '[t]he real, singing Negro derides the Negro who adopts the white man's religious ways in the same manner. They say of that type of preacher, "Why he don't preach at all. He just lectures." And the way they say the word "lecture" makes it sound like horse-stealing' (Hurston 1995e, 904).

at the level of form. The narrative breaks down into imagist fragments and an authoritative, quasi-scientific narrator provides brief snapshots of interrelated events: World War I, armistice, a '[w]orld gone money mad' and mass migration of African Americans to the northern cities in search of work (*J* 235). Speaking in Standard English, the narrator puts migration in its national and international context, in such a way as to challenge 'the premise that the worlds inscribed in [Hurston's] work must be mapped outside of national modernity, and mapped, instead, in a space characterized as "mythic", "spiritual", "nostalgic", or "anti-historical"' (Duck 2001, 265).

Adopting a transparent, even photographic, documentary technique, Hurston addresses the causes of migration, establishing connections between economic growth, migration and yearning for improved status created by life abroad as an African American soldier. Anonymous African American voices punctuate this detached, impressionistic historical account, communicating their personal experiences of discrimination and racism in modern America. An unnamed figure, for example, talks bitterly about treatment of black soldiers in the war: '[d]e black man ain't got no voice but soon ez war come who de first man dey shove in front? De nigger!' (*J* 233).[8]

In line with Eisenstein's description of a political meaning generated by juxtaposition, the speaker's isolated statement, with its unmistakable vernacular idiom, is imbued with political urgency because it is articulated in the midst of the narrator's historical overview and alongside various unnamed African American voices, who touch on such topics as the relative merits of Presidents Roosevelt and Wilson, and technology's place in the modern world. Coming from nowhere in the novel, this is a passage that refuses to settle on a single, authoritative perspective. Instead, a variety of discourses are mobilized in an effort to account for migration. In a sharp break with the social uplift envisaged by Alain Locke in *The New Negro*, enlightened individuals do not make an informed decision to move North, setting an example for others in the community; they simply conform to natural urges, following an unconscious herd instinct ('men moved like the great herds before the glaciers' (*J* 232)). An alternative, economic explanation is implied by Hurston's account of technology's insatiable appetite for more 'hands',

---

[8]   There is perhaps a sideways glance here to an earlier debate about the impact of African American soldiers on campaigns for racial equality, vividly captured in the pages of *The Crisis*. In the space of a year, Du Bois journeyed from the undiluted optimism of his famous July 1918 editorial 'Close Ranks', in which he implored African Americans to set aside their struggle for racial equality during a time of national crisis, towards a militancy forced upon him by continuing revelations that the United States military actively sought to maintain the colour line in Europe. Faced with evidence of entrenched racism, including an official document circulated to the French that demanded wholesale adoption of American racist attitudes towards black soldiers, Du Bois issued a second battle cry in May 1919: '[w]e *return*. We return *from fighting*. We return *fighting*. Make way for democracy!' (Carroll 2005, 52-3).

a description tinged with a 1930s awareness of the fragility of post-war boom ('the wheels and marts were hungry' (*J* 235)). But Hurston also makes room for various insiders' perspectives too, capturing the cultural repercussions of travel to the North, and even to Europe, in energetic code-switching that mixes a smattering of French with African American folkloric tropes: 'Blacker de berry sweeter de juice. Come tuh mah pick, gimme uh good black gal. De wine wuz sour, and Ah says parlez vous, hell!' (*J* 234).

Given that Hurston sounds an apocalyptic note throughout this passage, readers are left in little doubt of her anxiety about the effects of migration on the South. Yet, she does not express such reservations directly. Instead, readers are compelled towards a recognition that political and social marginalization persists, notwithstanding the sacrifices of black soldiers during the war and America's dependence on African American labour.

By recording one African American's view of W.E.B. Du Bois, Hurston takes further this exploration of the politics of form, raising questions about the political import of Harlem Renaissance literature:

> DuBois? Who is dat? 'Nother smart nigger? Man, he can't be smart ez Booger T.! Whut did dis DuBois ever do? He writes up books and papers, hunh? Shucks! dat ain't nothin', anybody kin put down words on uh piece of paper. Gimme da paper sack and lemme see dat pencil uh minute. Shucks! Writing! Man Ah thought you wuz talkin' 'bout uh man whut had done sumpin (*J* 234).

In accordance with Mae Gwendolyn Henderson's claim that 'simultaneity of discourse' is a common feature of African American women's writing, it is difficult to pin down Hurston's opinion here (Henderson 1990, 17). She overwrites her own voice with that of an informant, sharing narrative authority with an ordinary citizen, just as she does in *Mules and Men*. Such ventriloquy inserts this episode into a contemporary debate about the political significance of African American literature. As critics have often noted, particularly during the Harlem Renaissance, many writers were searching for an appropriate aesthetic format to represent African American life and culture, often clinging to an assumption that the arts could undermine racism. Most famously, in 'Criteria of Negro Art', published in *The Crisis* in 1926, Du Bois claimed that artists have a crucial role to play in the promotion of a world of 'truth and freedom' (Du Bois 1995, 512). For Du Bois, 'all art is propaganda' in the struggle for a social and political 'voice' (514): 'until the art of the black folk compels recognition they will not be rated as human' (Du Bois 1995, 515). This link between art and politics, which Christa Schwarz has termed the 'burden of representation' (2003, 32), was under discussion throughout the 1920s and beyond, and it often became a source of tension between writers, and even within a single author's work.[9]

9   In his provocative essay 'To Certain of our Philistines', Alain Locke contends that an excessive concern to 'compensate the attitudes of prejudice ... threatens a truly racial art

Hurston's speaker questions such arguments, imagining a practical alternative to cultural politics. For this man, the liberal arts are of little consequence to the southern folk when compared with practical benefits reaped from Booker T. Washington's investment in vocational education. In this context, writing and abstract debate seem an unnecessary distraction from the struggle for equality. Nevertheless, Hurston does not simply reject the political influence of art. Employing modernistic techniques of discordant juxtaposition, she crafts a highly individual portrait of the Great Migration, which substantially revises the conventions of the migration narrative identified by Farah Jasmine Griffin (1995, 3). Hurston departs from familiar generic tropes, such as the 'migrant's confrontation with the urban landscape' (64) and emphasis upon southern 'violence as the principal catalyst for migration', shifting attention to the effects of migration on southern communities (Griffin 1995, 18). Re-imagining generic conventions allows Hurston to contest prevailing ideas about migration, including Locke's equation of the Great Migration with uplift from 'medieval America to modern' (*N* 6).

Hurston's technique of breaking up the flow of familiar narrative forms is analogous to collage; she juxtaposes allusions and quotations, encouraging readers to rethink their assumptions. Reference to Egypt, for instance, brings to mind a variety of intertexts, including African American spirituals, which established a parallel between Hebrew enslavement and American slavery to articulate veiled resistance to white domination, and *Chicago Defender* advertisements that presented migration as 'The Flight out of Egypt' (Lemann 1991, 16). Hurston pursues this link between ancient Egypt and the American South to different effect, equating depopulation of the South with Moses' curse of death on Egypt's first-born sons (*J* 238). In other words, she revises familiar tropes to unsettle assumptions about migration.

Reference to Booker T. Washington's famous 'Atlanta Address', especially his description of southern African Americans as 'hands' who could either aid the southern economy or drag 'the load downward', suggests a caveat to any straightforward endorsement of Washington's economic pragmatism (1997, 596). Hurston's description of "'Goin' Nawth'" (*J* 238) formulates a tension between Washington's emphasis upon economic self-improvement and the pressures of modernity upon an African American population in the midst of migration. For Hurston, mythic accounts of a journey to '[t]he land of promise' (*J* 239) endorse a quest for economic success, threatening to mask continuing exploitation of African Americans labour, or 'muscled hands' (*J* 235). Applying Washington's vocabulary of 'hands', which was, perhaps, laced with subversive threat, to a description of the Great Migration, creates a sense of disjunction that confronts readers with the brutal reality of continuing economic exploitation of African Americans in the

---

with the psychological bleach of "lily-whitism"' (Locke 1983b, 161). Yet, in his landmark anthology *The New Negro*, he could not resist the idea that a significant African American contribution to American culture would ultimately lead to political emancipation and the forging of 'a new American attitude' (*N* 10).

1930s.[10] With its glancing allusions to, and subversion of, Washington's narrative of economic and social uplift, Hurston reminds us that a rhetoric of dehumanization underpins such discourse, an insight underscored by insistent repetition of the synecdoche 'hands'.

Although critics have often analysed Hurston's innovations with dialect, her technique of textual synthesis has received less attention. To address this gap, I have investigated Hurston's adaptation of the sermon form to fiction in *Jonah's Gourd Vine*. Attention to patterns of juxtaposition in the novel not only reveals Hurston's engagement with modernistic techniques; it also allows for an alternative intervention in continuing debates about the political import of her writing. In line with recent analysis of the juxtaposition of image and text in Harlem Renaissance texts, Hurston's innovation with form has political significance. However, this is a different kind of politics to the social realism prized by Richard Wright and Sterling A. Brown, who both raised concerns about Hurston's apparently apolitical stance.[11] Attention to the complex patterning of allusions in *Jonah's Gourd Vine* reveals that Hurston complicates assumptions about the role of African American writers, refusing to conform to Wright's 'blueprint' for the protest novel. Instead, she mines the open-ended sermon form to tackle such subjects as the Great Migration and cultural politics in an indirect, oblique fashion.

Moses and Nation-building: Zora Neale Hurston's *Moses, Man of the Mountain* and Edward Said's *Freud and the Non-European*

Attending to the formal qualities of *Jonah's Gourd Vine* reveals that Hurston's focus on specifically African American cultural forms is inflected by her involvement in the formal experimentation of transatlantic modernism. By the time Hurston wrote *Moses, Man of the Mountain*, in 1939, this international frame of reference had

---

[10]   In the 'Atlanta Address', 'hand' imagery is always ambivalent, suggesting at once racial separation and interdependence. When Washington states that '[i]n all things that are purely social we can be separate as the fingers, yet one as the hand in all things essential to mutual progress', he appears to accept the inevitability of segregation (1997, 515). Yet, his account of 'nearly sixteen millions of hands' who could make or break the southern economy exposes the South's utter dependence upon African American labour. See Baker (1987) for a discussion of Washington's 'liberating manipulation of masks' (1987, 25).

[11]   In his notorious review of *Their Eyes Were Watching God* in the *New Masses*, Richard Wright indicts Hurston for her failure to represent the realities of hunger, racism and violence in the South (Wright 1937, 25-6). These reservations about Hurston's avoidance of social realism were shared by many of her contemporaries. Sterling A. Brown's 1936 review of *Mules and Men*, for example, is underpinned by a similar anxiety: '[t]he tales ring genuine, but there seem to be omissions. The picture is too pastoral, with only a bit of grumbling about hard work, or a few slave anecdotes that turn the tables on old master' (Sollors 1990, 37). For Brown, Hurston's failure to depict the social inequalities of rural life tips the collection towards political conservatism.

expanded beyond technique to include subject matter as well. Any consideration of *Moses, Man of the Mountain*, a novel that rewrites the biblical story of Exodus, adding supplementary material from folktales, African American history, conjure stories and myths, must look beyond America. In revising the Moses story, Hurston opens out the narrative beyond its original frame of reference, making (oblique and explicit) points of comparison with American slavery, the rise of Nazism and European colonialism.

Hurston's method is analogous to découpage and assemblage: she uproots a familiar biblical narrative from its expected context, adding fragments derived from a variety of historical and cultural contexts. In this way, she demonstrates the story's flexibility, its potential as a vehicle for speaking about oppression across the globe. Even though the novel is structured according to a clearly defined sequential plot, unexpected juxtapositions create a sense of defamiliarization. Hurston's careful framing of *Moses* in the introduction, for instance, mentions both 'the common concept of Moses in the Christian world' and 'other concepts of Moses abroad in the world' (*M* xxiii). Such juxtapositions encourage readers to hold in view the biblical account of Moses, while introducing new narrative elements, which force them to reassess their preconceptions. These components, however, do not cohere into an integrated whole. Take, for example, the novel's opening, with its stark juxtaposition of an epigraph from Deuteronomy with an account of life in 'New Egypt' for the Hebrews under Pharaoh's rule. Elements of Hurston's description are derived from the Bible, but she inserts incongruous details, including a sketch of Pharaoh's secret police force, which owes much to the rise of totalitarianism in the 1930s. Such incongruent historical referents generate a sense of rupture and discontinuity.

A comparable technique of ahistoricist layering governs the treatment of Egyptian motifs and iconography in Harlem Renaissance visual art. Aaron Douglas, Loïs Mailou Jones and Charles Dawson, among others, updated ancient Egyptian motifs, incorporating them into modern cityscapes in such a way as to imply cultural continuities between Africa and African America. Douglas's *Building More Stately Mansions* (1944), for instance, is a painted collage of images taken from disparate contexts, including an Egyptian syrinx, a modern construction crane, a pagoda and a church. Reference to Egypt comes in the context of a layered, complex articulation of African American cultural identity, which proceeds by suggestion rather than explicit announcement to imply points of contact between ancient and modern, old and new, Africa and America.

As in these flexible renderings of Egyptian themes, Hurston's retelling of Exodus is a jumble of ancient and modern narrative elements, in which allusions to Sigmund Freud collide with references to the ancient Book of Thoth. As in 'Characteristics of Negro Expression', Hurston's collaging practice exposes contradictions in her thinking about race. Employing an international scope of reference that establishes points of contact between apparently disparate cultures, *Moses, Man of the Mountain* lays bare tensions inherent in Hurston's desire to celebrate African American culture while warning against the dangers of 'race consciousness'.

In exploring these issues, I want to make an unexpected juxtaposition of my own, a theoretical move that is, perhaps, in keeping with the eclectic spirit of Hurston's novel. To capture the implications of Hurston's rich layering of incongruent historical referents, including allusions to the Book of Thoth and Hitler's rise to power in 1930s Germany, I turn to Edward Said's *Freud and the Non-European* (2003), a critical text that assesses the Moses story as a nation-building narrative. Pairing Hurston and Said continues Said's project of seeing authors 'contrapuntally', as figures whose writings travel across temporal and cultural boundaries. And it also exposes imperialism as a neglected, if submerged, context for Hurston's response to nationalism in *Moses, Man of the Mountain*.

As a cultural critic, Edward Said's reputation rests, at least in part, upon his bold reinterpretations of canonical texts, especially his exposure of neglected connections between celebrated European literature and the spread of European imperialism. In his late work, *Freud and the Non-European* (2003), he adapts this transnational approach to Sigmund Freud's notoriously difficult treatise, *Moses and Monotheism*, in which Freud insists that Moses, the founder of Judaism, was an Egyptian. Exploring Freud's work in the context of contemporary Middle Eastern politics, Said juxtaposes the political realities of an Israeli state that 'took very specific legal and political positions' to 'seal off' Jewish identity from non-Jewish influences, with a founding narrative that places the religion's source outside the Jewish community (Said 2003, 43).[12]

For Said, such an argument has two main implications. First, he exposes any attempt to narrow Judaism into an exclusive, singular identity, or a 'nationalist or religious herd' (*F* 53), as a betrayal of the religion's pluralist history. Secondly, opening out his treatise from specific to general terms, he uses Freud's 'unresolved sense of identity' (*F* 55) as the basis for a critique of what he has referred to elsewhere as an 'identitarian consciousness': the belief that individuals can be labelled and defined strictly according to rigid categories of identity such as black and white, Western and Oriental (Said 1993, 330). Making a case against movements that try to simplify or purify, he argues that identity is always flawed and complicated. According to Said, this is the crucial point of Freud's insight: the theorization of identity as a kind of fissure can speak to other 'besieged identities as well', offering a narrative of human connectedness that crosses racial and national boundaries, even if it cannot mend broken identities in an act of 'utopian reconciliation' (*F* 54). Writing against the grain of unsullied originary sources and enclosed traditions, Said violates national, religious and racial borders, finding interconnection between groups where others seek to uphold separation.

The main focus of my analysis here is Hurston's representation of Moses as a figure who is of a different ethnic and cultural group from the Hebrews he liberates. Published in the same year that Freud's *Moses and Monotheism* appeared

---

[12]   References to Edward Said's *Freud and the Non-European* are abbreviated to *F*.

in English translation, Hurston's rewriting of the Moses story adapts the Book of Exodus into a collage-like form, adding supplementary material from folktales, African American history, conjure stories and myth. Taking Said's commentary on Freud as my starting point, I argue that Hurston's novel scrutinizes the dangers and ambiguities of nationalism. Hurston's treatment of nationalism can be contextualized against the backdrop of Boasian anthropology, which, as Barbara Foley and others have shown, sought to separate nation from race (Foley 2003, 155). But I wonder if Said's analysis of Freud might also offer a useful method for interpreting Hurston's 1939 novel. In particular, Said's postcolonial reading of Freud, which lays bare Freud's Eurocentric assumptions, can be mobilized to examine the anti-imperialist moments in *Moses, Man of the Mountain*.

This immediately raises the fraught issue of ahistoricism, triggering a series of questions about whether it is appropriate to establish conceptual links between writers from different periods, who are, in this case, also separated by gender and race. After all, the Palestinian migrant, Edward Said was a committed political activist, who not only sought to unmask overt and covert collaborations between politics and culture in his cultural criticism, but who also consistently attacked Zionism as a harmful manifestation of imperialism, calling for reconciliation between Jews and Palestinians. In contrast, the African American anthropologist and novelist Zora Neale Hurston, who is most famous for her fictional representations of the rural South in the 1930s, held complex, sometimes irreconcilable political views.

Hurston's work cannot be reduced to a unified whole: close analysis of her diverse *oeuvre*, which encompasses anthropological, autobiographical and fictional texts, shows that she 'simultaneously insisted upon substantive racial difference and no difference at all' (Wallace 1990, 174). Indeed, Hurston has often been attacked for her supposed conservatism. During her lifetime, she faced sustained criticism from male African American writers such as Richard Wright, Sterling A. Brown and Alain Locke for what they regarded as her evasion of racial responsibility, her failure to confront the hardships of poverty and racism in the American South through social realism.[13] More recently, the almost excessive

---

[13] The most famous example of this attitude is Richard Wright's review of *Their Eyes Were Watching God* in *New Masses*, in which he indicts Hurston for spiriting away contemporary hardships from her southern town of Eatonville. Likening her novel to the damaging tradition of 'ministrelsy', Wright criticizes Hurston's lack of political commitment, claiming that the novel 'carries no theme, no message, no thought' (Wright 1937, 25-6). These reservations about Hurston's departure from social realism towards what is often cast as a mode of pastoralism – or even utopianism – are echoed in the critical reception of Hurston's anthropological collection *Mules and Men*. For example, in his 1936 review, Alain Locke felt compelled to emphasize that Hurston's work does not mirror social reality: 'there is yet something too Arcardian about [her] ... work, considering the framework of contemporary American life and fiction. The depression has broken this peasant Arcady even in the few places where it still persisted, and while it is humanly interesting and

attention to Hurston's work in contemporary criticism has worried commentators such as Hazel Carby, Ann duCille and Michele Wallace, who have questioned what is at stake in such a reception. Carby, for instance, explains Hurston's popularity inside and outside the academy in political terms, claiming that her 'representation of African-American culture as primarily rural and oral' enables readers to retreat into a rural idyll, avoiding engagement with the realities of racism and inequality in contemporary American society (1994, 31).

My juxtaposition of these two writers is made more precarious by the fact that Said's conceptualization of nationalism grapples with the legacies of the Holocaust from an avowed Palestinian perspective. Said's theorization of the nation is thus shaped by the Nazi slaughter of millions of Jews, a reality that Hurston, writing in 1939, could not possibly know.

Yet, in spite of the many differences between these writers, it is instructive to read Said alongside Hurston because of their common interest in the myth of Moses as a nation-building story. Pairing *Moses, Man of the Mountain* with *Freud and the Non-European* continues Said's project of seeing authors 'contrapuntally', as 'figures whose writing travels across temporal, cultural and ideological boundaries' (*F* 24).[14] Said's concept of contrapuntality, elaborated most fully in *Culture and Imperialism*, challenges the idea that literature can be divided up into discrete cultural or national traditions. By developing a metaphor that conjures up an image of 'independently directed harmonizations and contacts' (Brennan 2005, 48), Said remains alert to the interactions between 'views and experiences that are ideologically and culturally closed to each another', such as imperialism and resistance to it (Said 1993, 37). Thus, he famously reads *Mansfield Park* with C.L.R. James and Eric Williams, giving emphasis to historical realities that are silenced in Jane Austen's novel (Said 1993, 95-116).

In *Freud and the Non-European*, Said puts Freud's work 'into contact with cultural, political and epistemological formations undreamed of by … its author', interpreting Freud's insights about Jewish identity in the light of Israel's nationalist policies after 1948 and post-World War II decolonization (*F* 25). In other words, he extends Freud's insights beyond a narrow European perspective, opening up Freud's ideas to an understanding of later, global historical concerns. Reading Hurston's novel through *Freud and the Non-European* might be read as an extension of this project, an attempt to discover how Said's thoughts about the narrowly defined notions of identity that circumscribe individuals in the Middle East and the colonial context might illuminate Hurston's exploration of African American identity in the 1930s. If, as Said claims, Freud is 'an overturner and a

---

refreshing enough, it is a critical duty to point out that it is so extinct that our only possible approach to it is the idyllic and the retrospective' (Sollors 1990, 61).

[14]   The most striking examples of this 'contrapuntal' approach occur in *Culture and Imperialism*: Said reads Jane Austen's *Mansfield Park* in the light of British imperialism, and Joseph Conrad's *Heart of Darkness* alongside contemporary postcolonial writers like V.S. Naipaul and Tayib Salih.

re-mapper of accepted or settled geographies and genealogies' who 'lends himself especially to rereading in different contexts' (*F* 27), what insights do his treatise on identity and nationalism provide with regard to Hurston's representation of nation-building in *Moses, Man of the Mountain*?

My concern is not simply to establish a direct line of influence between Freud and Hurston. As Robert Hemenway notes, Hurston may well have encountered Freud's ideas about Moses' Egyptian heritage in the psychoanalytical journal *Imago*, which published the first two chapters of *Moses and Monotheism* in 1937 (1980, 257). Given her close association with the German-speaking Franz Boas and his circle, which included figures with a keen interest in Freudian psychoanalysis such as Alfred L. Kroeber, it seems likely that Hurston was conversant with Freud's controversial claims that Moses was an Egyptian and that his monotheistic religion was in fact based upon the religious beliefs of a heretical Egyptian ruler called Ikhnaton (Hegeman 1999, 83-5). There are certainly some intriguing connections between Freud and Hurston's representations of Moses, most notably a shared refusal 'to set aside truth in favour of supposed national interests' (Freud 1939, 3). Nevertheless, an awareness of Said's discussion of Freud shadows forth an alternative interpretation of both Hurston and Freud, foregrounding an analysis of imperialism that remains marginal to Freud's 1939 study.[15]

Reading *Moses, Man of the Mountain* through Said adds to a growing body of work that places Hurston in an international frame, a critical trend that represents a break with the dominant critical paradigm of the 1970s and 1980s, which tended to privilege her as a custodian of an 'authentic' African American culture.[16] This move beyond the confines of American race politics into a broader, international context is not a new thing. Deborah E. McDowell's introduction to the 1991 edition of the novel, for instance, demonstrates that '[t]he shadow of Nazism is cast from the beginning of *Moses, Man of the Mountain*' (1991, xv). More recently, in separate studies of *Moses, Man of the Mountain*, Barbara Johnson and Melanie J. Wright have developed McDowell's suggestive approach, offering a sustained analysis of the novel's engagement with European events. Paying detailed attention to Hurston's pointed comparison between Pharaoh as a dictator who justifies his victimization of the Hebrews through a newly invigorated race-based nationalism and Moses' formation of a nation founded on miscegenation, they interpret *Moses, Man of the Mountain* as a critique of events in Germany leading up to World War II. Taking a rather different approach, Delia Caparoso Konzett has demonstrated

---

[15]   Said's key insight in *Freud and the Non-European* is his recognition that Freud speaks of empire in a way that locates it safely in the past. While Freud presents Moses as an imperial ruler who wants to build an 'empire', his argument is played out without any reference to contemporary European colonialism (Freud 1939, 32).

[16]   The classic example of this approach is Alice Walker's important collection of essays *In Search of Our Mothers' Gardens*, which presents Hurston as an exceptional figure who maintained a deep affinity with the folk culture of the South at a moment when her contemporaries were 'still infatuated with things European' (1983, 85).

Hurston's commitment to exploring cultural continuities across the African diaspora. Konzett argues that Hurston's Moses is a self-conscious amalgamation of African, African American and Caribbean myths: he is both the great liberator and nation-builder represented in southern U.S. spirituals, and a mystical figure derived from African American and Caribbean hoodoo culture, associated with magic and shamanism (Konzett 2002a, 107).

Recourse to Edward Said develops this critical trend, bringing into focus the way in which Hurston's adaptation of the Moses myth strains towards an international perspective. Hurston's tale of emancipation, freedom and nation-building exceeds national and historical boundaries: her Hebrews speak in African American dialect, but straightforward allegory is undermined by rich layering of incongruent historical referents, including allusions to the ancient Book of Thoth, Hitler's rise to power in Germany in the 1930s, and parallels with the exploitation of colonized peoples in the early twentieth century. In line with Laura E. Donaldson's claim that Hurston rewrites the Exodus story with an anticolonial slant, the pairing of Said and Hurston underlines how imperialism provides a neglected context for Hurston's novel (Donaldson 1992, 105). This strand of the novel is most prominent in Hurston's sustained investigation of monuments as a vehicle for the formation of national identity.

While my comparative approach offers a framework for considering Hurston's engagements with nationalism, it is important to recognize the limitations of this ahistorical method. Such a reading must be supplemented by contextualization of the diverging concerns of two writers who are separated by gender, race and several generations. Important resonances in *Moses, Man of the Mountain* are missed if we fail to contextualize Hurston's representation of nation-building in the light of debates about nationalism during the Harlem Renaissance. In *Spectres of 1919: Class and Nation in the Making of the New Negro*, Barbara Foley argues that many Harlem Renaissance writers expressed a blind faith in nationalism as a 'fundamentally transformative politics' that could 'emancipate those bearing the yoke of oppression and exploitation' (2003, viii). Few African American writers could resist the lure of nationalist arguments as a means of combating racism, but, as Foley astutely points out, by countering "bad", race-based nationalism with "good", democratic or anti-racist cultural nationalism, writers like Alain Locke sometimes unwittingly repeated the essentialism they intended to challenge (2003, ix).

To date, there has been little discussion of Hurston's work in these critical conversations. Part of my aim in this chapter is to suggest that *Moses*, a novel centrally concerned with the pitfalls – and perhaps the inescapability – of nationalism, must be inserted into this debate.[17] Given that Franz Boas fought against racism on both sides of the Atlantic and was a key influence on Hurston, one important strand of my discussion will be to consider the complexity of Hurston's engagement with his pronouncements on nationalism.

---

[17]   See Dawahare (2003); Foley (2003).

Testing the Limits of 'national faith'

With this proviso in mind, I will now consider how Hurston and Said recast the Moses story in exploring the dangers of nationalism. Both writers consider the relationship between race and religion as the basis for nationalist identification in order to dispute narrow nationalisms that exclude certain groups from full citizenship. Said places his discussion in a specific historical context, posing questions about Jewishness as a vehicle for citizenship in Israel after 1948. Describing Israel as a state for Jews in which non-Jews 'were juridically made foreigners', he describes a slippage between the categories of religion and race, suggesting that the privileging of any category of identity as absolute can result in intolerance, dogmatism and fanaticism (*F* 42). In the case of Israel, he argues that the formation of a state in which one community was set above all others resulted in 'a re-schematization of races and peoples' that repeated the binary logic of colonialism where one race or people was viewed as fully human while others were regarded as less than human (*F* 41).

For Said, Freud's concept of identity as complex and flawed offers a route out of such binary thinking, a challenge to 'any doctrinal attempt that might be made to put Jewish identity on a sound foundational basis, whether religious or secular' (*F* 45). Said's use of the word 'doctrinal' is important because he implies that the blind faith he associates with religion is also a characteristic of racial or 'secular' categories that assign individuals the status of insider or outsider, essentializing identity while denying the realities of hybridity. It is worth pausing for a moment to note that Jacqueline Rose underlines this connection between nationalism and religious faith in *The Question of Zion*. Accounting for the affective dimensions of national identity, she locates Israeli nationalism in the context of a Zionist tradition of messianism, arguing that '[w]ith the birth of Israel, nationalism became the new messianism – the aura of the sacred, with all its glory and tribulations, passed to the state' (Rose 2005, 8)

Hurston also explores the dangers of '[n]ational faith' to question singular nationalist identities, although, in distinction to Said, her representations are not tethered to a specific context, but rather allude to the dangers of race-based nationalism in more general terms (Rose 2005, 83). In *Moses, Man of the Mountain*, Pharaoh is a tyrant responsible for the development of a 'new order', a nationalistic 'New Egypt' founded upon the exclusion and victimization of the Hebrews, who have been 'driven out of their well-built homes and shoved further back into Goshen', the segregated Hebrew quarter (*M* 1-2). Pharaoh's nationalism is underpinned by racism: he justifies his exploitation of Hebrews as slaves and his murder of their baby sons by presenting them as polluters of the organic 'body of Egypt' (*M* 20).

In a move that echoes Said's assumption that religion is often anti-democratic, Hurston aligns his race-based nationalism with religious rhetoric: Pharaoh justifies his subjugation of the Hebrews by claiming it as divinely sanctioned. In an extended passage that presents Pharaoh's words in indirect speech to underline his excessive power, he puts racism beyond the realms of rationality, insisting that he can speak for the gods: '[t]he gods were forbidden the boundaries of Goshen' (*M* 21).[18]

In their reinterpretations of the Moses story, both Hurston and Said indict such theological national identities as being dangerous ideologies that work to oppress those groups regarded as 'foreigners' or 'aliens'. They employ a technique reminiscent of collage, uprooting a familiar narrative from its expected context, creating new juxtapositions in the process. Writing against enduring binaries that divide individuals according to such hierarchies of difference as colonizer and colonized, black and white, civilized and primitive, Hurston and Said undercut the notion of cultural purity in the biblical story, exposing the multiple origins of Hebrew culture.

This should be interpreted as a political gesture, a challenge to the fundamentally static binaries of identity that Said has described as 'the hallmark of imperialist cultures' (1993, xxviii). Thus, Said purposefully selects the metaphor of excavation to describe Freud's unearthing of Egyptian and Arabian antecedents for Jewish religious identity. He then sets this layered conception of identity against the manipulation of archaeology that both Palestinians and Israelis use to legitimate exclusive, nationalist identities by way of 'reconstructing the past and inventing tradition' (*F* 49). In this way Said can come to contend that the interconnections between Arabic, Egyptian and Jewish culture have been repressed in an effort to simplify and purify national identity. A process of excavation is required, Said argues, in order to uncover the realities of cultural interdependence. Indeed, Said's contemporary re-articulation of Freud's arguments about the non-European origins of Judaism must be read as a challenge to the construction of exclusive Jewish and Palestinian histories in the Middle East.

In an analogous way, Hurston's rewriting of the Moses story as a whole is underpinned by a deliberate endeavour to open out the story's sources, allowing for non-Jewish influences. As in Freud's accommodation of non-Jewish sources for Judaism, Hurston counters the antagonism described in the Book of Exodus between Egypt and Israel and polytheism and monotheism, thereby undermining the biblical representation of Judaism as a complete rejection of Egyptian culture and religion. A distinctive aspect of this acknowledgement of diverse cultural sources is Hurston's representation of Moses as a great hoodoo man, a theme that preoccupied her throughout her career.[19] In her introduction, Hurston signals that

---

[18]   In his recent article 'National Socialism and Blood-Sacrifice in Zora Neale Hurston's *Moses, Man of the Mountain*', Mark Christian Thompson interprets the irrationality of Pharaoh's divine rule as an allusion to Hitlerism (2004, 395-415).

[19]   In *Jonah's Gourd Vine*, for instance, John Pearson's chief opponent in the church, Reverend Harris, celebrates Moses as 'de greatest hoodoo man dat God ever made' (*J* 231). In her account of the origins of hoodoo in *Mules and Men*, Hurston revises the Bible to assert that Moses' power grew from his association with an African hoodoo man: 'Moses never would have stood before the Burning Bush, if he had not married Jethro's daughter. Jethro was a great hoodoo man' (*MM* 184). Such examples reveal the symbolic force that

it was interest in the unrecorded tales of Moses that exist '[w]herever the children of Africa have been scattered by slavery' that prompted her to write the novel (*M* xxiv). This fascination with versions of the Moses story that are 'scattered' across the African diaspora builds upon her anthropological study *Tell My Horse* (1938), in which she explains that 'wherever the Negro is found, there are traditional tales of Moses and his supernatural powers that are not in the Bible, nor can they be found in any written life of Moses' (1990b, 116).

Her anthropological writings on hoodoo, which include the second section of *Mules and Men* and an essay for *The Journal of American Folklore* entitled 'Hoodoo in America', provide further clues about the motivations for this emphasis on hoodoo. In 'Hoodoo in America', Hurston marks hoodoo as a unique cultural product of the African diaspora: she explains that hoodoo is the African American term for 'African magic practices and beliefs' that have been grafted onto 'characteristics of the prevailing religious practices' in America to create a unique set of beliefs and rituals (1931, 317-18). Yet, as Hurston explains in her investigation of hoodoo in *Mules and Men*, this is a marginalized or 'suppressed religion' (*MM* 183). Occupying a position analogous to Judaism in *Moses, Man of the Mountain*, it is often concealed by believers because '[i]t is not the accepted theology of the Nation' (*MM* 185). This association between hoodoo and undocumented cultural transmissions is underlined in *Mules and Men* when Hurston highlights a direct connection between orality and hoodoo: '[b]elief in magic is older than writing. So nobody knows how it started' (*MM* 183).

Given this declaration that to pinpoint the origins of marginalized oral cultures of the African diaspora is not possible, it comes as no surprise that Hurston, in *Moses, Man of the Mountain*, holds in view a multiplicity of sources, without constructing a hierarchy of importance between them. Oral culture is simply one important strand of the culture the Hebrews will inherit. For example, Moses receives his early education from a stableman, Mentu, who teaches him about the richness of oral storytelling and has 'answers in the form of stories for nearly every question that Moses asked' (*M* 38). Mentu expands Moses' horizons, encouraging him to listen to nature and translating for him the talk of animals, birds and plants so that he can imagine ways of thinking and behaving that exist outside the structures of the Egyptian court.

Precisely because of this association of orality with plural cultural origins, Hurston adds a new ingredient to the plot of the Moses story: Moses' quest to read the Book of Thoth. It is the servant Mentu who first relates the tale of the Book of Thoth, communicating the importance of both oral and written knowledge. Although he is illiterate, Mentu provides clear instructions regarding the location of this legendary book of knowledge that lies in the middle of the river at Koptos. Written by the god Thoth, who was worshipped by the Egyptians as the creator

---

the figure of Moses carries in Hurston's fiction and anthropology. At the very least, he becomes a vehicle through which to intervene in debates about religious, and even political, leadership.

of the world, a master of magic spells, the inventor of writing and the originator
of mathematics (Bernal 1991, 141), this book promises knowledge of conjure. Its
readers will be able to understand the talk of animals, 'enchant the heavens, the
earth, the abyss, the mountain, and the sea', enter the spirit world and discover
the 'secrets of the deep' (*M* 53). Mentu stresses that the 'wisdom' contained in
the Book of Thoth is distinct from the bookish 'learning' of the Egyptian priests
(*M* 54). The book springs from Egyptian culture, but, rather like Judaism in the
Bible and hoodoo in the American South, it occupies a marginal position in relation
to the dominant religion.

     Later in the novel, Moses makes the journey to Koptos and, in a description
that resonates with Said's archaeological metaphor of excavation to suggest the
recovery of cultural knowledge that has been repressed or denied, he employs
workmen to dig into the river only to discover a book protected by numerous
charms. After he has defeated the immortal snake that guards the site, he literally
drinks in the words of the book, absorbing them into his physical body in an
attempt to stave off further cultural forgetfulness: '[w]hen he had read the book,
he took a new piece of papyrus and copied the words of the book on it. Then he
washed off the writing with beer and drank the beer for then he knew he would
never forget what he had read' (*M* 120). After Moses drinks the beer, he consumes
the wisdom of Egypt, and Africa is figured as a source of wisdom and literacy. In
this way, Hurston adapts a foundational legend that represents the revolutionary
development of Judaism out of the polytheism of Egypt; instead, Moses' spiritual
power is predicated upon a fusion of Egyptian and Hebrew culture (he learns from
Egyptian gods, a Hebrew servant and Jehovah).

     To underline these connections, Hurston deftly balances multiple cultural
sources. Melanie J. Wright has argued that the description of Moses swallowing
a book places the story in a specifically African American context, echoing the
'experience of hoodoo conjurer Marie Leveau and the importance attached to
books (especially the Bible) as part of the paraphernalia of voodoo and hoodoo'
(2003, 57). However, I would suggest that Hurston is casting her net much wider,
given that there is also a clear biblical source for this incident. In the Book of
Revelations, John eats the angel's book in order to become a gifted prophet who,
like Moses, experiences personal suffering as a result of his position as leader:
'And I took the little book out of the angel's hand, and ate it up; it was in my mouth
as sweet as honey: and as soon as I had eaten it, my belly was bitter' (10.10).

     Through these knotted allusions, Hurston broadens the scope of the Moses story,
muddying notions of cultural provenance and drawing attention to intersection
and complication. Thus, her representation of the Book of Thoth as simply another
source of Moses' power, which is neither derived from nor assigned a different
value to Moses' God-given powers, is based upon an understanding of the Bible
that recognizes influences from diverse cultures, without privileging either oral
or written forms. In distinction to the biblical account of Moses as the founder
of a culturally exclusive monotheism, Hurston describes a mysterious fusion of
Egyptian and Hebrew cultural strands, celebrating the hoodoo power of Thoth

or Hermes Trismegistos, founder of the very religion that Moses of the Bible so strongly opposed (Assmann 1997, 36).

A Comparative Moses?

On one level, this is no more than to say that both Hurston and Said reveal that cultural identity is always composite: challenging the notion of 'some cheap, pre-given sameness' (Gilroy 2000a, 133), they reach towards 'the possibility of a more generous and pluralistic vision of the world' (Said 1993, 277). Much of the disruptive force of these narratives is derived from a collaging of allusions from diverse cultural traditions, which reveals unexpected points of contact to mount 'an argument against purity, newness, and unlimited progress' (Levin 1989, xix-xx). However, their respective challenges to the separation of humanity into 'autonomous tribes, narratives, cultures' become more conflicted when Hurston and Said take the myth of Moses beyond its specific context, opening up the narrative of the Hebrews' liberation to the exploration of linked, analogous oppressions that overlay their descriptions of African American and Palestinian experiences (Said 1993, 330).

In Said's case, this search for parallels is a direct challenge to Israel's marginalization of Palestinians. He indicts Israel for defining Jewishness as a prerequisite for citizenship, which he interprets as 'a parodistic re-enactment' of the racist logic 'that had been so murderous' in Nazi Europe (*F* 41). Said is careful to acknowledge the particular horrors of the Holocaust, but he warns against an exceptionalist view of Jewish history; instead, he notices a binary logic of racial separation and difference common to Nationalist Socialism and Zionism, with its 'binary opposition Jew-versus-non-European' (*F* 40-41). In his forceful emphasis upon historical parallels, Said could certainly be accused of underplaying the differences 'between industrial genocide and ethnic transfer', but his rhetoric is polemical and emotive (Rose 2005, 145). He grapples with the contradictions of Israeli nationalism, talking about 'the suffering of the Jewish people and the violence of the Israeli state in the same breath' (Rose 2005, xiv).

Hurston's implicit comparison of the plight of the Jews in Germany in the 1930s with that of African Americans marginalized by systems of disenfranchisement and segregation is guided by a less explicit political argument. As Deborah E. McDowell has noted, in *Moses* Hurston makes striking parallels between the Third Reich and the slaves in Goshen who are under surveillance by the secret police, and made into 'aliens' in their own country (McDowell 1991, xv). The Nuremberg laws of 1935, for instance, reduced Jews to the status of aliens: a certificate of descent, popularly called *Ariernachweis*, or Aryan certificate, was a precondition for German citizenship, and Jews were subsequently excluded from medical practice, education and marriage or sexual relations with Aryan Germans by law (Stackelberg 1999, 146). The Hebrews of Hurston's novel are also denied citizenship by legislative acts: 'Hebrews were disarmed and prevented from becoming citizens of Egypt, they found out that they were aliens, and from one new decree to the next they sank lower and lower' (*M* 2).

Moreover, the novel's opening account of Rameses' rise to power in a 'New Egypt' echoes Hitler's seizure of power in 1933 (*M* 1). For Hurston, Pharaoh's (and Hitler's) 'intensified nationalism' (56) depends upon a racist scapegoating of the Hebrews as 'enemy-prisoners' who exist within the nation's borders (*M* 60): his renewal of Egyptian identity, defined by militarism and religion, depends on the exclusion of the Hebrews from these very activities. Furthermore, Hurston not only suggests parallels between the geographical separation of the races in Goshen, Germany and the Jim Crow South; she also interrogates the means through which racist ideologies are upheld, describing Egyptian spectacles that bestow military aggression with sacred power, likening Pharaoh to 'the sun-god' (*M* 47).

In the light of this concern Hurston has over Nazism and American race politics, Barbara Johnson, Laura E. Donaldson and Melanie J. Wright have argued that Hurston's reworking of the Moses story to query notions of racial purity is written 'with an eye to Germany' (Wright 2003, 67). According to Wright, Hurston launches a polemic against 'both American racism and the Nazi program' (2003, 69) while Johnson argues that Hurston undermines the ideology that underpins Hitler's thinking, 'questioning the grounding of nationhood on racial identity' (1997, 21). Like Edward Said, she reimagines the narrative of Moses to create a fissure at the heart of national identity.

Throughout the novel, Hurston lays stress upon the cultural and ethnic differences between Moses and the Hebrews: when talking to God, Moses always describes his followers as 'your people' and never my people (*M* 195); he finds Hebrew 'ways' 'strange' (*M* 200); and, in a pointed reference to the novel's opening description of the Hebrews' marginalized position in Egypt, he feels like an 'alien' among them (*M* 206). Much hangs on this sustained distinction between Moses' cultural outlook and that of the people he leads. For one thing, Hurston prises apart essentialist equations of race with nation, claiming that something other than racial affiliation holds these people together.[20]

As Melanie J. Wright has convincingly argued, Hurston's emphasis upon the racial hybridity of the Hebrew nation derives some of its political punch from Boasian anthropology, which consistently sought to separate race and nation

---

[20]   Hurston undermines the notion of Israel as a homogeneous racial group, which is posited in the Bible from the moment Moses slays an Egyptian overseer because he has killed 'an Hebrew, one of his [Moses'] brethren' (Exodus 2.11). Instead, from the outset, Israel is a nation composed of diverse racial groups. When the Israelites pack up to leave Egypt '[a] great horde of mixed-blooded people grabbed up their things and joined the hosts of Israel' (*M* 182). Racial mixing becomes a distinctive marker of Israelite identity, which Moses struggles to preserve in the face of opposition. This emphasis on common humanity as the basis for nationality rather than the fear and prejudice that insists upon racial distinctiveness foreshadows Said's warning against the desire to make national or racial identity exhaustive.

(Wright 2003, 60-61). In contrast to the evolutionists, who arranged cultures into 'a time series' demonstrating the progress of humanity from simple to complex civilization, Boas accounted for differences in populations by identifying the historical processes of contact as the vehicle of cultural change (1938, 177). Boas's key work, *The Mind of Primitive Man* gathers historical examples of racial mixing from across the globe in order to expose how the contention that 'national characteristics are due to racial descent' is a damaging ideological construct, based upon prejudice rather than scientific fact (1938, 253).

However, it is my assertion that Barbara Johnson, Laura E. Donaldson and Melanie J. Wright's insistence upon the subversiveness of *Moses, Man of the Mountain* threatens to smooth over the complexities of Hurston's attitude to nationalism. These ambiguities stem, at least in part, from her attempt to adumbrate a line of connection between the marginalization of African Americans and colonized peoples in the extensive European empires that spanned the globe in the early twentieth century. Given Wright's emphasis on 'Hurston's intellectual debt to Boas' (2003, 60), it is worth pointing out that Hurston's anti-imperialism stands in marked contrast to Boas's equivocal pronouncements upon colonialism in his essay 'Colonies and the Peace Conference' (1919). In that essay, Boas's sharp criticism of European greed and racism is blunted by both his refusal to condemn the system of colonialism and his plea for Germany to be allowed to maintain its place as an imperial power (1919a, 247).

My focus on imperialism chimes with Said's argument that reading a historical writer in the context of present concerns 'reopens and challenges what seems to have been the finality of an earlier figure of thought', dramatizing 'latencies' in their work that have been overlooked (*F* 25). Reading Hurston's novel through the filter of Said's *Freud and the Non-European* renders visible the text's engagement with the issue of colonial exploitation, which Hurston presents in general rather than specific terms. Moreover, in one of the few moments when she comments directly on the rise of Hitler, in a section from the 1941-42 manuscript of her autobiography *Dust Tracks on a Road*, Hurston locates her discussion of Hitler's invasion of Holland in the context of colonial oppression.[21] While condemning Hitler as 'a bandit' (792), she indicts European and American hypocrisy: Germany has attracted censure because 'it is not cricket to enslave one's own kind' yet it is perceived as being legitimate to exploit non-Europeans in the colonies of Africa and Asia (Hurston 1995d, 790). Hurston makes her criticism of Nazism clear, but she insists that it must be viewed in a global context where empire-building is deemed an index of 'civilization': 'I hear people shaking with shudders at the thought of Germany collecting taxes in Holland. I have not heard a word against Holland collecting one twelfth of poor people's wages in Asia' (1995d, 792).

---

[21]   The most overtly political sections of the 1941-42 manuscript of *Dust Tracks* were cut because Hurston's editors considered her commentary too anti-American to be published after Pearl Harbor.

Hurston's commentary on World War II tacitly reinforces my approach since it suggests that any interpretation of *Moses, Man of the Mountain* must negotiate with the context of Nazism and imperialism. Given this, I will now explore the ways in which Hurston's novel engages with the issue of global imperialism.

The most obvious reference to colonialism occurs in Hurston's cool diagnosis of the motivations and effects of nationalist-inspired war in Pharaoh's 'New Egypt'. Departing from biblical sources to draw on Josephus's *Jewish Antiquities* (Wright 2003, 49), Hurston reveals to us the ideological thinking that underpins Egypt's aggressive military campaigns in Ethiopia and elsewhere:

> Inside the royal palace affairs went on unconscious of the legends of Goshen. The Pharaoh had his programs, national and international. At home he worked to reorganize the county into a unit intensely loyal to the new regime. Externally he strove to bulwark the country against outside attack. Force was his juices and force was his meat. It was his boast that his reign should make it so that outsiders trembled when they breathed the mighty name of Egypt. The very rims of the earth should bear the spread wings of the Hawk-god Horus, who signified the sun in Egypt and should bear its light to all the world (*M* 36).

Hurston unearths a close connection between what we might call Pharaoh's cartographic attitude, his all-consuming awareness of spatial boundaries between inside and outside, national and international, palace and Hebrew ghetto, and his twin policies of cultural imperialism and military aggression. As Hurston implies through her sustained, almost obsessive, focus on the mindset of division and enclosure in the Egyptian palace (she repeats the word 'inside' at the beginning of four consecutive paragraphs), Pharaoh's power seems to rest on his ability to divide and rule. He constructs literal and symbolic borders between Egyptians and 'outsiders'; the court and the people; and, as we have already seen, he segregates the slave population in the ghetto of Goshen.

Yet, with no little irony, Hurston reveals that the ultimate effect of such a foreign policy is to blur the distinction between insider and outsider: when the Egyptian armies return from war, they bring 'slaves in hordes' and the streets teem 'with strange nationalities and tongues. From the Sudan, all Asia and Greece' (*M* 57). Contrary to the logic of enclosure, which lends the Pharaoh's palace a somewhat claustrophobic feel, imperialism consolidates the mixture of cultures on a global scale.

As well as countering Pharaoh's reductive fetishization of a pure national identity, Hurston makes two important points that shape her discussion of imperialism throughout the novel. First, her focus on Pharaoh's construction of spatial hierarchies that justify his military, economic and cultural exploitation of non-Egyptian peoples suggests a parallel between the treatment of the Hebrew slaves within Egypt's borders and the colonization of foreign lands. Indeed, in a section from the manuscript of *Dust Tracks*, Hurston made this connection more explicit, speaking of colonialism as 'mov[ing] the slave quarters farther away from the house' (1995d, 793). Secondly, it is clear that Hurston's description of imperialism as a sacred project has implications for the formation of Israel as a religious nation. Pharaoh aims to impose his religion – which, as we have already seen, is fundamental to his authoritarian rule – upon the rest of the world. In this sense, Hurston echoes Freud, who, in *Moses and Monotheism*, makes a connection between the development of Egyptian monotheism and its expansionist ambitions, arguing that an all-powerful God could be seen as 'the reflection of a Pharaoh autocratically governing a great world empire' (1939, 80).

If Pharaoh is associated with an imperialism presented in rather sweeping terms as military aggression and religious dominance, it is clear that this model of rule, in which a leader dominates people of a different ethnic and cultural group, haunts Hurston's representation of Moses. Could it be that Hurston's representation of the ethnic difference between leader and people is not wholly positive? Faced with overwhelming evidence of racial oppression in America and the colonies, and the shadow of anti-Semitism spreading across Europe, perhaps Hurston could not take refuge in the kind of utopian attitude to humanist nationalism that both Wright and Johnson describe in their accounts of *Moses, Man of the Mountain*?

Hurston departs from a Boasian model in her sustained analysis of the complex consequences of cultural or racial difference between leader and people. Throughout his career, Boas sought to challenge 'imperialistic nationalism' (1919b, 236) by drawing attention to the gap between dangerous myths of racial purity and scientific fact. Making clear his opposition to the 'imperialistic tendencies' of modern nationalism (236), Boas fleshed out an alternative concept of 'nationality', which celebrated the mixing of 'distinct racial elements' (232) as a challenge to 'unwholesome uniformity of thought' (1919b, 237). In Boas's hands, the blasting of 'essentialist equations of race with nation' takes on a radical, even utopian, character (Foley 2003, 155).

Given this context, it is entirely plausible to read Hurston's novel as a celebration of cultural and racial diversity, as Melanie J. Wright has done. Notwithstanding the validity of such interpretations, an approach that places undue emphasis upon the novel's subversiveness overlooks Hurston's attention to negative consequences that stem from the cultural differences between Moses and the people he leads.[22]

---

[22] My argument here is informed by recent scholarship which grapples with the contradictions of Boas's legacy. There is no doubt that Boas's emphasis upon the prevalence of racial mixing was underpinned by an anti-racist agenda to counter ill-informed prejudice and 'much-read propaganda' with scientific and historical facts (1925, 89). Through his broad cultural appeal in widely disseminated journals and public speeches, Boas embarked on a mission to educate the general American public about the centrality of racial crossing to human development. Yet, recent studies by Barbara Foley and Julia E. Liss have addressed the conceptual limitations of Boas's thinking on race. According to Foley, Boas's tendency to analyse racism in emotional or psychological terms means that he never gets to grips with 'the material foundations of racism' (Foley 2003, 153). More pertinent to this analysis Foley's sharp analysis of the tensions that animate Boas's thinking on the relationship

Moses is associated with the kind of cultural nationalism that Boas advocates but, as he insists upon national adoption of prescribed religious and cultural values, he begins to resemble an imperial ruler who 'conceived the plan of founding a new empire, of finding a new people, to whom he could give the religion that Egypt disdained' (Freud 1939, 32).

Memorials and Nationalism

Consequently, it is possible to detect an undertow of anxiety about Moses' extensive power over the Hebrews, even though he is often represented as an idealized leader who sacrifices his own personal wishes for the communal good. At certain points in the text, there are striking parallels between Moses' leadership, which frequently disregards protest or dissent, and that of the tyrannical Pharaoh, who is associated with policies of enslavement, oppression and imperialism, especially through his programme of building monuments.

A chain of representations of memorials in *Moses* creates a faultline in the text that complicates any idealization of Moses' leadership. From the beginning of the novel, memorials are associated with Pharaoh's dictatorship and his oppression of the Hebrews. Not only are the Hebrews forced into backbreaking labour in the stone quarries and brickyards, producing beautiful cities that glorify Pharaoh, but, as Pharaoh tells a gathering of Hebrew elders, their position as a 'people without monuments' is one of the many justifications for their enslavement (*M* 22). Characterizing them as 'a people who honor nobody' and forget their 'benefactors as soon as possible after the need is past', he plans to make them 'work and work and work and work' until they 'have paid in a measure for [their] crimes against Egypt' (*M* 22). When one of the assembled slaves complains that Pharaoh is overlooking cultural difference, disregarding the fact that Hebrews, unlike Egyptians, do not 'trust' their 'memories to stones', Pharaoh only becomes even more unreasonable (*M* 22).

Through the trope of memorials, Hurston gestures towards a long, global history, in which people deemed to be 'alien' or other have been exploited to produce what Jan Morris has called the 'stones of empire', monuments of grandeur and permanence that serve a political and aesthetic purpose, creating a visual embodiment of imperial confidence and power.[23] Hurston not only alludes to the unacknowledged role of black slave labour in the creation of an American prosperity, which was, in W.E.B. Du Bois's words, 'built upon a groan' (1996,

---

between race and culture: 'his Herderian definition of culture as folk genius implied an essentialist notion of group collectivity that threatened to let in through the ontological back door the linkage of culture with race that had been ushered out the epistemological front door' (2003, 156).

[23]   I borrow this phrase from Jan Morris, *Stones of Empire: The Buildings of the Raj* (1983).

102); she also focuses on the values of empire as expressed in material objects, bringing to mind British colonial architecture of the early twentieth century, which operated as a kind of propaganda that often reinforced the racial hierarchies that underpinned colonialism.

Hurston was not unaware of this link between monumental histories and colonial power. In a passage excised from *Dust Tracks*, she speaks of colonialism in unspecific terms, occurring in 'a place way off where the people do not look like him [the ruler]', and drawing attention to the role that 'unforgetting stone' plays in the construction of an image of benign, masterful rule (1995d, 790). Describing images that manipulate religious iconography, Hurston shows that imperial rhetoric emphasizes a divine mission to rule and enlighten, obscuring the realities of violent subjugation and the ruthless pursuit of profit (1995d, 790).

Although Hurston underestimates the complexity and variety of colonial rule across the globe, her description does have particular resonance for British India. For example, in 1911, Edwin Lutyens designed the city of New Delhi, with its famous orchestration of space and its careful arrangement of housing according to racial and class hierarchies, to convey 'the idea of a peaceful domination and dignified rule over the traditions and life of India by the British Raj' (Evenson 1989, 146). Hurston reduces colonialism to the shorthand of caricature. Nevertheless, there is a serious point behind her tactic of juxtaposition. In a move that recalls Said's metaphor of contrapuntality, she brings to light different but comparable histories in which racial hierarchies and divisions have wreaked havoc, and privileges have been monopolized by one race at the expense of another.

Given these associations, it seems important that Moses is linked with such monuments throughout his leadership of Israel. Despite the Hebrews' beliefs about the inappropriateness of stone memorials, Moses goes to great lengths to construct memorials that consolidate a coherent, unifying national identity forged through sharing a common culture, history and project for the future. In a move that foreshadows Benedict Anderson's influential theory that the nation is first and foremost 'an imagined political community', held together by the individual's belief that they are part of a collective, Hurston depicts the strategies Moses adopts to create a national consciousness (Anderson 1983, 6). In his account of the emergence of the modern nation-state, Anderson highlights the novel and the newspaper as media through which individuals could '"think" the nation', but Moses makes comparable use of ritual and memorial (Anderson 1983, 28). Encouraging the Hebrews to preserve artifacts that will bolster their national history, such as manna, Moses shows a deep understanding of the need for a shared history and religion, and common memorials, myths and habits.

It is difficult to miss the Boasian character of Moses' nationalism. Although Boas was highly critical of an 'imperialistic nationalism' that was so often characterized by 'the lust of dominion', he did not believe that nationalism should be dispensed with altogether (1919b, 236). Instead, in keeping with other Boasians, he argued that cultural nationalism could be 'one of the most fruitful sources of cultural progress' (236), as long as sufficient effort was made to preserve diversity within unity.[24]

By contrast, Hurston offers a more ambivalent portrayal of cultural nationalism in *Moses, Man of the Mountain*. In fact, it is when Moses imposes memorials upon a people who have traditionally carried their memories through an oral culture that he begins to resemble Pharaoh in his insistence upon a narrow conception of identity. In Moses' hands, memorials serve the interests of his religious state: his monumental histories take on the characteristics of the 'official nationalism' that Anderson presents as 'a conscious, self-protective *policy*, intimately linked to the preservation of imperial-dynastic interests' (Anderson 1983, 145).

The tensions inherent in Hurston's stance lead me to suggest that recent accounts of *Moses, Man of the Mountain* as a radical text which shatters racial essentialism by articulating a 'new vision of national identity ... based on dislocation and difference' do less than justice to the complexity of Hurston's position (Konzett 2002a, 108).[25] Given Andrew Warnes's investigation of the ways in which Hurston's writings 'lay contemporary ideological or epistemological assumptions bare' (2006, 380), it is imperative to resist the temptation to resolve contradictions that animate Hurston's work.

Sustained attention to this association between Moses and memorials demonstrates that he has set himself the project of converting national heterogeneity into a religious and cultural homogeneity that echoes 'New Egypt'. Moses emphasizes a notion of the common good that takes precedence over the interest of individuals, but this ends up being antithetical to pluralism. He attains unity through the expulsion of everything that would threaten his narrow religious vision for the nation.

He is willing to sacrifice individuals for the good of the state, including those who deign to question his authority, such as Miriam and Aaron. In view of Moses' belittling attitude towards Miriam during her lifetime, his response to her death seems politically expedient:

---

[24]   This distinction between "positive" and "negative" kinds of nationalism is common in Boasian anthropology. In *Patterns of Culture*, for instance, Ruth Benedict echoes Boas's sentiments: '[w]hat really binds men together is their culture – the ideas and the standards they have in common. If instead of selecting a symbol like common blood heredity and making a slogan of it, the nation turned its attention rather to the culture that unites its people, emphasizing its major merits and recognizing the different values which may develop in a different culture, it would substitute realistic thinking for a kind of symbolism which is dangerous because it is misleading' (1935, 11-12).

[25]   Recent critical studies of *Moses, Man of Mountain* have tended to assert its radical credentials. Laura E. Donaldson, for instance, contends that the novel 'clears a new imaginative space for the oppositional and *différant* knowledge of the new mestiza' (Donaldson 1992, 114-15).

Moses called a halt and told the people what it meant to lose a patriot like Miriam. The young ones were told what the old ones had forgotten – all about those days back in Egypt when the house of the prophetess Miriam was the meeting place of all those who were willing to work for freedom…. The people all listened and thought it was a great speech. They even mourned when Moses ordered them to mourn for thirty days. … So Moses buried her with a big ceremony and ordered a great tomb of rocks to be piled up over her grave (*M* 265).

Hurston's description of Moses' attempt to fix down the referents of Hebrew history must be seen as a moment of stress, which treads the razor-thin line between a leader who acts without a mandate on the community's behalf and a tyrant who abuses his power. Such anxieties are undoubtedly compounded by ethnic and cultural differences between leader and people, which are, at this moment, redolent of Pharaoh's cultural imperialism. As in Hurston's representation of Egypt, the act of memorial is associated with the exercise of considerable power by a leader: like Pharaoh, Moses 'orders' the Hebrews to start building work, and he imposes a particular narrative history upon 'all' of them, even though he mocked Miriam's claims that she was a 'prophetess' during her lifetime.

This connection with Pharaoh is underlined by Hurston's use of free indirect discourse, which not only recalls Pharaoh's speech to the Hebrews 'using his own sacred voice and lips' (*M* 19), but also highlights Moses' god-like power, his careful separation of himself from 'the people'. More insidious is Moses' use of the word 'patriot',[26] which suggests that his memorial is inspired by a nationalism that can be placed alongside that of Pharaoh's oppressive state.[27] In Moses' speech, Miriam is constructed as symbolic carrier of national identity, but she is denied an

---

[26]   It is difficult to read this episode without mentioning Hurston's sustained interest in political leadership, which spans her fictional and anthropological writings. It is telling that Moses describes Miriam as a 'patriot'. In *Tell My Horse*, Hurston uses this word to indict corrupt Haitian politicians who mask their self-serving ambition behind rousing speeches. She writes: '[t]hese talking patriots, who have tried to move the wheels of Haiti on wind from their lungs, are blood brothers to the empty wind bags who have done so much to nullify opportunity among the American Negroes' (Hurston 1990b, 75). Creating an understated parallel between Moses (who elicits the people's obedience through his persuasive rhetoric) and political leaders who exploit oral dexterity for political ends, Hurston implies that her portrait of Moses' leadership should not only be compared with her fictional representations of such flawed leaders as Jody Starks in *Their Eyes Were Watching God* and John Pearson in *Jonah's Gourd Vine*, but also with her anthropological writings, which articulate a more direct political commentary on contemporary events. See Melanie J. Wright for a detailed discussion of Hurston's interventions in 'debates concerning African American leadership and communal development' (Wright 2003, 66).

[27]   Given Hurston's taste for what Alice Gambrell calls 'self-revision' (1997, 115), it is worth interpreting this scene in conjunction with Hurston's earlier representation of that other patriarchal leader with a passion for public speeches, Jody Starks in *Their Eyes Were Watching God* (1986 [1937]). Reading Moses' speech alongside Jody's manipulation

active role in shaping the emergent nation-state. As Floya Anthias and Nira Yuval-Davis have pointed out, nationalist discourses often cast women in a symbolic or metaphoric role, and Hurston reveals that Moses' state is no exception: his project of monument-building is explicitly linked to the exercise of patriarchal power.

In attending to the autocratic elements of Moses' rule, Hurston's imaginative revision of the Bible foreshadows a text by Edward Said that offers an unusual interpretation of the Exodus story. In his review of Michael Walzer's *Exodus and Revolution*, which is reprinted in *Blaming the Victims*, Said argues that the potential for tyrannical rule is inherent in the biblical story because of its investment in the idea of a chosen people. Said makes the case that Moses' transformation into a Pharaoh-like dictator is an inevitable consequence of what he calls the 'irreducibly sectarian premises of Exodus' (167), which permit some to 'believe that history – the world of societies and nations, made by men and women – vouchsafes certain peoples the extremely problematic gift of "Redemption"' (1988, 177). Against the backdrop of nationalist struggles that aimed for political independence, Said holds up the Exodus story as a reminder of the dangers posed by narrow, chauvinistic nationalisms that privilege cultural insiders over outsiders.

In accordance with Said's provocative thesis, Hurston's version of the Exodus story is alert to the underside of Moses' strategy to forge cultural unity among the Hebrews. Associations of Moses with monumental history suggest a caveat to any reading of *Moses, Man of the Mountain* as a straightforward rejection of singular nationalism. In a sequence supplementary to the Bible, Moses kills the Levite Aaron when his refusal to abandon Egyptian values threatens Moses' plans for the Hebrews. Explaining to Aaron his motives for slaughtering him, Moses emphasizes that Aaron views power in Egyptian terms, prizing status, pomp and hierarchy, but he has failed to understand the emergent symbols of national identity: 'You didn't see the significance of the Ark of the Covenant nor the Tent of Testimony. All you saw was the gold and silver vessels and the robes and the power that goes with it. No, Aaron, you can't go over there and make a fool out of Israel's graves' (*M* 274). On one level, there are clear justifications for Moses' actions: he needs the Hebrews to abandon Egyptian values and embrace Hebrew attitudes. Yet, it is striking that Hurston draws attention to symbols of national consciousness that Aaron does not interpret appropriately.

The implication is that the influence of Egyptian notions of statehood and hierarchy must be quashed so that Moses can construct a coherent national consciousness through art and culture. For Moses, a circumscription of identity is necessary in order to formulate national consciousness: oral cultures are abandoned in favour of the more easily interpreted cultural signs of architecture and religious ritual. In contrast to the provisional identities celebrated by Said, it seems that Hurston is aware that fixity of identity is very hard to escape.

---

of public speeches to reinforce his position as undisputed leader of the community raises questions about the extent of Moses' self-interest.

In other words, Hurston does not simply pit the "bad" race-based nationalism of Hitler and Pharaoh against the "good" cultural nationalism of Moses; she reveals that both nationalisms set limits and prescribe behaviour, and even require sacrificial victims. In this context, the slaughtered Aaron, like Miriam, is to become one of the symbols of Hebrew national identity: 'God has built you a pyramid greater than Pharaoh, and generations of Israelites will make pilgrimages to the grave of Aaron, the patriot. God will remember your sacrifice and guard your memories' (*M* 275). Even if this speech is interpreted as an appeal to Aaron's ego, which has been so heavily influenced by Egyptian ideas, there is something troubling about Moses' manipulation of history to construct a hagiography of 'patriots': guarding memories seems dangerously close to manipulating them. Hurston's symbolic linkage of the oppressive state of Egypt with Israelite national consciousness through the trope of memorials raises concerns about the powers of a single leader, particularly in the context of a world that was becoming familiar with totalitarianism and imperial exploitation.

Attention to the trope of memorials in *Moses* suggests that there is in fact a noticeable distance between Said and Hurston in their engagements with nationalism. In *Freud and the Non-European*, Said claims Freud's thinking on identity as a model for exploring the shared concerns of widely dispersed marginalized groups. He does not underplay the difficulties posed by imagining identity as a flaw or a break, but he moves from particularity towards the universal, arguing that Freud's insights resonate beyond Jewish experience. Said presents himself as a diagnostician of identity, an analyst who takes a long, global and historically informed perspective; but I think that Hurston's fictional exploration of nationalism is embroiled in the very predicament of tribal or universal identity that Said describes.

In line with Andrew Warnes's recent analysis of Hurston's '[s]plit desires' for 'a Toomeresque America beyond race' and a 'nourishing narrative of African American survival', *Moses* oscillates between a yearning for humanist connectedness and a weary awareness of enduring racial hierarchies that constrain individual agency (Warnes 2006, 379). Indeed, by 1945, Hurston openly articulated the viewpoint that is so ambiguously seeded through her novel. In a letter to Carl Van Vechten on 12 September 1945, she describes Moses as 'a dictator' who 'did not care a fig for those Hebrew people' (Kaplan, 2002, 529). Presenting her ideas in the context of a broader discussion of anti-Semitism, Hurston contends that 'Moses had worked out an idea for a theocratic government, and the Hebrews were just so the available laboratory material' (Kaplan 2002, 529). In describing Moses as a 'dictator', Hurston implies that it is Moses' ethnic difference from the Hebrews (he is not of the people) that allows him to treat the Hebrews like 'material' rather than 'people'. For Hurston, the enduring nature of 'Race Consciousness' undermines any utopianism about a nation held together through shared cultural and religious heritage rather than race (1995d, 784).

Reading Hurston's *Moses, Man of the Mountain* alongside Edward Said's *Freud and the Non-European* brings to the surface the complexity of Hurston's treatment of nationalism. Cutting across temporal borders to expose connections and affiliations reveals Hurston and Said as figures mindful of unquestioned identity politics. Both writers use their representation of Moses to open out cultural identity beyond the confines of a separatist or triumphalist nationalism. Yet Hurston's fictional rendering of the 'fissure' at the heart of collective identity and her attempt to find a way to recognize difference that does not necessarily entail domination, break down at those moments when she struggles to irrevocably separate nation from race. In a perceptive reading of the novel, Delia Caparoso Konzett has shown that the Hebrews override Moses' multiracial vision for the nation, fixating upon their leader's Egyptian origins and his wife's racial difference during moments of crisis and strife (Konzett 2002a, 109). However, it is my contention that this resurfacing of racial identity is not only a preoccupation of the community that Hurston represents; her narrative also bears the signs and strains of her own struggle against the racialist thinking which was so deeply ingrained in early twentieth-century American culture. At certain points in the text, the ideal of ethnic and cultural difference between leader and people collapses into anxiety about the possibility for exploitation, a concern associated with imperialism through the trope of memorials.

Conclusion

Hurston is not, as Alice Walker maintains, a genius who manages to transcend historical context; instead, her texts are animated by tensions that stem from early twentieth-century American realities. Analysis of Hurston's collage method, in which cultural fragments are reassembled in new contexts, allows for a sustained investigation of such contradictions. Attending to patterns of juxtaposition in *Jonah's Gourd Vine* reveals that Hurston's celebration of an autonomous, organic folk culture is inflected by her engagement with aesthetic possibilities opened up by what Sieglinde Lemke has termed 'primitivist modernism'. Approaching *Moses, Man of the Mountain* as a version of collage captures the profound instability of Hurston's attempt to update the Exodus story for a modern audience. Wheeling between past and present, Hurston brings into contact different historical periods and cultural worlds. In doing so, she exposes unexpected affiliations and affinities that contest the separatist logic of Jim Crow. At the same time, she never loses sight of the particularity of African American experience. Such demands leave their mark on the novel. Consequently, it is hardly surprising that *Moses* mounts a case against racialist thinking while refusing to relinquish investment in the idea of a chosen people who must, ultimately, adhere to prescribed cultural norms and values.

Conclusion

In *Charleston* (c. 1928), an illustration for Paul Morand's *Black Magic*, Aaron Douglas reproduces a scene familiar from much visual culture and literature of the Jazz Age. Layering silhouetted figures, abstract motifs and geometric patterns, he captures, in its dynamics, a jazz performance in a cabaret. Any celebration of African American cultural vibrancy, however, is cut short by the spectre of racial violence. Douglas introduces a lynching rope into this relaxed scene: using a sharp white line, he positions it at the centre of the painting.

Such jarring juxtapositions and leaps of tone are a characteristic pose in Aaron Douglas's art. This painted collage, with its superimposed images and stylized figures, derives much of its power from suggestion rather than explicit comment. As in Jacob Lawrence's later, more famous image for *The Migration of the Negro Series* (panel 15), '[t]he most striking object, the hanging body, is striking by its absence' (Griffin 1995, 13). Interpreting such omissions brings viewers face to face with the murdered bodies that haunt American consciousness. Indeed, it is difficult to look at Douglas's painting without thinking of Sterling A. Brown's extraordinary poem 'Cabaret', in which a description of well-fed, privileged white patrons in a Chicago Black and Tan cabaret is intercut with disturbing snapshots of deplorable poverty and racism in the South, a reality that never registers in the consciousness of the '[r]ich, flashy, puffy-faced' customers (Brown 1980, 111).

No Harlem Renaissance artist is more important to this study than Aaron Douglas. Although he does not employ the literal assemblage of disparate materials, his art is governed by a collage sensibility. Douglas's signature style rests upon a technique of superimposing various thematic layers and abstract motifs. Moreover, he often stages jarring incongruity, which forces viewers to reassess their assumptions about African American life and history. The collage-like texture of Douglas's images, which draws inspiration from black vernacular culture and modernist formal experimentation, also encapsulates the mutual interplay of ideas and styles between the Harlem Renaissance and Euro-American modernism that has been so central to my analysis. Richard J. Powell, for instance, notes that '[f]rom exposure to visual modernism via teacher-mentor Winold Reiss, to the many opportunities in 1920s Manhattan for seeing avant-garde art (especially from France and Germany), Douglas was both ideally situated and intellectually poised to take the universal, distilling spirit of contemporary art and design into the visionary sphere of the New Negro' (2007, 62). Like the Harlem Renaissance writers who have featured in this study, Douglas recasts modernist aesthetics from an African American cultural and historical perspective. As Susan Earle explains: '[h]is work was a radical act that opened doors for African American artists in Harlem and beyond in the 1920s and 1930s, inviting dialogue with international modernism that put African American life, labor, and freedom, along with African traditions and motifs, at its center' (2007, 5).

Given that the Harlem Renaissance was an interdisciplinary movement, which witnessed unprecedented collaboration between African American visual artists, musicians, writers and dancers, it is hardly surprising to see a flow of styles across diverse media. Until quite recently, accounts of the Harlem Renaissance have tended to focus on literature, paying insufficient attention to its multimedia scope. There are, of course, some notable exceptions to this trend, including Richard J. Powell and David A. Bailey's exhibition catalogue, *Rhapsodies in Black: Art of the Harlem Renaissance* (1997), which interprets the Harlem Renaissance as a cultural movement that included film, photography, literature, book illustration, music and sculpture. In the past few years, Martha Jane Nadell and Anne Elizabeth Carroll have pioneered a new approach to the period, looking at dynamic interplay between word and image in the pages of key Harlem Renaissance texts. After these foundational studies, it is now possible to ask pointed questions about the relationship between visual art and literature in the New Negro Renaissance, and even to mine visual art for a critical method through which to interpret literary form.

A fascination with visual art among Harlem Renaissance writers is suggested by a proliferation of fictional characters in New Negro novels who are trying to make their mark as artists. Take, for instance, Angela Murray in Jessie Fauset's *Plum Bun* or Wallace Thurman's dark tale of thwarted artistic ambition, *Infants of the Spring*. Beyond this thematic interest in the figure of the artist, several writers sought to introduce the immediacy of visual culture into the literary sphere. Hurston's concept of 'hieroglyphics', for example, accords with a broader modernist turn towards expression that falls somewhere in between visual and written communication (1995b, 831). Elsewhere Toomer's impressionistic portrayal of urban life in *Cane* bears the imprint of Alfred Stieglitz's photography, with its crisp, angular lines. And, of course, the splashes of colour – dusk, crimson, violet – that connect disparate pieces in the collection owe much to Toomer's sustained engagement with Georgia O'Keeffe's dynamic use of colour.[1] Such interest in transposing modernistic visual experimentation onto the page stems, at least in part, from Toomer's immersion in New York avant-garde circles.

Taking these formal and thematic connections as its point of departure, *The Collage Aesthetic in the Harlem Renaissance* has drawn inspiration from visual art to develop a set of reading practices for interpreting the patterning of cultural fragments in selected Harlem Renaissance texts. The collage aesthetic, of course, appears in various guises in works by Toomer, Hurston and Locke. Hurston, for instance, focuses on the "glue" that holds African American culture together, while Toomer orchestrates unsynthesized fragments, creating a collage of voices and perspectives that never settles into a coherent whole. Notwithstanding

---

[1]   See Nadell (2001) for a more sustained discussion of the influence of modernist visual culture on *Cane*.

these differences, visual collage, with its potential for jarring discontinuity and integrative representation, offers a flexible framework for examining the authors' formal choices, not least because they all deployed an aesthetic method of appropriation and reformulation.

Visual culture, however, is not the only source for my collage concept. The early twentieth century saw a burgeoning preoccupation with 'patterns of culture'; Boasian anthropologists, in particular, pioneered a new methodology and critical vocabulary for investigating cultural difference. One element of this interest in the culture concept involved formulating visual metaphors that sought to capture a dynamic process of cultural development. To this end, Boasian anthropologists conceived of culture in spatial terms, speaking of it as 'a multiplicity of converging and diverging lines' (Boas 1974a, 34), a 'thing of shreds and patches' (Lowie 1949, 428) and a 'mosaic' (Sapir 1963, 326), to mention only a few. This spatial culture concept, with its shift of focus from race and evolutionism to culture, impacted upon Harlem Renaissance thought.

Such concepts of culture crossed disciplinary lines. In particular, as Michael A. Elliott has pointed out, new modes of cultural description 'played a critical role in shaping the broader American culture of words' (2002, xii). Not only did a number of prominent New Negro intellectuals formulate their own models of cultural development, elaborating upon (and sometimes resisting) Boasian ideas. There is also a close, if complex, connection between thematic collage form and the move that Boas makes from a linear, chronological narrative of evolutionary progress towards '*synchronic* (and culturally specific) description and analysis' (Elliott 2002, 20). As Michael A. Elliott explains, 'the shift from cultural evolution (which understood culture as a uniform, global process) to Boasian culture (which understood culture as an aggregation of the practices and beliefs specific to a particular group) involved a radical change in the *narrative* organization of knowledge about group-based alterity' (Elliott 2002, xxiii). Given this strong link between ideas of cultural difference and narrative form, Boasian anthropology offers a valuable framework for exploring formal choices in Harlem Renaissance texts.

One aspect of collage form that comes into sharp focus when analysed with reference to these two cultural contexts is the politics of collage. Several modernist visual artists emphasized the subversive potential of collage technique. Much of the disruptive force of modernist collage, they noted, derives from its capacity to shock, its rearrangement of familiar elements to challenge preconceptions. Relatedly, Boas conceived of his description of cultures as 'a development from diverse sources which are gradually worked into a single cultural unit' as a means of intervening in contemporary political debates about such topics as immigration and miscegenation (Boas 1940, 217).

In the hands of African American practitioners collage form moved beyond the generalized stance of opposition embodied by white avant-garde figures such as Picasso. Consequently, it is important not to lose sight of the particularity of African American collage forms. As Coco Fusco insists, tactics of cultural recycling carry a specific political significance for writers of colour as they grapple with a history of cultural marginalization:

> [t]he strategy of taking elements of an established or imposed culture and throwing them back with a different set of meanings is not only key to guerilla warfare; the tactics of reversal, recycling, and subversive montage are aesthetics that form the basis of many twentieth-century avant-gardes. Nonetheless, a more profound understanding of the influences affecting many artists of color demands that we also perceive their connections to the semiotics characteristic of the colonial condition. Syncretism, or the fusion of different forms of belief or practice, enabled disempowered groups to maintain their outlawed or marginalized traditions. It also paved the way for a host of cultural recycling methods that infuse old icons with new meanings (1995, 34).

With Fusco's timely reminder ringing in our ears, I want to emphasize the subversive potential of collage form for Harlem Renaissance writers. Locke uses the anthology form in *The New Negro* to reconfigure democracy, highlighting the need for African American 'culture-citizenship'. In *Cane*, Toomer tears apart the 'whitewashed' façade of American history, revealing the interracial quality of American culture. In *Moses, Man of the Mountain*, Hurston pursues this link between formal innovation and historical unveiling to different effect, recasting the Moses story to address such issues as leadership, colonialism and nationalism. Ultimately, patterning of diverse cultural sources in these works becomes a means of challenging dominant accounts of American history, a way of reflecting on racial, cultural and national identity with implications for the present.

There are, of course, already a number of metaphors that have been used to analyse the political implication of African American authors' formal choices. Many of these metaphors – the blues aesthetic, the jazz aesthetic, the quilt and Signifyin(g), to mention just a few – are derived from black vernacular culture. Such emphasis accords with a broad tendency in African American studies to focus on vernacular culture as a privileged site of authentic expression and cultural resistance. There is no doubt that Harlem Renaissance writers drew heavily on vernacular forms and styles in their work, transforming received generic conventions in the process. In this respect, the strategies of appropriation and revision that I have described accord with Henry Louis Gates's magisterial account of Signifyin(g), in which African American writers modify (and critique) Euro-American cultural codes through repetition 'with a signal difference' (1988a, xxiv).

My formulation of the collage aesthetic, however, moves away from the exclusionary logic of cultural nationalism, which has, at times, privileged vernacular culture at the expense of other literary, visual and theoretical models. In fact, collage may be useful as a metaphor precisely because it makes space for a vernacular aesthetic without restricting our understanding of African American texts to an exclusive focus on such styles. Furthermore, since my approach is historically specific, growing as it does from a direct engagement with transatlantic modernist expression, it strives to avoid the pitfalls of generalization. Interpreting the stylistic choices made by Locke, Toomer and Hurston in their specific context – particularly in the light of Boasian anthropology – guards against a postmodern tendency to 'depoliticize the act of appropriation by abstracting it from its historical context' (Fusco 1995, 70).

Since collage is a cross-media term, it encapsulates the teeming diversity of Harlem Renaissance texts during an interdisciplinary movement when writers incorporated a mixture of cultural elements into their writings. With its jagged edges, collage registers what Ralph Ellison later termed 'the fragmentizing effects of American social processes' on African Americans, especially the violent cultural dislocation caused by transatlantic slavery (Ellison 1994, 691). But collage, with its potential to create new wholes from scraps, also highlights an enduring tradition of African American resistance through cultural improvisation. Finally, this approach introduces a sense of pictorial space into discussions of literary form. This allows for a more precise mapping of the relationships between fragments in a textual whole, encompassing such effects as temporal disruption, correspondence, fusion, dislocation, masking, contamination, rupture, synthesis and surprise.

Much of my analysis has been devoted to the politics of form. Yet, the political implications of collage form remain dormant without 'the active and activating consciousness of the reader' (Fish 1980, 83). Active interpretation is crucial in verbal collage because its identification often relies upon a reader's ability to decode intertextual fragments (Adamowicz 1998, 15). Since textual collage proceeds by juxtaposition, readers must actively engage with the material, supplying emotions and ideas. This is, at once, collage form's strength and its weakness. To grasp the significance of disparate fragments, readers must become active interpreters, filling in silences and fleshing out suggestions. Such formal moves break down any sense of distance, forcing readers to immerse themselves in the text and inhabit alternative viewpoints. At several points during this study, I have compared such multiple perspectives with the double take viewers must perform when viewing collage, an unsettled (and unsettling) mode of perception that flickers between detailed observation of individual fragments and a long-distanced view that registers the reformulation of appropriated materials into a new whole. At the very least, these unsettled, even disorientating, perspectives carry the potential to complicate unquestioned assumptions.

Nevertheless, it is also important to acknowledge the limitations of a politics that relies so heavily upon reader participation. Even a brief glance at the reception history of such texts as *Mules and Men*, *The New Negro* and *Cane* reveals that readers often overlooked, or disregarded, the political implication that was apparently hard-wired into Harlem Renaissance collage forms. To take only the most striking example, Toomer's arresting critique of racial determinism in *Cane* largely escaped sustained critical attention until the 1990s.

Reading is a motif that runs through the pages of this book. Not only are texts like *Mules and Men* and *Cane* populated with internal audiences who offer alternative perspectives. I have also been centrally concerned with the question of how we read collage, especially with reference to concepts of reading space (distance and proximity). Indeed, one of the most surprising elements of this project has been the extent to which my focus on collage form has required me to shift my attention from author to reader. Such analysis responds to a tension between authorial control and the apparent randomness of collage form. On the one hand, the complex, patterned structure of *Cane* and *The New Negro* is a product of authorial (or editorial) control, which has been orchestrated to generate specific effects. On the other, the democratic openness of collage form, in which examples are left to speak for themselves without explanations or mediating frameworks, creates space for active reader involvement.

Interest in implied audiences in Harlem Renaissance writing is gathering pace, as demonstrated by two recent works in particular: Mark Whalan's fascinating account of Toomer's 'attempts to craft a multiracial audience for *Cane*' (2007, 209) and Katharine Capshaw Smith's searching discussion of sophisticated modes of address employed in New Negro children's literature in an effort to reform 'the adult reading over the shoulder of the child' (2006, xx). Taken together with these studies, *The Collage Aesthetic in the Harlem Renaissance* opens up new areas for discussion, especially with regard to changing constructions of readership during the Harlem Renaissance.

Nowhere is the dynamic relationship between collage form and readership better seen than in *The Crisis*. A regular column entitled 'The Outer Pocket' printed extracts from readers' letters, often identifying correspondents according to their gender, race, region, age and profession. To some extent, the column functioned as a marketing tool, drawing attention to the magazine's diverse readership in an attempt to attract new subscriptions.[2] Yet, Du Bois's orchestration of readers' comments also takes on an explicitly political dimension. Letters included in the

---

[2]   Such aims are evident in 'Echoes from Around the World' (October 1929), which announces 'plans to extend widely [the magazine's] circulation, so that many more thousands may share its service and the darker peoples of the world feel its beneficent influence'. What stands out in this advert is the international scope of *The Crisis*'s readership. To underline the magazine's commitment to marginalized peoples across the globe, a message of encouragement 'To the American Negro' from Gandhi is printed alongside testimonials from named readers living in specific locations across the globe. A white southerner based in Long Island describes *The Crisis* as 'the one magazine among the dozen on my table that I read cover to cover'. One of the 'few Colored Doctors practising in London', who keeps a copy of the magazine in his waiting room, comments that 'it is surprising to note how many people become interested in it'. A student based in the United States, who describes herself as a 'Zulu woman from Natal, South Africa', commends the magazine 'for the fine interpretation [it is] giving of Africa'. While it is difficult to ascertain whether these letters are genuine, there is certainly a link between construction of an implied readership and collage form. Taken together, these juxtaposed endorsements trumpet the magazine's cosmopolitan credentials, a move that is, at least in part, shaped by a pressing need to reach new audiences during a period of economic recession.

April 1917 column, for instance, demonstrate his inclusive editorial approach to 'The Outer Pocket'. Making room for conflicting opinions from readers of various backgrounds and political persuasions, he records responses to two short stories about lynching printed in a previous issue. While the shocking account of violence prompts one correspondent to renew his subscription, a reader from Boston describes the subject matter as 'extremely ill-advised material for colored readers' (Du Bois 1917, 286). Eschewing direct commentary on individual letters, Du Bois juxtaposes them in such a way as to expose prejudices or limitations of perspective.

The lively letters pages in *The Crisis* draw attention to a complex, differentiated audience who engage actively with the magazine's contents. At the same time, the layout of 'The Outer Pocket', with its sharp juxtapositions and carefully identified correspondents, invites readers to adopt a critical, sceptical attitude. Such texts push us to develop a more complicated interpretive framework for thinking about the relationships between formal choices, reader intervention and authorial control.

Bibliography

Abrams, M.H. (1953) *The Mirror and the Lamp: Romantic Theory and the Critical Tradition*. New York: Oxford University Press.

Adamowicz, Elza (1998) *Surrealist Collage in Text and Image: Dissecting the Exquisite Corpse*. Cambridge: Cambridge University Press.

Allison, Alexander W. et al, eds (1983) *The Norton Anthology of Poetry*. New York: Norton.

Anderson, Benedict (1983) *Imagined Communities: Reflections on the Origin and Spread of Nationalism*. London: Verso.

Anderson, Paul Allen (2001) *Deep River: Music and Memory in Harlem Renaissance Thought*. Durham: Duke University Press.

Anthias, Floya and Nira Yuval-Davis, eds (1989) *Woman-Nation-State*. Basingstoke: Macmillan.

Assmann, Jan (1997) *Moses the Egyptian: The Memory of Egypt in Western Monotheism*. Cambridge, MA: Harvard University Press.

Babcock, Barbara (1992) '"Not in the Absolute Singular": Re-Reading Ruth Benedict', *Frontiers: A Journal of Women's Studies* 12(3): 39-77.

Baker, Houston A., Jr. (1987) *Modernism and the Harlem Renaissance*. Chicago: University of Chicago Press.

Baker, Houston A., Jr. (1991) *Workings of the Spirit: The Poetics of Afro-American Women's Writing*. Chicago: University of Chicago Press.

Baker, Lee D. (1998) *From Savage to Negro: Anthropology and the Construction of Race, 1896-1954*. Berkeley: University of California Press.

Barkan, Elazar and Ronald Bush, eds (1995) *Prehistories of the Future: The Primitivist Project and the Culture of Modernism*. Stanford: Stanford University Press.

Basalla, Susan Elizabeth (1997) 'Family Resemblances: Zora Neale Hurston's Anthropological Heritage', unpublished doctoral thesis, Princeton University.

Benedict, Ruth (1935) *Patterns of Culture*. London: Routledge and Kegan Paul.

Berman, Avis (1980) 'Romare Bearden: "I Paint Out of the Tradition of the Blues"', *Art News* 79, December: 60-66.

Bernal, Martin (1991) *Black Athena: The Afroasiatic Roots of Classical Civilization: Volume One, The Fabrication of Ancient Greece, 1785-1985*. London: Vintage.

Bernal, Martin (2001) *Black Athena Writes Back: Martin Bernal Responds to His Critics*, ed. David Chioni Moore. Durham: Duke University Press.

Birch, Anthony A.H. (1993) *The Concepts and Theories of Modern Democracy*. London: Routledge.

Boas, Franz (1910) 'The Real Race Problem', *The Crisis*, December: 22-5.

Boas, Franz (1919a) 'Colonies and the Peace Conference', *The Nation*, 15 February: 247-49.

Boas, Franz (1919b) 'Nationalism', *The Dial* 65, 8 March: 232-7.

Boas, Franz (1921) 'The Problem of the American Negro', *The Yale Review* 10, January: 384-95.

Boas, Franz (1925) 'What is a Race?', *The Nation* 120(3108), 28 January: 89-91.

Boas, Franz (1929 [1925]) *Anthropology and Modern Life*. London: Allen and Unwin.

Boas, Franz (1938 [1911]) *The Mind of Primitive Man*. New York: Macmillan.

Boas, Franz (1940) *Race, Language and Culture*. New York: Macmillan.

Boas, Franz (1966 [1911]) *Introduction to Handbook of American Indian Languages*. Lincoln: University of Nebraska Press.

Boas, Franz (1974a [1904]) 'The History of Anthropology', in George W. Stocking, Jr. (ed.) *A Franz Boas Reader: The Shaping of American Anthropology, 1883-1911*, pp. 23-36. Chicago: University of Chicago Press.

Boas, Franz (1974b [1887]) 'The Principles of Ethnological Classification', in George W. Stocking, Jr. (ed.) *A Franz Boas Reader: The Shaping of American Anthropology, 1883-1911*, pp. 61-7. Chicago: University of Chicago Press.

Boas, Franz (1974c [1889]) 'The Aims of Ethnology', in George W. Stocking, Jr. (ed.) *A Franz Boas Reader: The Shaping of American Anthropology*, pp. 67-71. Chicago: University of Chicago Press.

Boas, Franz (1974d [1889]) 'On Alternating Sounds', in George W. Stocking, Jr. (ed.) *A Franz Boas Reader: The Shaping of American Anthropology*, pp. 72-7. Chicago: University of Chicago Press.

Boas, Franz (1974e [1899]) 'Fieldwork for the British Association, 1888-1897', in George W. Stocking, Jr. (ed.) *A Franz Boas Reader: The Shaping of American Anthropology*, pp. 88-107. Chicago: University of Chicago Press.

Boas, Franz (1974f [1905]) 'The Mythologies of the Indians', in George W. Stocking, Jr. (ed.) *A Franz Boas Reader: The Shaping of American Anthropology*, pp. 135-48. Chicago: University of Chicago Press.

Boas, Franz (1974g [1906]) 'The Outlook for the American Negro', in George W. Stocking, Jr. (ed.) *A Franz Boas Reader: The Shaping of American Anthropology*, pp. 310-16. Chicago: University of Chicago Press.

Boas, Franz (1974h [1909]) 'Race Problems in America', in George W. Stocking, Jr. (ed.) *A Franz Boas Reader: The Shaping of American Anthropology*, pp. 318-30. Chicago: University of Chicago Press.

Bourne, Randolph (1996 [1916]) 'Trans-National America', in Werner Sollors (ed.) *Theories of Ethnicity: A Classical Reader*, pp. 93-108. New York: New York University Press.

Brennan, Timothy (2005) 'Resolution', in Homi Bhabha and W.J.T. Mitchell (eds) *Edward Said: Continuing the Conversation*, pp. 43-55. Chicago: University of Chicago Press.

Brockelman, Thomas P. (2001) *The Frame and the Mirror: On Collage and the Postmodern*. Evanston: Northwestern University Press.

Brooks, Van Wyck (1968a [1915]) 'America's Coming-of-Age', in Claire Sprague (ed.) *Van Wyck Brooks, The Early Years: A Selection from his Works, 1908-1921*, pp. 79-158. New York: Harper and Row.

Brooks, Van Wyck (1968b [1918]) 'On Creating a Usable Past', in Claire Sprague (ed.) *Van Wyck Brooks, The Early Years: A Selection from his Works, 1908-1921*, pp. 219-26. New York: Harper and Row.

Brown, Sterling A. (1980) 'Cabaret', in Michael S. Harper (ed.) *The Collected Poems of Sterling A. Brown*, pp. 111-12. Evanston: TriQuarterly Books.

Budge, E.A. Wallis (1920) *An Egyptian Hieroglyphic Dictionary*. London: Murray.

Bunzl, Matti (1996) 'Franz Boas and the Humboldtian Tradition: From *Volksgeist* and *Nationalcharakter* to an Anthropological Concept of Culture', in George W. Stocking, Jr. (ed.) *Volksgeist as Method and Ethic: Essays on Boasian Ethnography and the German Anthropological Tradition*, pp. 17-78. Madison: University of Wisconsin Press.

Bürger, Peter (1984) *Theory of the Avant-Garde*. Minneapolis: University of Minnesota Press.

Callahan, John F., ed. (1994) *The Collected Essays of Ralph Ellison*. New York: Modern Library.

Calverton, V.F. (1925) 'The Latest Negro', *The Nation* 121(3156), 30 December: 761-2.

Carby, Hazel (1994) 'The Politics of Fiction, Anthropology, and the Folk: Zora Neale Hurston', in Geneviève Fabre and Robert O'Meally (eds) *History and Memory in African-American Culture*, pp. 28-44. New York: Oxford University Press.

Carr, Helen (2000) 'Imagism and Empire', in Howard J. Booth and Nigel Rigby (eds) *Modernism and Empire*, pp. 64-92. Manchester: Manchester University Press.

Carroll, Anne Elizabeth (2005) *Word, Image, and the New Negro: Representation and Identity in the Harlem Renaissance*. Bloomington: Indiana University Press.

Cather, Willa (1996 [1918]) *My Àntonia*. London: Everyman.

Ching, Barbara and Gerald W. Creed, eds (1997) *Knowing Your Place: Rural Identity and Cultural Hierarchy*. New York: Routledge.

Clifford, James (1988) *The Predicament of Culture: Twentieth-Century Ethnography, Literature, and Art*. Cambridge, MA: Harvard University Press.

Cohen, Joshua (1996) 'Procedure and Substance in Deliberative Democracy', in Seyla Benhabib (ed.) *Democracy and Difference: Contesting the Boundaries of the Political*, pp. 95-119. Princeton: Princeton University Press.

Coleridge, Samuel Taylor (1983 [1797-98]) 'Kubla Khan', in Alexander W. Allison et al (eds) *The Norton Anthology of Poetry*, pp. 564-5. New York: Norton.

Cowan, Bainard and Jefferson Humphries, eds (1997) *Poetics of the Americas: Race, Founding, and Textuality*. Baton Rouge: Louisiana State University Press.

Curl, James Stevens (1994) *Egyptomania. The Egyptian Revival, A Recurring Theme in the History of Taste*. Manchester: Manchester University Press.

Davis, Angela Y. (1999) *Blues Legacies and Black Feminism: Gertrude 'Ma' Rainey, Bessie Smith, and Billie Holiday*. New York: Vintage.

Davis, Gerald L. (1985) *I Got the Word in Me and I Can Sing It, You Know: A Study of the Performed African-American Sermon*. Philadelphia: University of Pennsylvania. Press.

Davis, Christina (1994) 'An Interview with Toni Morrison', in Danille Taylor-Guthrie (ed.) *Conversations with Toni Morrison*, pp. 223-33. Jackson: University Press of Mississippi.

Dawahare, Anthony (2003) *Nationalism, Marxism, and African American Literature between the Wars: A New Pandora's Box*. Jackson: University Press of Mississippi.

Diedrich, Maria and Werner Sollors, eds (1994) *Black Columbiad: Defining Moments in African American Literature and Culture*. Cambridge, MA: Harvard University Press.

Dijkstra, Bram (1969) *Cubism, Stieglitz, and the Early Poetry of William Carlos Williams: The Hieroglyphics of a New Speech*. Princeton: Princeton University Press.

Donaldson, Laura E. (1992) *Decolonizing Feminisms: Race, Gender, and Empire-Building*. Chapel Hill: University of North Carolina Press.

Dos Passos, John (1963 [1922]) 'Off the Shoals', in William Wasserstrom (ed.) *A Dial Miscellany*, pp. 106-11. New York: Syracuse University Press.

Douglas, Ann (1995) *Terrible Honesty: Mongrel Manhattan in the 1920s*. New York: Noonday Press.

Du Bois, W.E.B. (1910a) 'Editorial: N.A.A.C.P.', *The Crisis*, December: 16-17.

Du Bois, W.E.B. (1910b) 'Editorial: The Inevitable', *The Crisis*, December: 21.

Du Bois, W.E.B. (1912) 'Editorial: The Gall of Bitterness', *The Crisis*, February: 153.

Du Bois, W.E.B., ed. (1917) 'The Outer Pocket', *The Crisis*, April: 286.

Du Bois, W.E.B. (1920) *Darkwater: Voices from within the Veil*. New York: Harcourt, Brace.

Du Bois, W.E.B. (1928) 'The Browsing Reader', *The Crisis*, June: 202, 211.

Du Bois, W.E.B. (1995 [1926]) 'Criteria of Negro Art', in David Levering Lewis (ed.) *W.E.B. Du Bois: A Reader*, pp. 509-15. New York: Henry Holt.

Du Bois, W.E.B. (1996 [1903]) *The Souls of Black Folk*. Harmondsworth: Penguin.

Duck, Leigh Anne (2001) '"Go there tuh know there": Zora Neale Hurston and the Chronotype of the Folk', *American Literary History* 13(2): 265-94.

duCille, Ann (1993) *The Coupling Convention: Sex, Text, and Tradition in Black Women's Fiction*. Oxford: Oxford University Press.

Earle, Susan (2007) 'Harlem, Modernism, and Beyond: Aaron Douglas and His Role in Art/History', in Susan Earle (ed.) *Aaron Douglas: African American Modernist*, pp. 5-51. New Haven: Yale University Press.

Early, Gerald, ed. (1991) *My Soul's High Song: The Collected Writings of Countee Cullen, Voice of the Harlem Renaissance*. New York: Doubleday.

(1929) 'Echoes from Around the World', *The Crisis*, October: n.p.

Edwards, Brent Hayes (2003) *The Practice of Diaspora: Literature, Translation, and the Rise of Black Internationalism*. Cambridge, MA: Harvard University Press.

Elliott, Michael A. (2002) *The Culture Concept: Writing and Difference in the Age of Realism*. Minneapolis: University of Minnesota Press.

Ellison, Ralph (1994) 'The Art of Romare Bearden', in John F. Callahan (ed.) *The Collected Essays of Ralph Ellison*, pp. 684-93. New York: Modern Library.

Evenson, Norma (1989) *The Indian Metropolis: A View Toward the West*. New Haven: Yale University Press.

Fabian, Johannes (1983) *Time and the Other: How Anthropology Makes its Object*. New York: Columbia University Press.

Fabre, Geneviève and Michel Feith, eds (2001) *Jean Toomer and the Harlem Renaissance*. New Brunswick: Rutgers University Press.

Fabre, Geneviève and Michel Feith, eds (2001) *Temples for Tomorrow: Looking Back at the Harlem Renaissance*. Bloomington: Indiana University Press.

Fabre, Geneviève and Robert O'Meally, eds (1994) *History and Memory in African-American Culture*. New York: Oxford University Press.

Faulkner, Peter, ed. (1986) *A Modernist Reader: Modernism in England 1910-1930*. London: Batsford.

Feith, Michel (2001) 'The Syncopated African: Constructions of Origins in the Harlem Renaissance (Literature, Music, Visual Arts)', in Geneviève Fabre and Michel Feith (eds) *Temples for Tomorrow*, pp. 51-72. Bloomington: Indiana University Press.

Fiedler, Leslie A. (1968) *The Return of the Vanishing American*. London: Jonathan Cape.

Fish, Stanley E. (1980 [1970]) 'Literature in the Reader: Affective Stylistics', in Jane P. Tompkins (ed.) *Reader-Response Criticism: From Formalism to Post-Structuralism*, pp. 70-100. Baltimore: Johns Hopkins University Press.

Foley, Barbara (1998) '"In the Land of Cotton": Economics and Violence in Jean Toomer's *Cane*', *African American Review* 32(2): 181-98.

Foley, Barbara (2003) *Spectres of 1919: Class and Nation in the Making of the New Negro*. Urbana: University of Illinois Press.

Frank, Waldo (1919) *Our America*. New York: Boni and Liveright.

Frank, Waldo, Lewis Mumford, Dorothy Norman, Paul Rosenfeld and Harold Rugg, eds (1975 [1934]) *America and Alfred Stieglitz: A Collective Portrait*. New York: Aperture.

Franke, Astrid (1999) 'Struggling with Stereotypes: The Problems of Representing a Collective Identity', in Leonard Harris (ed.) *The Critical Pragmatism of Alain Locke: A Reader on Value Theory, Aesthetics, Community, Culture, Race, and Education*, pp. 21-38. Lanham: Rowman and Littlefield.

Frazier, E. Franklin (1966 [1939]) *The Negro Family in the United States*. Chicago: University of Chicago Press.

Freud, Sigmund (1939) *Moses and Monotheism*, trans. Katherine Jones. New York: Vintage.

Fulton, DoVeanna S. (2006) *Speaking Power: Black Feminist Orality in Women's Narratives of Slavery*. New York: State University of New York Press.

Fusco, Coco (1995) *English is Broken Here: Notes on Cultural Fusion in the Americas*. New York: New Press.

Gambrell, Alice (1997) *Women Intellectuals, Modernism and Difference: Transatlantic Culture, 1919-1945*. Cambridge: Cambridge University Press.

Gates, Henry Louis, Jr. (1988a) *The Signifying Monkey: A Theory of African-American Literary Criticism*. Oxford: Oxford University Press.

Gates, Henry Louis, Jr. (1988b) 'The Trope of a New Negro and the Reconstruction of the Image of the Black', *Representations* 24: 129-55.

Gates, Henry Louis, Jr. and K.A. Appiah, eds (1993) *Zora Neale Hurston: Critical Perspectives Past and Present*. New York: Amistad.

Gates, Henry Louis, Jr. and Nellie Y. McKay, eds (1997) *The Norton Anthology of African American Literature*. New York: Norton.

Gates, Henry Louis, Jr. and Gene Andrew Jarrett, eds (2007) *The New Negro: Readings on Race, Representation, and African American Culture, 1892-1938*. Princeton: Princeton University Press.

Gatewood, Willard B. (1990) *Aristocrats of Color: The Black Elite, 1880-1920*. Bloomington: Indiana University Press.

Genette, Gérard (1997) *Paratexts: Thresholds of Interpretation*, trans. Jane E. Lewin. Cambridge: Cambridge University Press.

Gidley, Mick, ed. (1992) *Representing Others: White Views of Indigenous Peoples*. Exeter: University of Exeter Press.

Gillis, John R., ed. (1994) *Commemorations: The Politics of National Identity*. Princeton: Princeton University Press.

Gilroy, Paul (1993) *The Black Atlantic: Modernity and Double Consciousness*. London: Verso.

Gilroy, Paul (2000a) *Between Camps: Race, Identity and Nationalism at the End of the Colour Line*. London: Allen Lane.

Gilroy, Paul (2000b) *Against Race: Imagining Political Culture Beyond the Color Line*. Cambridge, MA: Belknap Press of Harvard University Press.

Godden, Richard (1997) *Fictions of Labor: William Faulkner and the South's Long Revolution*. Cambridge: Cambridge University Press.

Goldman, Jane (2004) *Modernism, 1910-1945: Image to Apocalypse*. Basingstoke: Palgrave.

Gordon, Deborah (1990) 'The Politics of Ethnographic Authority: Race and Writing in the Ethnography of Margaret Mead and Zora Neale Hurston', in Marc Manganaro (ed.) *Modernist Anthropology: From Fieldwork to Text*, pp. 146-62. Princeton: Princeton University Press.

Graff, Gerald (1987) *Professing Literature: An Institutional History*. Chicago: University of Chicago Press.

Grammer, John M. (2004) 'Plantation Fiction', in Richard Gray and Owen Robinson (eds) *A Companion to the Literature and Culture of the American South*, pp. 58-75. Oxford: Blackwell.

Gray, Richard and Owen Robinson, eds (2004) *A Companion to the Literature and Culture of the American South*. Oxford: Blackwell.

Gray, Thomas (1983 [1751]) 'Elegy Written in a Country Churchyard', in Alexander W. Allison et al (eds) *The Norton Anthology of Poetry*, pp. 463-6. New York: Norton.

Griffin, Farah Jasmine (1995) *"Who Set You Flowin'?": The African-American Migration Narrative*. Oxford: Oxford University Press.

Grossman, James R. (1989) *Land of Hope: Chicago, Black Southerners, and the Great Migration*. Chicago: University of Chicago Press.

Gubar, Susan (1997) *Racechanges: White Skin, Black Face in American Culture*. New York: Oxford University Press.

Guibernau, Montserrat (1999) *Nations Without States: Political Communities in a Global Age*. Malden: Blackwell.

Handler, Richard (1990) 'Boasian Anthropology and the Critique of American Culture', *American Quarterly* 42(2): 252-73.

Harris, Leonard, ed. (1989) *The Philosophy of Alain Locke: Harlem Renaissance and Beyond*. Philadelphia: Temple University Press.

Harris, Leonard, ed. (1999) *The Critical Pragmatism of Alain Locke: A Reader on Value Theory, Aesthetics, Community, Culture, Race, and Education*. Lanham: Rowman and Littlefield.

Harrison, Beth (1996) 'Zora Neale Hurston and Mary Austin: A Case Study in Ethnography, Literary Modernism, and Contemporary Ethnic Fiction', *MELUS* 21(2): 89-106.

Harrison, Ira E. and Faye V. Harrison, eds (1999) *African-American Pioneers in Anthropology*. Urbana: University of Illinois Press.

Hatch, Gary Layne (1996) 'Logic in the Black Folk Sermon: The Sermons of Rev. C.L. Franklin', *Journal of Black Studies* 26(3): 227-44.

Hegeman, Susan (1999) *Patterns for America: Modernism and the Concept of Culture*. Princeton: Princeton University Press.

Helbling, Mark (1999a) *The Harlem Renaissance: The One and the Many*. Westport: Greenwood Press.

Helbling, Mark (1999b) 'African Art and the Harlem Renaissance: Alain Locke, Melville Herskovits, Roger Fry, and Albert C. Barnes', in Leonard Harris (ed.) *The Critical Pragmatism of Alain Locke: A Reader on Value Theory, Aesthetics, Community, Culture, Race, and Education*, pp. 53-84. Lanham: Rowman and Littlefield,

Hemenway, Robert E. (1980) *Zora Neale Hurston: A Literary Biography*. Urbana: University of Illinois Press.

Henderson, Mae Gwendolyn (1989) 'Speaking in Tongues: Dialogics, Dialectics, and the Black Woman Writer's Literary Tradition', in Cheryl A. Wall (ed.) *Changing Our Own Words: Essays on Criticism, Theory, and Writing by Black Women*, pp. 16-37. London: Routledge.

Hernández, Graciela (1995) 'Multiple Subjectivities and Strategic Positionality: Zora Neale Hurston's Experimental Ethnographies', in Ruth Behar and Deborah A. Gordon (eds) *Women Writing Culture*, pp. 148-65. Berkeley: University of California Press.

Herskovits, Melville J. (1985 [1928]) *The American Negro: A Study in Racial Crossing*. Westport: Greenwood Press.

Hill, Lynda Marion (1996) *Social Rituals and the Verbal Art of Zora Neale Hurston*. Washington DC: Howard University Press.

Hoffman, Frederick J., Charles Allen, Carolyn F. Ulrich, eds (1947) *The Little Magazine: A History and A Bibliography*. Princeton: Princeton University Press.

Hoffman, Katherine, ed. (1989) *Collage: Critical Views*. Ann Arbor: UMI Research Press.

Holloway, Karla F.C. (1987) *The Character of the Word: The Texts of Zora Neale Hurston*. New York: Greenwood Press.

Hopkins, Pauline E. (1905) *A Primer of Facts Pertaining to the Early Greatness of the African Race and the Possibility of Restoration by its Descendants*. Cambridge, MA: Hopkins.

Huggins, Nathan Irvin (1971) *Harlem Renaissance*. New York: Oxford University Press.

Huggins, Nathan Irvin, ed. (1976) *Voices from the Harlem Renaissance*. New York: Oxford University Press.

Hughes, Langston (1993 [1940]) *The Big Sea*. New York: Hill and Wang.

Hughes, Robert (1991) *The Shock of the New: Art and the Century of Change*. London: Thames and Hudson.

Hurston, Zora Neale (1931) 'Hoodoo in America', *The Journal of American Folklore* 44: 317-417.

Hurston, Zora Neale (1976 [1929]) 'The Sermon', in Nathan Huggins (ed.) *Voices from the Harlem Renaissance*, pp. 239-44. New York: Oxford University Press.

Hurston, Zora Neale (1986 [1937]) *Their Eyes Were Watching God*. London: Virago.

Hurston, Zora Neale (1987 [1934]) *Jonah's Gourd Vine*. London: Virago.

Hurston, Zora Neale (1990a [1935]) *Mules and Men*. New York: Harper Perennial.

Hurston, Zora Neale (1990b [1938]) *Tell My Horse: Voodoo and Life in Haiti and Jamaica*. New York: Harper Perennial.

Hurston, Zora Neale (1991 [1939]) *Moses, Man of the Mountain*. New York: Harper Perennial.

Hurston, Zora Neale (1995a [1928]) 'How it Feels to be Colored Me', in Cheryl A. Wall (ed.) *Zora Neale Hurston: Folklore, Memoirs, and Other Writings*, pp. 826-9. New York: Library of America.

Hurston, Zora Neale (1995b [1934]) 'Characteristics of Negro Expression', in Cheryl A. Wall (ed.) *Zora Neale Hurston: Folklore, Memoirs, and Other Writings*, pp. 830-46. New York: Library of America.

Hurston, Zora Neale (1995c [1934]) 'Spirituals and Neo-Spirituals', in Cheryl A. Wall (ed.) *Zora Neale Hurston: Folklore, Memoirs, and Other Writings*, pp. 869-74. New York: Library of America.

Hurston, Zora Neale (1995d [1942]) *Dust Tracks on a Road*, in Cheryl A. Wall (ed.) *Zora Neale Hurston: Folklore, Memoirs, and Other Writings*, pp. 557-808. New York: Library of America.

Hurston, Zora Neale (1995e [n.d.]) 'The Sanctified Church', in Cheryl A. Wall (ed.) *Zora Neale Hurston: Folklore, Memoirs, and Other Writings*, pp. 901-5. New York: Library of America.

Hurston, Zora Neale (1995f [1950]) 'What White Publishers Won't Print', in Cheryl A. Wall (ed.) *Zora Neale Hurston: Folklore, Memoirs, and Other Writings*, pp. 950-55. New York: Library of America.

Hurston, Zora Neale (1999) 'Heaven', in Pamela Bordelon (ed.) *Go Gator and Muddy the Water: Writings by Zora Neale Hurston from the Federal Writers' Project*, pp. 109-10. New York: Norton.

Hutchinson, George (1993) 'Toomer and American Racial Discourse', *Texas Studies in Literature and Language* 35(2): 226-50.

Hutchinson, George (1995) *The Harlem Renaissance in Black and White*. Cambridge, MA: Belknap Press of Harvard University Press.

Ickringill, Steve, ed. (1990) *Looking Inward, Looking Outward: From the 1930s through the 1940s*. Amsterdam: VU University Press.

(1977 [1930]) *I'll Take My Stand: The South and the Agrarian Tradition by Twelve Southerners*. Baton Rouge: Louisiana State University Press.

Irwin, John T. (1980) *American Hieroglyphics: The Symbol of the Egyptian Hieroglyphics in the American Renaissance*. New Haven: Yale University Press.

Iser, Wolfgang (1980 [1974]) 'The Reading Process: A Phenomenological Approach', in Jane P. Tompkins (ed.) *Reader-Response Criticism: From Formalism to Post-Structuralism*, pp. 50-69. Baltimore: Johns Hopkins University Press.

Jacknis, Ira (1996) 'The Ethnographic Object and the Object of Ethnology in the Early Career of Franz Boas', in George W. Stocking, Jr. (ed.) *Volksgeist as Method and Ethic: Essays on Boasian Ethnography and the German Anthropological Tradition*, pp. 185-214. Madison: University of Wisconsin Press.

Jacobs, Harriet (1997 [1861]) 'Incidents in the Life of a Slave Girl', in Henry Louis Gates, Jr. and Nellie Y. McKay (eds) *The Norton Anthology of African American Literature*, pp. 209-45. New York: Norton.

Jacobs, Karen (2001) *The Eye's Mind: Literary Modernism and Visual Culture.* Ithaca: Cornell University Press.

Jirousek, Lori (2004) '"That Commonality of Feeling": Hurston, Hybridity, and Ethnography', *African American Review* 38(3): 417-27.

Johnson, Barbara (1993) 'Thresholds of Difference: Structures of Address in Zora Neale Hurston', in Henry Louis Gates, Jr. and K.A. Appiah (eds) *Zora Neale Hurston: Critical Perspectives Past and Present*, pp. 130-40. New York: Amistad.

Johnson, Barbara (1997) 'Moses and Intertextuality: Sigmund Freud, Zora Neale Hurston, and the Bible', in Bainard Cowan and Jefferson Humphries (eds) *Poetics of the Americas: Race, Founding, and Textuality*, pp. 15-29. Baton Rouge: Louisiana State University Press.

Johnson, James Weldon ed. (1958 [1922]) *The Book of American Negro Poetry.* New York: Harcourt, Brace and World.

Johnson, James Weldon (1961 [1927]) *God's Trombones: Seven Negro Sermons in Verse.* New York: Viking Press.

Jones, Robert B., ed. (1996) *Jean Toomer: Selected Essays and Literary Criticism.* Knoxville: University of Tennessee Press.

Joseph, Philip (2002) 'The Verdict from the Porch: Zora Neale Hurston and Reparative Justice', *American Literature* 74(3): 455-83.

Joyce, James (1960 [1916]) *A Portrait of the Artist as a Young Man.* London: Cape.

Kadlec, David (2000a) *Mosaic Modernism: Anarchism, Pragmatism, Culture.* Baltimore: Johns Hopkins University Press.

Kadlec, David (2000b) 'Zora Neale Hurston and the Federal Folk', *Modernism/ Modernity* 7(3): 471-85.

Kallen, Horace M. (1996 [1915]) 'Democracy versus the Melting-Pot: A Study of American Nationality', in Werner Sollors (ed.) *Theories of Ethnicity: A Classical Reader*, pp. 67-92. New York: New York University Press.

Kaplan, Carla, ed. (2002) *Zora Neale Hurston: A Life in Letters.* New York: Doubleday.

Kerman, Cynthia Earl and Richard Eldridge (1987) *The Lives of Jean Toomer: A Hunger for Wholeness.* Baton Rouge: Louisiana State University Press.

King, Desmond (2000) *Making Americans: Immigration, Race, and the Origins of the Diverse Democracy*, Cambridge, MA: Harvard University Press.

King, Richard H. and Helen Taylor, eds (1996) *Dixie Debates: Perspectives on Southern Cultures.* New York: New York University Press.

Kinnamon, Keneth (1997) 'Anthologies', in William L. Andrews, Frances Smith Foster and Trudier Harris (eds) *The Oxford Companion to African American Literature*, pp. 22-8. New York: Oxford University Press.

Kirschke, Amy Helene (1995) *Aaron Douglas: Art, Race, and the Harlem Renaissance.* Jackson: University Press of Mississippi.

Konzett, Delia Caparoso (2002a) *Ethnic Modernisms: Anzia Yezierska, Zora Neale Hurston, Jean Rhys, and the Aesthetics of Dislocation*. New York: Palgrave Macmillan.

Konzett, Delia Caparoso (2002b) "'Getting in Touch with the True South": Pet Negroes, White Crackers, and Racial Staging in Zora Neale Hurston's *Seraph on the Suwanee*', in Samina Najmi and Rajini Srikanth (eds) *White Women in Racialized Spaces: Imaginative Transformation and Ethical Action in Literature*, pp. 131-46. Albany: State University of New York Press.

Krupat, Arnold (1992) *Ethnocriticism: Ethnography, History, Literature*. Berkeley: University of California Press.

Larsen, Nella (1995 [1928, 1929]) *Quicksand and Passing*. London: Serpent's Tail.

Lauret, Maria (1996) "'I've got a right to sing the blues": Alice Walker's Aesthetic', in Richard H. King and Helen Taylor (eds) *Dixie Debates: Perspectives on Southern Cultures*, pp. 51-66. New York: New York University Press.

Lawal, Babatunde (2002) 'The African Heritage of African American Art and Performance', in Paul Carter Harrison, Victor Leo Walker II and Gus Edwards (eds) *Black Theatre: Ritual Performance in the African Diaspora*, pp. 39-63. Philadelphia: Temple University Press.

Leininger-Miller, Theresa (2001) *New Negro Artists in Paris: African American Painters and Sculptors in the City of Light, 1922-1934*. New Brunswick: Rutgers University Press.

Lemann, Nicholas (1991) *The Promised Land: The Great Black Migration and How It Changed America*. New York: Knopf.

Lemke, Sieglinde (1998) *Primitivist Modernism: Black Culture and the Origins of Transatlantic Modernism*. New York: Oxford University Press.

Levin, Kim (1989) 'Foreword', in Katherine Hoffman (ed.) *Collage: Critical Views*, pp. xix-xx. Ann Arbor: UMI Research Press.

Levine, Lawrence W. (1977) *Black Culture and Black Consciousness: Afro-American Folk Thought From Slavery to Freedom*. New York: Oxford University Press.

Lévi-Strauss, Claude (1985) *The View from Afar*, trans. Joachim Neugroschel and Pheobe Hoss. Oxford: Blackwell.

Lewis, David Levering, ed. (1994) *The Portable Harlem Renaissance Reader*. Harmondsworth: Penguin.

Lewis, David Levering, ed. (1995) *W.E.B. Du Bois: A Reader*, New York: Henry Holt.

Lewis, David Levering (1997 [1979]) *When Harlem was in Vogue*. New York: Oxford University Press.

Lhamon, W.T. (1998) *Raising Cain: Blackface Performance from Jim Crow to Hip Hop*. Cambridge, MA: Harvard University Press.

Lindsay, Vachel (1970 [1922]) *The Art of the Moving Picture*. New York: Liveright.

Liss, Julia E. (1995) 'Patterns of Strangeness: Franz Boas, Modernism, and the Origins of Anthropology', in Elazar Barkan and Ronald Bush (eds) *Prehistories of the Future: The Primitivist Project and the Culture of Modernism*, pp. 114-30. Stanford: Stanford University Press.

Liss, Julia E. (1998) 'Diasporic Identities: The Science and Politics of Race in the Work of Franz Boas and W.E.B. Du Bois, 1894-1919', *Cultural Anthropology* 13(2): 127-66.

Locke, Alain, ed. (1925a) 'Harlem, Mecca of the New Negro', *Survey Graphic* 6(6).

Locke, Alain, ed. (1925b) *The New Negro: An Interpretation*. New York: Boni.

Locke, Alain (1983a [1928]) 'Beauty Instead of Ashes', in Jeffrey C. Stewart (ed.) *The Critical Temper of Alain Locke: A Selection of his Essays on Art and Culture*, pp. 23-5. New York: Garland Press.

Locke, Alain (1983b [1925]) 'To Certain of our Philistines', in Jeffrey C. Stewart (ed.) *The Critical Temper of Alain Locke*, pp. 161-2. New York: Garland Press.

Locke, Alain (1983c [1935]) 'The Eleventh Hour of Nordicism: Retrospective Review of the Literature of the Negro for 1934', in Jeffrey C. Stewart (ed.) *The Critical Temper of Alain Locke*, pp. 227-35. New York: Garland Press.

Locke, Alain (1983d [1924]) 'The Concept of Race as Applied to Social Culture', in Jeffrey C. Stewart (ed.) *The Critical Temper of Alain Locke*, pp. 423-31. New York: Garland Press.

Locke, Alain (1989a [1942]) 'Who and What is "Negro"?', in Leonard Harris (ed.) *The Philosophy of Alain Locke*, pp. 207-28. Philadelphia: Temple University Press.

Locke, Alain (1989b [1949]) 'Frontiers of Culture', in Leonard Harris (ed.) *The Philosophy of Alain Locke*, pp. 229-36. Philadelphia: Temple University Press.

Locke, Alain, ed. (1992a [1925]) *The New Negro: Voices of the Harlem Renaissance*. New York: Touchstone.

Locke, Alain (1992b) *Race Contacts and Interracial Relations: Lectures on the Theory and Practice of Race,* ed. Jeffrey C. Stewart. Washington, DC: Howard University Press.

Lorini, Alessandra (1999) *Rituals of Race: American Public Culture and the Search for Racial Democracy*. Charlottesville: University of Virginia Press.

Lorini, Alessandra (2001) '"The Spell of Africa is Upon Me": W.E.B. Du Bois's Notion of Art as Propaganda', in Geneviève Fabre and Michel Feith (eds) *Temples for Tomorrow: Looking Back at the Harlem Renaissance*, pp. 159-76. Bloomington: Indiana University Press.

Lott, Eric (1993) *Love and Theft: Blackface Minstrelsy and the American Working Class*. New York: Oxford University Press.

Lowe, John (1994) *Jump at the Sun: Zora Neale Hurston's Cosmic Comedy*. Urbana: University of Illinois Press.

Lowell, Amy (1986 [1915]) 'Preface to *Some Imagist Poets*', in Peter Faulkner (ed.) *A Modernist Reader: Modernism in England 1910-1930*, pp. 53-5. London: Batsford.

Lowie, Robert H. (1949 [1921]) *Primitive Society*. London: Routledge and Kegan Paul.

Mackert, Michael (1994) 'Franz Boas' Theory of Phonetics', *Historiographia Linguistica* 21(3): 351-84.

MacLean, Nancy (1994) *Behind the Mask of Chivalry: The Making of the Second Ku Klux Klan*. New York: Oxford University Press.

Mandelbaum, David G., ed. (1963) *Selected Writings of Edward Sapir in Language, Culture and Personality*. Berkeley: University of California Press.

Manganaro, Marc, ed. (1990) *Modernist Anthropology: From Fieldwork to Text*. Princeton: Princeton University Press.

Manganaro, Marc (2002) *Culture, 1922, The Emergence of a Concept*. Princeton: Princeton University Press.

Massa, Ann (1970) *Vachel Lindsay: Fieldworker for the American Dream*. Bloomington: Indiana University Press.

Maxwell, William J. (1997) '"Is it True What They Say About Dixie?": Richard Wright, Zora Neale Hurston, and Rural/Urban Exchange in Modern African-American Literature', in Barbara Ching and Gerald W. Creed (ed.) *Knowing Your Place: Rural Identity and Cultural Hierarchy*, pp. 71-104. New York: Routledge.

McDowell, Deborah E. (1991) 'Lines of Descent/Dissenting Lines', in Zora Neale Hurston, *Moses, Man of the Mountain*, pp. vii-xxii. New York: Harper Perennial.

McKay, Nellie Y. (1984) *Jean Toomer, Artist: A Study of His Literary Life and Work, 1894-1936*. Chapel Hill: University of North Carolina Press.

Mead, Margaret (1969 [1928]) *Coming of Age in Samoa: A Study of Adolescence and Sex in Primitive Societies*. Harmondsworth: Penguin.

Meisenhelder, Susan Edwards (1999) *Hitting a Straight Lick with a Crooked Stick: Race and Gender in the Work of Zora Neale Hurston*. Tuscaloosa: University of Alabama Press.

Mencke, John G. (1979) *Mulattoes and Race Mixture: American Attitudes and Images, 1865-1918*. Ann Arbor: UMI Research Press.

Mercer, Kobena, ed. (2005) *Cosmopolitan Modernisms*. Cambridge, MA: MIT Press.

Mercer, Kobena (2005) 'Romare Bearden, 1964: Collage as Kuntswollen', in Kobena Mercer (ed.) *Cosmopolitan Modernisms*, pp. 124-45. Cambridge, MA: MIT Press.

Michaelsen, Scott (1999) *The Limits of Multiculturalism: Interrogating the Origins of American Anthropology*. Minneapolis: University of Minnesota Press.

Mickell, Gwendolyn (1999) 'Feminism and Black Culture in the Ethnography of Zora Neale Hurston', in Ira E. Harrison and Faye V. Harrison (eds) *African-*

American Pioneers in Anthropology, pp. 51-69. Urbana: University of Illinois Press.

Morgan, Marcyliena (1998) 'More than a Mood or an Attitude: Discourse and Verbal Genres in African-American Culture', in Salikoko S. Mufwene, John R. Rickford, Guy Bailey and John Baugh (eds) *African-American English: Structure, History, and Use*, pp. 251-81. London: Routledge.

Morris, Jan with Simon Winchester (1983) *Stones of Empire: The Buildings of the Raj*. Oxford: Oxford University Press.

Morrison, Toni (1989) 'A Bench by the Road', *World: Journal of the Unitarian Universalist Association* 3(1): 4-5, 37-41.

Mufwene, Salikoko S., John R. Rickford, Guy Bailey and John Baugh, eds (1998) *African-American English: Structure, History, and Use*. London: Routledge.

Nadell, Martha Jane (2001) 'Race and the Visual Arts in the Works of Jean Toomer and Georgia O'Keeffe', in Geneviève Fabre and Michel Feith (eds) *Jean Toomer and the Harlem Renaissance*, pp. 142-61. New Brunswick: Rutgers University Press.

Nadell, Martha Jane (2004) *Enter the New Negroes: Images of Race in American Culture*. Cambridge, MA: Harvard University Press.

Nora, Pierre (1994) 'Between Memory and History: *Les Lieux de Mémoire*', in Geneviève Fabre and Robert O'Meally (eds) *History and Memory in African-American Culture*, pp. 284-300. New York: Oxford University Press.

North, Michael (1994) *The Dialect of Modernism: Race, Language and Twentieth-Century Literature*. New York: Oxford University Press.

North, Michael (1999) *Reading 1922: A Return to the Scene of the Modern*. New York: Oxford University Press.

Odum, Howard W. (1925) 'The New Negro', *Modern Quarterly* 3, October-December: 127-8.

Oliver, Paul (1969) *The Story of the Blues*. London: Barrie and Radcliff the Cresset Press.

Olsson, Anders (2000) *Managing Diversity: The Anthologization of 'American Literature'*. Uppsala: Uppsala University Press.

Ong, Walter (1982) *Orality and Literacy: The Technologizing of the Word*. London: Methuen.

Ovington, Mary White (1911) *Half a Man: The Status of the Negro in New York*. London: Longmans, Green.

Owen, Wilfred (1983 [1920]) 'Dulce Et Decorum Est', in Alexander W. Allison et al (eds) *The Norton Anthology of Poetry*, p. 1037. New York: Norton.

Phillips, Ulrich B. (1948 [1929]) *Life and Labor in the Old South*. Boston: Little, Brown.

Poggi, Christine (1992) *In Defiance of Painting: Cubism, Futurism, and the Invention of Collage*. New Haven: Yale University Press.

Powell, Richard J. (1997) *Black Art and Culture in the Twentieth Century*. London: Thames and Hudson.

Powell, Richard J. (2007) 'The Aaron Douglas Effect', in Susan Earle (ed.) *Aaron Douglas: African American Modernist*, pp. 53-73. New Haven: Yale University Press.

Powell, Richard J. and David. A. Bailey, eds (1997) *Rhapsodies in Black: Art of the Harlem Renaissance*. Berkeley: University of California Press.

Richards, David (1994) *Masks of Difference: Cultural Representations in Literature, Anthropology and Art*. Cambridge: Cambridge University Press.

Rose, Jacqueline (2005) *The Question of Zion*. Princeton: Princeton University Press.

Rusch, Frederik L., ed. (1993) *A Jean Toomer Reader: Selected Unpublished Writings*. New York: Oxford University Press.

Sapir, Edward (1963 [1919]) 'Culture, Genuine and Spurious', in David G. Mandelbaum (ed.) *Selected Writings of Edward Sapir in Language, Culture and Personality*, pp. 308-31. Berkeley: University of California Press.

Said, Edward W. (1988) 'Michael Walzer's *Exodus and Revolution*: A Canaanite Reading', in Edward W. Said and Christopher Hitchens (eds) *Blaming the Victims: Spurious Scholarship and the Palestinian Question*, pp. 161-78. London: Verso.

Said, Edward W. (1993) *Culture and Imperialism*. London: Vintage.

Said, Edward W. (2003) *Freud and the Non-European*. London: Verso.

Savage, Kirk (1994) 'The Politics of Memory: Black Emancipation and the Civil War Monument', in John R. Gillis (ed.) *Commemorations: The Politics of National Identity*, pp. 127-49. Princeton: Princeton University Press.

Savage, Kirk (1997) *Standing Soldiers, Kneeling Slaves: Race, War, and Monument in Nineteenth-Century America*. Princeton: Princeton University Press.

Scarborough, Dorothy (1925) 'From Cotton Field and Levee to the Streets of Harlem: Negro Work Songs and Spirituals and New Negro Ways', *The New York Times Book Review*, 20 December: 19, 27.

Schuyler, George (1998 [1931]) *Black No More*. London: X Press.

Schwartzman, Myron (1990) *Romare Bearden: His Life and Art*. New York: Abrams.

Schwarz, A.B. Christa (2003) *Gay Voices of the Harlem Renaissance*. Bloomington: Indiana University Press.

Scruggs, Charles (1997) 'The Photographic Print, the Literary Negative: Alfred Stieglitz and Jean Toomer', *Arizona Quarterly* 53(1): 61-89.

Scruggs, Charles and Lee VanDemarr (1998) *Jean Toomer and the Terrors of American History*. Philadelphia: University of Pennsylvania Press.

The Seven Arts, 2 vols, New York: AMS Reprint, [n. d.].

Sherwood, Yvonne (2001) *A Biblical Text and its Afterlives: The Survival of Jonah in Western Culture*. Cambridge: Cambridge University Press.

Smith, Katharine Capshaw (2006) *Children's Literature of the Harlem Renaissance*. Bloomington: Indiana University Press.

Smitherman, Geneva (1977) *Talkin and Testifyin: The Language of Black America*. Boston: Houghton Mifflin.

Sollors, Werner (1986) *Beyond Ethnicity: Consent and Descent in American Culture*. New York: Oxford University Press.

Sollors, Werner (1990) 'Anthropological and Sociological Tendencies in American Literature of the 1930s and 1940s: Richard Wright, Zora Neale Hurston, and American Culture', in Steve Ickringill (ed.) *Looking Inward, Looking Outward: From the 1930s through the 1940s*. pp. 22-75. Amsterdam: VU University Press.

Sollors, Werner, ed. (1996) *Theories of Ethnicity: A Classical Reader*. New York: New York University Press.

Sollors, Werner (1997) *Neither Black Nor White Yet Both: Thematic Explorations of Interracial Literature*. New York: Oxford University Press.

Sprague, Claire, ed. (1968) *Van Wyck Brooks, The Early Years: A Selection from his Works, 1908-1921*. New York: Harper and Row.

Stackelberg, Roderick (1999) *Hitler's Germany: Origins, Interpretations, Legacies*. London: Routledge.

Staller, Natasha (2001) *A Sum of Destructions: Picasso's Cultures and The Creation of Cubism*. New Haven: Yale University Press.

Stearns, Harold, ed. (1922) *Civilization in the United States: An Inquiry by Thirty Americans*. New York: Harcourt, Brace.

Stein, Gertrude (1990 [1909]) *Three Lives*. Harmondsworth: Penguin.

Stewart, Jeffrey C., ed. (1983) *The Critical Temper of Alain Locke: A Selection of his Essays on Art and Culture*. New York: Garland Press.

Stewart, Jeffrey C. (1989) *To Color America: Portraits by Winold Reiss*. Washington, DC: Smithsonian Institution Press.

Stocking, George W., Jr., ed. (1974) *A Franz Boas Reader: The Shaping of American Anthropology, 1883-1911*. Chicago: University of Chicago Press.

Stocking, George W., Jr., ed. (1996) *Volksgeist as Method and Ethic: Essays on Boasian Ethnography and the German Anthropological Tradition*. Madison: University of Wisconsin.

Stovall, Tyler (1996) *Paris Noir: African Americans in the City of Light*. Boston: Houghton Mifflin.

Sundquist, Eric J. (1983) *The Hammers of Creation: Folk Culture in Modern African-American Fiction*. Athens: University of Georgia Press.

Sundquist, Eric J. (1993) *To Wake the Nations: Race in the Making of American Literature*. Cambridge, MA: Belknap Press of Harvard University Press.

Tate, Claudia (1994) 'Toni Morrison', in Danille Taylor-Guthrie (ed.) *Conversations with Toni Morrison*, pp. 156-70. Jackson: University Press of Mississippi.

Taylor-Guthrie, Danille, ed. (1994) *Conversations with Toni Morrison*. Jackson: University Press of Mississippi.

Thompson, Mark Christian (2004) 'National Socialism and Blood-Sacrifice in Zora Neale Hurston's *Moses, Man of the Mountain*', *African American Review* 38(3): 385-415.

Toomer, Jean (1993 [1923]) *Cane*. New York: Boni and Liveright.

Toomer, Jean (1996a [1924]) 'The Negro Emergent', in Robert B. Jones (ed.) *Jean Toomer: Selected Essays and Literary Criticism*, pp. 47-54. Knoxville: University of Tennessee Press.

Toomer, Jean (1996b [1928]) 'The Crock of Problems', in Robert B. Jones (ed.) *Jean Toomer: Selected Essays and Literary Criticism*, pp. 55-9. Knoxville: University of Tennessee Press.

Toomer, Jean (1996c [1929]) 'Race Problems and Modern Society', in Werner Sollors (ed.) *Theories of Ethnicity: A Classical Reader*, pp. 168-90. New York: New York University Press.

Torgovnick, Marianna (1990) *Gone Primitive: Savage Intellects, Modern Lives*. Chicago: University of Chicago Press.

Trachtenberg, Alan (1989) *Reading American Photographs: Images as History, Mathew Brady to Walker Evans*. New York: Hill and Wang.

Turner, Darwin T. (ed.) (1988) *Jean Toomer's Cane: An Authoritative Text, Backgrounds, Criticism*. New York: Norton.

Van Vechten, Carl (2007 [1925]) 'Uncle Tom's Mansion', in Henry Louis Gates, Jr. and Gene Andrew Jarrett (eds) *The New Negro: Readings on Race, Representation, and African American Culture, 1892-1938*, pp. 223-7. Princeton: Princeton University Press.

Veneciano, Jorge Daniel (2004) 'Louis Armstrong, Bricolage, and the Aesthetics of Swing', in Robert O'Meally, Brent Hayes Edwards and Farah Jasmine Griffin (eds) *Uptown Conversations: The New Jazz Studies*, pp. 256-77. New York: Columbia University Press.

Walker, Alice (1983) *In Search of Our Mother's Gardens: Womanist Prose*. London: Women's Press.

Walker, Alice (1983a [1976]) 'Saving The Life that is Your Own: The Importance of Models in the Artist's Life', in Alice Walker, *In Search of Our Mother's Gardens*, pp. 3-14. London: Women's Press.

Walker, Alice (1983b [1979]) 'Zora Neale Hurston: A Cautionary Tale and A Partisan View', in Alice Walker, *In Search of Our Mother's Gardens*, pp. 83-92. London: Women's Press.

Walker, Alice (1983c [1975]) 'Looking for Zora', in Alice Walker, *In Search of Our Mother's Gardens*, pp. 93-116. London: Women's Press.

Wall, Cheryl A., ed. (1995a) *Zora Neale Hurston: Folklore, Memoirs, and Other Writings*. New York: Library of America.

Wall, Cheryl A. (1995b) *Women of the Harlem Renaissance*. Bloomington: Indiana University Press.

Wall, Cheryl A. (2005a) *Worrying the Line: Black Women Writers, Lineage, and Literary Tradition*. Chapel Hill: University of North Carolina Press.

Wall, Cheryl A. (2005b) 'Zora Neale Hurston's Essays: On Art and Such', *The Scholar and Feminist Online* 3(2), n. p.

Wallace, Michele (1990) *Invisibility Blues: From Pop to Theory*. London: Verso.

Walters, Keith (1999) '"He can read my writing but he sho' can't read my mind": Zora Neale Hurston's Revenge in *Mules and Men'*, *Journal of American Folklore* 112(445): 343-71.

Wardi, Anissa J. (2003) *Death and the Arc of Mourning in African American Literature*. Gainesville: University Press of Florida.

Warnes, Andrew (2006) 'Guantanamo, Eatonville, Accompong: Barbecue and the Diaspora in the Writings of Zora Neale Hurston', *Journal of American Studies* 40(2): 367-89.

Washington, Booker T. (1997 [1901]) 'Up from Slavery', in Henry Louis Gates and Nellie Y. McKay (eds) *The Norton Anthology of African American Literature*, pp. 490-521. New York: Norton.

Wasserstrom, William, ed. (1963) *A Dial Miscellany*. New York: Syracuse University Press.

West, Genevieve (2005) *Zora Neale Hurston and American Literary Culture*. Gainesville: University Press of Florida.

Whalan, Mark (2007) *Race, Manhood, and Modernism in America: The Short Story Cycles of Sherwood Anderson and Jean Toomer*. Knoxville: University of Tennessee Press.

White, John (2004) 'Southern Music', in Richard Gray and Owen Robinson (eds) *A Companion to the Literature and Culture of the American South*, pp. 185-202. Oxford: Blackwell.

Whitman, Walt (1994a [1855]) 'Song of Myself', in Nina Baym et al (eds) *The Norton Anthology of American Literature, Volume One*, pp. 2048-90. New York: Norton.

Whitman, Walt (1994b [1871]) 'Democratic Vistas', in Nina Baym et al (eds) *The Norton Anthology of American Literature, Volume One*, pp. 2170-73. New York: Norton.

Williams, Vernon J., Jr. (1996) *Rethinking Race: Franz Boas and his Contemporaries*. Lexington: University Press of Kentucky.

Williamson, Joel (1995) *New People: Miscegenation and Mulattoes in the United States*. Baton Rouge: Louisiana State University Press.

Wilson, Anthony (2003) 'The Music of God, Man, and Beast: Spirituality and Modernity in *Jonah's Gourd Vine'*, *The Southern Literary Journal* 35(2): 64-78.

Wright, Melanie J. (2003) *Moses in America: The Cultural Uses of Biblical Narrative*. Oxford: Oxford University Press.

Wright, Richard (1937) 'Between Laughter and Tears', *New Masses*, 5 October: 25-6.

Young, Robert J.C. (1995) *Colonial Desire: Hybridity in Theory, Culture, and Race*. London: Routledge.

Index

African American labour 86, 87, 88-9, 137, 162, 163-4, 180
African American sermons 114, 127, 151-60
African art 10, 13-14, 51, 52, 159
African diaspora 3-4, 115, 116, 130, 135-6, 158-9, 170, 173
'Aims of Ethnology, The' (Boas) 38, 143-4
America and Alfred Stieglitz: A Collective Portrait (Frank et al.) 61
Anderson, Benedict 77, 181-2
Anderson, Paul Allen 72, 116, 150
anthologies 50-55, 58-61, 69, 73, 76-7
anthropology *see* Boasian anthropology
Anthropology and Modern Life (Boas) 25, 26, 122
Arens, Egmont 134; *see also* hieroglyphics; Stieglitz
Art of the Moving Picture, The (Lindsay) 133n, 134-5
Ascent of Ethiopia, The (Jones) 13-14, 136-7
Aspects of Negro Life: From Slavery Through Reconstruction (Douglas) 11-13, 93
assimilation
    Boas on 26-7, 45-6
    Herskovits on 36-7
    Hurston on 121-2
    in *The New Negro* 66-9
audience
    implied audiences in *The Crisis* 44-5, 192-3
    Hurston on 125-8
    in *Jonah's Gourd Vine* 159-60; *see also* reading; reception
'Avey' (Toomer) 93-4, 103

Baker, Houston A., Jr. 3, 17, 76-7, 99, 119
Baker, Josephine 159
Bearden, Romare 11, 80-81, 85
'Becky' (Toomer) 82-3, 87

Benedict, Ruth 34, 118, 144, 182n
Bernal, Martin 116, 135
biblical allusions
    in *Jonah's Gourd Vine* 152-6, 159-60
    in *Moses, Man of the Mountain* 165, 170, 174-5, 176n
    in *Mules and Men* 142-3
'Blood-Burning Moon' (Toomer) 88-9, 103n
blues 14-15, 81, 88, 156, 190
Boas, Franz 2, 17, 19-48
    and *Cane* 80, 99-108
    and Hurston 118-23, 141-5, 154-5, 169, 170, 176-7, 179-80, 181-2, 189
    influence on *The New Negro* 55-6, 64-9
    on language development 22-4
    on miscegenation 24-7, 45-7
    on nationalism 31-2, 33-4, 176-7
    spatial culture concept 19-21, 27-34; *see also* individual works
Boasian anthropology 2, 17, 19-48, 55-6, 64-9, 80, 99-108, 118-23, 141-8, 154-5n, 169, 170, 176-7, 179-80, 181-2, 189
'Bona and Paul' (Toomer) 87, 98
Book of American Negro Poetry, The (ed. Johnson) 59-60
Bourne, Randolph 15-16, 30, 63, 72, 106-7
'Box Seat' (Toomer) 84, 101, 102
Braque, Georges 80
Breton, André 6
Brockelman, Thomas P. 9, 90
Brooks, Van Wyck 15-16, 58-9, 62-3, 92, 98
Brown, Sterling A. 140, 164, 187
Building More Stately Mansions (Douglas) 137, 165
Bürger, Peter 4-5

'Cabaret' (Brown) 187
Calverton, V.F. 59, 75-6